ERRATA

Caption for Figure 3.1 (p. 34)

(a) The Sun as a Pulsator. The coronal radiation pattern of the solar eclipse of May 28, 1919. (b) Radiation Pattern of a Violin at 1000 Hz. Oriented along AB with neck at A and chin rest at B (after H.F. Olson). (c) The Electron as a Pulsator. Diffraction waves caused by resonances and anti-resonances and an electron (a material particle) demonstrates its wave- and light-like character in passing through a thin metallic plate.

Caption for Figure 3.2 (p. 48)

Modulated Waves from the Moon to an Elementary Particle of Matter (Quantum Wave Packet). **A.** Continuously observed tides at Avonmouth, England, for one month, show the lunar semi-diurnal wave (carrier) modulated by the (signal) wave of the lunar fortnightly cycle. These are gravitational-intensity waves, released — as with all energy — through "time windows." **B, C, D.** Amplitude-Modulated Electromagnetic Waves as used in Radio and Television Broadcasting. **E.** The Wave Packet of a Material Particle (after Rojansky's *Quantum Mechanics*). This picture is borne out by observations, and the figure shows a typical wave packet, representing an amplitude-modulated, double-sideband wave produced by a "signal" whose modulating effect is very great everywhere except over a small range centered on the particle. The particle's velocity is simply, then, the velocity at which the minimal modulating effect travels. The figure shows the particle at a momentary position. For any particle of mass m and velocity v, its most prominent wavelength (associated with the particle's overwhelmingly most probable position) is given by h/mv where h is Planck's universal constant, and the corresponding frequency is mv^2/h. This concept provides a resolution of the so-called particle-wave "paradox." The modulation is caused by interference patterns among waves of probability, or fluctuations of likelihood, of position and momentum. Such interference reduces amplitudes to almost zero except where the particle (wave packet) is. E.K. Kennard was the physicist who, on the basis of the ideas of Louis de Broglie and Erwin Schrödinger, first introduced the key idea of a wave-packet. Through the 1950s they were also called "Kennard packets." That they were also *modulated waves* soon became clear.

DESTINY AND CONTROL IN HUMAN SYSTEMS

Frontiers in Systems Research:
Implications for the social sciences

The objective of the series is to develop a rich resource of advanced literature devoted to the implications of systems research for the social sciences. The series includes monographs and collections of articles suitable for graduate students and researchers in academia and business, including rewritten Ph.D. dissertations. No undergraduate textbooks or reference books are included. Quality, originality, and relevance with respect to the objectives of the series will be used as primary criteria for accepting submitted manuscripts. The present volume concludes this series.

Destiny and Control in Human Systems

Studies in the
Interactive Connectedness
of Time (Chronotopology)

Charles Musès, M.A., Ph.D.

Kluwer-Nijhoff Publishing
a member of the Kluwer Academic Publishers Group

Boston-Dordrecht-Lancaster

To those far-seeing ones of the near and distant past—many of them anonymous—whose searching for and finding the meaning of human experience we all pursue even further, knowing as they did that the quest is eminently worthwhile.

Distributors for North America:
KLUWER ACADEMIC PUBLISHERS
190 Old Derby Street
Hingham, MA 02043, U.S.A.

Distributors Outside North America:
Kluwer Academic Publishers Group
Distribution Centre
P. O. Box 322
3300AH Dordrecht, The Netherlands

Library of Congress Cataloging in Publication Data

Muses, Charles Arthur
  Destiny and control in human systems.

  (Frontiers in systems research)
  Bibliography: p. 192
  Includes index.
  1. Time. 2. System theory. 3. Social systems.
I. Title. II. Series.
BD638.M85   1984   003   84-5780
ISBN 0-89838-156-8

Printed in the United States of America

Contents

Acknowledgments

For stimulating conversation and correspondence with Ralph Abraham, John Casti, Paul Halmos, Marco Schützenberger, Stephen Smale and Eugene Wigner—and also with Joseph Campbell, Francis Huxley, Christiane de Montet, Jeffrey Burton Russell, and Mary Woodlee. To all my appreciation, as well as to the fine artist who did the final illustrations,* Rockne Chandler Beeman.

Sincere thanks to Series Editors John Casti and George Klir and to Philip Jones, former Director of the American office of Kluwer-Nijhoff, for their vision in making the publication of this book—a project and development of several years—now possible. And a large vote of gratitude to Christiane for putting up with me throughout long, arduous writing and for her intelligence and dedication in working so well with difficult copy under difficult circumstances.

---

*For Figs. 2.1, 2.2, 3.4, 3.7, 3.8, 3.9, 3.10, 3.11, 4.1, 4.2, 4.3, 4.4, 4.5 and 5.1, as well as Table 4.3.

Note to the Reader

Just as a medicine that does not cure illness of the body is vain, so the philosophy that does not heal distress of the mind is useless.

—Pythagoras

That all our ills, or at least the majority of them, occur from a wrongful changing and action of the mind, will not, I believe, be denied by any true physician.

—Flavius Claudius Julianus (Oration to Hera, *ca.* 360)

*Alpha continues to begin
Omega is refreshed at every end.*

—Wallace Stevens (1949)

"Human" rather than "social" appears on the title page because we would not wish to confine ourselves solely to institutions but also address the experience of human beings, who alone make institutions possible. Indeed, the more the human factor is neglected or denigrated in an institution— political or economic—the more speedily such institutions will fail; and history is strewn with the skeletons of such failures.

This book will not be concerned with repeating either the already well known or the otherwise available.* Rather we shall, appropriately for this Frontiers Series, concentrate on those facts and connections that lead most readily, geodesically if you will, to new and useful viewpoints and findings. Time is an ultimate frontier.

These pages were written for all those with lively interests in the workings, events, and situations of the world in interpenetrating contexts including that of personality. It was written as well for system scientists who wish to incorporate the importance of timing and psychosocial factors in their system models and in their basic paradigms as well. The general or interdisciplinary

---

*There is in fact a plethora, almost *ad nauseam*, of general works that more or less recount the history of men's sustained puzzlement over time from Augustine on, and the more the modern puzzlements concerning time *measurements* using signals of finite speed between moving systems, and the pitfalls that might exist for the unwary. But as to discussions of the nature of time itself, much less its qualitative aspects, the reader, like Omar before him, is ushered out through the same door wherein he went. Indeed one editor of a book of that genre went so far as to issue in his preface a disclaimer to have resolved anything or to have given any answers, so sure was he of their absence in what he nevertheless was asking his readers to spend their time on.

reader would probably first read the prologue, chapters 2, 4, 5, and the epilogue.

Many are interested in time, both for itself and its social and psychological implications, without being technically trained in the manipulation of mathematical notation. Hence for the sake of the interdisciplinary readership also addressed, technical mathematical expressions have been largely avoided.

The references (numbered in square brackets) are designed not as bibliography per se, but primarily to include work that may be of contingent value or contain passages cited in the text. Though all the chapters address subtopics, in the case of chapter 3 the subsections are substantially independent.

It should be noted that while on occasion mathematics enters importantly into the discussion, this book is not about mathematical systems theory. In fact, one of its underlying postulates is that mathematics is sometimes insufficient, and perhaps even inappropriate for problems peculiar to systems theory and practice, and that other symbolic languages must be deployed for sufficiently rich and applicable results.*

If you desire full use of the book you should see the notes, which often contain an excursus on substantive points that the flow of the text would not accommodate despite their value. This book has made for exciting research and writing, now shared with you.

C.M.
Côte d'Azur, 1983

---

*See, for example, section 4.2; also, a supplement (embodying mathematical tools relevant to chrontopology) originally written for this book but omitted because of publisher's space considerations will appear separately.

PROLOGUE

[Time speaks] *I, that please some, test all. . . .*
It is in my power
To o'erthrow law and in one self-born hour
To plant and o'erwhelm custom.

—Shakespeare (*Winter's Tale*, iv,1)

Time is not a clock, or a calendar. Time is an eroding,
infinite mystery—in fact a son of a bitch.

—Preston Jones (*Texas Trilogy*)

In 1980 I was asked by a friend and colleague (John Casti), and then kindly invited by the editor (George Klir) of this series on Frontiers in Systems Research, to do a book on the nature and implications of the time parameter, a project that had occupied me several years. Given the further fact that this book was to be addressed to a varied audience of interdisciplinary scientists and informed general readers, I was aware of the novelty and difficulty of the task. The challenge, however, was a creative one and the theme close to the heart of human achievements (and problems!) in this climactic, fast-paced century of centuries so outstanding for both its triumphs and its tragedies, so bristling with timing-crises.

The following pages, then, summarize the results of a still ongoing pursuit of that most hidden and powerful of realities, Time. It is the author's intent that those results, suitably compressed for a book of standard Series size, remain accessible to even those general readers who nonetheless feel the fascination and sense the depths of the subject.

As a scientific field, chronotopology is new. It constitutes a modern facet of systems theory (and practice)—one dealing with what we call chrono-topological systems, or simply *chronosystems*, which signally include those characterized by the essential presence of human personality, human perceptions, and human planning or time-scheduling. Thus most all systems, even ecological ones in our nature-manipulated era, are seen to be chronosystems or to have prime chronotopological components. The active presence of human awareness is impossible to disconnect from time, because its prime movers are *desires* and *plans* (implementations of desiderata); and these essentially depend on time for their dénouement.

Without further ado, we launch the quest with Shakespeare's ever appropriate question, What see you else in the dark abysm of time? (*Tempest*, i,2). Since such predictive power lies at the heart of all scientific endeavor, the contribution of chronotopology to system theory is of large potential import.

DESTINY AND CONTROL
IN HUMAN SYSTEMS

1 INTRODUCTION: SYSTEM THEORY AND CHRONOTOPOLOGY[1]

When contrasted with narrower, axiomatic, and necessarily more subjective ways (because of axiom choices and hence possible omissions), the inductive and phenomenological nature of Ludwig von Bertalanffy's and George Klir's general approach to system theory turns out to be a candidate broad enough to accommodate the nature of time (e.g. see R. Orchard's exposition of Klir [1]), the arts[2] [3, p. 16] and hence the whole range of psychosocial phenomena. Therefore this is the indicated general systems approach and philosophy most relevant to chronotopology. Only much later would enough be known to smugly write down a closed axiom set beforehand—with *hindsight*. And even then, that may well be a risky business because nature in her full gamut of powers and possibilities has a history of being extremely surprising to human presumption. Even mathematics is open-ended and is an *experimental* science which Oliver Heaviside profoundly and first clearly grasped as the nineteenth century closed, and which Kurt Gödel clinched for the twentieth. Such infinite open-endedness is *a fortiori* true of all the other less formalized sciences, and for system science par excellence. The moral is: work, observe, and record. Only in such an enlightenedly objective and inspired, inductive fashion will system science really make strides into rich applicability. This book is a call for such diligent observation in a new and potentially very significant field: chronotopology.

Time, one of the most anciently recorded [4] of human experiences, has also been one of the most mysterious and obdurate for analysis, and has remained so. That principal parameter of the vast cosmic system in which we are embedded remains as recalcitrant as ever. Space is more amenable, yet time holds the trump cards in the game of cosmic process. So we must push on further. To do so, we now consider the notion and corresponding entity of a *system*.

1.1 Time and Nonlinear Systematics: Chronotopological Systems (Chronosystems)[3]

Time, we know, enters very basically into systems theory, a system being any combination of human and non-human elements that functions more or less organismically, in relation to a given environment, in the interests of some end or enterprise, which may be only mere survival itself as in the case of parasitic organisms and systems. Indeed, survival as *sole* end is the primary definition of a parasitic system, biological or bureaucratic as the case may be. We can now give a more analytic definition of a *system* within the purview of this book. The usual definition is narrower, and results when certain of our conditions are restricted or trivialized.

By way of preliminary to a more comprehensive definition, the term *trajectory* denotes simply some space/time[4] path of changing states undergone by the system. It is understood that transitions (along some trajectory) from state to state would have associated probabilities and that a system trajectory involving $t_0 \rightarrow t_2$, where $t_2 - t_0$ is a time interval, will also carry the system through the state $x(t_1)$, where t_1 lies between t_0 and t_2 in time, and $x(t)$ is the state associated with time t, all times being consistently measured. Note that "t" phenomenologically can be either the moment following upon the lapse of time interval $t - t_0$, or else that interval itself, which are two quite different experiences, answering geometrically to a point and a line, respectively. One may distinguish these denotations by the usage of "at" and "after" time t.

Now the definition of a chronosystem can be given in terms of the following operational elements:

1. Given the initial state and future inputs, trajectories to future times exist which, however, need not be unique; and single trajectories may have branch points. Thus future outputs need not be unique, nor even necessarily expressible in ordinary (real) numbers; that is, they may be multiple and possibly expressible only in terms of hypernumbers.[5]

2. The start of a given trajectory may be *before* $t = t_0$ and the first state of such a trajectory need not be $x(t_0)$. That is, causes from before the initial epoch are admitted; although the most manageable chronotopological systems implicitly contain the possible futures of all such past effects within the nature of the *initial* state $x(t_0)$, even though the trajectory began before that epoch.

3. State trajectories, though ordinarily continuous, may contain discontinuities.

4. A trajectory may depend on *future* inputs (which are only potentialities at present) as well as on the initial state $x(t_0)$—which itself may summarize *prior* inputs in terms of activating memories of the past—all acting in the present so as to affect the future still further by *feedforward*.

It should be noted that the fourth portion of the definition of a chronosystem makes it clear that while perhaps such systems can be simulated in some manner, they cannot be compassed by deterministic or even stochastic mathematics, since conventional predictive theories, as Norbert Wiener ever has stressed, depend solely upon the *past*, while here we confront *present* outputs that in some measure depend on *future* values of the input. We shall indeed see, in chapter 3 and beyond, that in chronosystems there is in general no unique future because of options and alternatives (free choice), although there are at time constraints for being able to exercise these prerogatives optimally or at all.

A corollary to all this is that mathematics need not be sufficient to represent chronosystems, thus making clear the important fact that mathematics (a linear, nonqualitative language) is not the essence of system-theoretical methodology. What is the essence is an organismic and qualitative viewpoint, represented as precisely and appropriately as possible by the use of whatever symbol system, linear or not, may be pressed into service. The error of monolithically identifying systems analysis with mathematical analysis was exposed with clarity (and considerable acerbity) by David Berlinski [8], but his barbs fall harmlessly to the ground once the fact is grasped that the mathematical symbol system is not the essence of systems theory. In thus indirectly helping to make this vital fact clear, he performed an historical and scientific service to the subject, rendered with intellectual honesty.

It is thus seen that a chronotopological system or chronosystem is at least nonlinear[6] and is in general much more complex than the more restricted definition of a system ordinarily used. In that simple (but far less applicable) definition, the initial state $x(t_0)$ is all one requires to predict a deterministically unique state for any future time t, in which future outputs are always expressible in real numbers. Moreover, the trajectories of such simplified systems are everywhere continuous and never can be affected by potential future inputs. In other words, in nonchronotopological system theory, the time parameter is merely quantitative and is essentially symmetric, passive, plastic, and colorless, whereas in chronotopological system theory it is asymmetric, active, elastic (or inherently energy-containing), and qualitatively—not merely quantitatively—specifiable. When those enhancements are relinquished, the chronotopological definition of a system degenerates into that of the simpler systems usually considered, which do not do justice to the actual world and hence fall short in their predicted outcomes.

1.2 The Human Factor Cannot be Neglected with Impunity

The more simplistic view works quite well, however, when a system has only inanimate components, though even then it has been increasingly found that assumptions of linearity must be broadened to include the pervasive nonlinearities found even in the purely physical world, let alone its biological and psychosocial contexts. That fact is not really surprising when we consider that even the differential equations leading to the surface of so simple an object as an ellipsoid are nonlinear, as I pointed out as early as 1962 in a lecture at Ravello for the School of Theoretical Physics of the University of Naples. Thereafter, nonlinearity became a big thing and all the previously linear people (e.g., J. Lions who was with me at Ravello) began writing books on it. But nonlinearity per se, without insight into the *nature* of time and awareness components of a system, is also futile in the long and even sometimes the short run. There is no substitute for living insight.

When we encounter the human factor in our systems and still try to force them into an un-chronotopological straightjacket, we are then truly in for a host of unpleasant surprises in the form of erroneous predictions—a fact discussed in a seminar on surprise in systems theory that I conducted in October 1982 at the International Institute for Applied Systems Analysis (IIASA) in Vienna [9].

The two elements of (1) personality variations and potentials and (2) human reaction patterns and their relations to time structures are the two most neglected factors in systems theory today. Continued neglect will lead to more and more serious discrepancies in predictions as these factors, by way of global social change at increasing rates, become inescapably more prominent. What is currently least discussed, much less treated, in systems theory—except for the most elementary physical systems where those factors are either obviously predictable or else quite absent or uncalled for—are *optimal timing* and *personality dynamics*. Both of these factors are deeply engaged in chronotopology and hence in the theory of chronotopological systems, as we shall see more explicitly later.

1.3 Systematics and Phenomenology

In currently understandable terms, the thrust of this book is necessarily what Edmund Husserl well termed the "crisis of twentieth century science," appearing in the increasingly evident fact that naively smug scientism (with its assumption that physically oriented science and technology is all sufficient) is finding itself unable to determine humanity's authentic position in the scheme of things or to direct history sensibly. A corollary of that fact is our exponentially increasing social unrest reflected in economic malaise and political dilemma.

Under these circumstances, to cite Joseph Kockelman's paraphrase of Husserl [10], the world "to an ever-growing degree becomes an artificial world . . . in which less and less [of the natural] is left over. . . . Man, too, becomes an artificial object which is no more than a product of his own scientific projects. . . . In its main lines this seems to be the core of what Husserl calls 'the deprivation of meaning' " that more and more forces itself upon the attention of current humanity as the greatest socio-anthropological obstacle in the way of deeper development of humanity and indeed of science itself.

These pages are an endeavor to show a prime direction in which our world-view needs to deepen in order to remedy our situation: clearly addressing *the profound questions raised by the nature of time* and seeking out their meaning for humanity and how we can use the answers gleaned. Ancient Egypt, the civilization that lasted some four thousand years—longer than any other as a cultural-geographical whole with a characteristic system of basic values and doctrine, paid profound attention to this question.[7]

The following pages can thus constitute a needed corrective to the omissive scientism that had so long neglected the anguishes and joys of the human heart as an ultimate scientific datum for any valid world-view. So in a practical as well as theoretic sense, this book appropriately appears in a series devoted to the frontiers of the social sciences.

The developmental biologist Hans Speeman, on the closing page of his last great work, "Experimental Contributions to a Theory of Development," clearly observed that time and again the very biological data had forced him scientifically to use expressions that referred to psychological rather than physical analogues. He next acutely notes that this "must mean more than a poetic image," and then develops his conclusion:

> It must mean that these processes of development [embryological and genetic], like all biological processes, whether or not they are at one time resolved into chemical and physical processes and can be constructed from them, at their most fundamental basis bear a similarity with those very living processes of which we possess the most intimate knowledge, the *psychic*.[8]
>
> It must mean that we ourselves . . . solely in the interests of the progress of our exact basic sciences, should not forego the advantage of our position between both [physical and psychic] worlds. This recognition is now dawning in many places and I believe my experiments have taken a step toward this new and high aim.

1.4 Needed Metamorphosis in Science

But phenomenology is not enough. It is clear of course that a purblind science, lost in endless circles of carelessly shifting phenomena, is manifestly powerless to break out of that circle. But so is the mere raising of a critique against it, however well directed, as was the phenomenological critique starting with Husserl.

Indeed, the two endeavors taken together literally come to nothing and zero each other out. A third term is needed—a new standpoint and deeper foundation on which to build a better and more profound science, more attuned to the whole meaning and significance of humanity in this universe— a science that then incorporates not only knowledge but wisdom, which peculiarly applies to the knowledge of time's potential harvests and how best to garner them for the longest term welfare for all. There is no wisdom without such knowledge of time. And what science then becomes is like the winged imago to the crawling larva.

Of course there are still those who would not look through Galileo's telescope for fear of seeing Jupiter's moons, clutching prejudgments of what is deemed "impossible," often with destructively paranoid intensity. And there are those who, similarly, without a shred of their own study or investigation of the matter, still blindly cry "No" when they would begin to see that qualitative developments in time can be predicted from environmental determinants. For such obstructionists there is really only Max Planck's remedy: they will have to die and allow a new generation not so afflicted to succeed.

But this book is for those who are not yet willing to ossify intellectually, and are not afraid personally to investigate even at the expense of having to forego past prejudices in the face of new realizations. Those realizations that we will be discussing forthwith have to do with a new view of time: as a self-resonating system of qualitative interconnections and self-connectivity—in other words, with what we have previously named *chronotopology* [11]. It studies the manifold interrelationships that flow into and affect the present from both past and future. As a necessary preparation for those considerations we shall first look at the most general idea of what a language is— a means of conveying meanings through some syntactic symbol-system operating in real time.

A preliminary consideration of syntactic systems as such is a necessary step in arriving at a language capable of discussing the as yet largely unfamiliar concepts intrinsically entrained by chronotopological considerations. Such a development is all the more needed because those concepts, to be efficiently handled, require their own language, as we shall especially see in chapter 4, in order to avoid confusingly long and round-about verbal circumlocutions in ordinary language, much as if one would translate into words a comparatively simple mathematical expression such as

$$d/dt(t^2 + 1)^{-1/2} \text{ or } (x^3 - y)^{2/5}.$$

In the following pages there will be little attempt to re-hash unresolved or halting efforts of the past to unravel the meaning of time. Only so much of that enterprise, remote or contemporary, will be considered which contains hints of viable concepts, at least hints developable and applicable to understanding the nature of the world and cosmic system in which we find ourselves, as well as the nature of those selves in that system. We shall view only those ideas that were and still are, in one direction or another, probingly suggestive in shedding light upon the meaning of experience. Note that apart from such ideas, the enterprise of history is in large part purely archival, with all the irrelevance to life that that implies.

Notes

1. The science of the nature and self-connectivity of time and hence the study, among other things, of literally the future (later see also section 3.15).

2. Confirming that Klir's instinct and scope in including the arts were sound and appropriate, we cite one of the few really great mathematicians of the twentieth century, Marston Morse: "Mathematics is an art, and as an art chooses beauty and freedom. It is an aid to technology, but it is not a part of technology. It is a handmaiden of the arts, but it *not for this reason* an art. Mathematics is an art because its mode of discovery and its inner life are like those of the arts" [2] (emphasis ours). And as we will see, mathematics itself is not the last word in system theory.

3. As noted in the prologue, all systems having human components are chronosystems, an explicit definition of which will be presently given.

4. Note that we have not used the usual hyphenated "space-time" as that device of Hermann Minkowski's genius, though performing signal service in rendering vectors and tensors more compact and homogeneous, is at bottom artificial and omissive, since it not only does not do justice to phenomenological reality but in fact distorts and misrepresents it. The sins of a reductive "space-time" come back to haunt it, however, and we find in all books of sufficiently advanced physics important caveats as to the "distinctive nature of the time dimension," or words to that effect. The insightful mathematical physicist Hermann Weyl was never under any illusions about this important fact, and ever since the first edition of his *Space Time Matter* in 1918, he saw that time had a very different dimensional character from space, even mathematically speaking. We shall discuss these matters in more detail in the announced Supplement in the section on negative dimensions—which are not *ex*tension as are spatial dimensions, but *in*tension. Their intentional character links them closely with the nature of time.

5. A term introduced by us some years ago and since adopted in the literature. The first hypernumber beyond the reals is $\sqrt{-1}$, called i; the second is ε, defined by $\varepsilon^2 = +1$ but $\varepsilon \neq \pm 1$, and introduced by us in a 1971 NASA seminar at Ames Research Center.

6. The basic problem in general linear programming is the *optimization* problem: i.e., to minimize a given (continuous) linear form with respect to a given set of initial or boundary conditions. When the applied significance of such a linear form concerns the extent of error or derivation in some context, the problem becomes one of approximation or control theory. When, instead of a linear form to minimize, we have a (convex) *functional*, a function whose arguments are also functions, we then have a general *nonlinear* optimization or control problem.

7. *Vide* chapter 5.

8. Mind, *psyche*, as we noted some years ago, is that which uniquely both engenders awareness as verb or action and orders awareness as noun or result.

2 SYNTACTIC LANGUAGES: THE SYMBOLIC AND THE DIABOLIC

This chapter might be subtitled "Symbolic Systems," without which no other system theory is possible. The human species has been variously called *homo sapiens*, the wise—a bit on the unmerited side; or *homo faber*, the builder and maker—not sufficiently characteristic since beavers and orioles construct excellent living quarters, and bees, wasps, and termites do well as architects. Considerably more relevant is *homo symbolens*,[1] the human as a symbolizing animal, for in this we have no peers on earth. The more pathological side is then *homo diabolicus*, a possible psycho-subspecies of diabolizing ones, and we shall say more of that presently.

The antiquity of *homo symbolens* was underscored after Alexander Marshack read the June 1962 report in *Scientific American* by Jean de Heinzelin of the University of Ghent, on the groupings of tally scratches or notches on a bone fragment from a site at Ishango (Congo region, upper Nile) dating from *ca*. 6500 B.C.E. Heinzelin conjectured they pertained to some "arithmetical game." But Marshack had the bright idea of counting the numbers of marks in each grouping and thereby was able to announce that they were not a game but rather represented a tally of six lunar months. Marshack then confirmed this analysis from reindeer, bison, and raptor bones going back to late paleolithic times (*ca*. 35,000 B.C.E.), noting that lunar phases[2] as well as numbers of days were noted in terms of spacings

9

between groups or sub-groups of notches [4]. Thus the sophistication of using both marks and empty spaces as symbols is already attested some forty thousand years ago. There is also some further and more modern history to be stated.

After de Heinzelin's widely publicized article had drawn specific attention to the non-random groupings and clearly numerical markings on the mesolithic Ishango bone, Marshack's subsequent (since 1964) [5] counts of lines on incised mesolithic and paleolithic bones and stone tallies showed—not surprisingly in the light of M. Baudoin's 1916 findings [6]—that lunar time reckoning goes back to at least through 25,000 B.C.E. Marshack's intuitions and comparisons, occasionally forced and less convincing when his allowances become too conveniently elastic, nonetheless did show that lunar phases were definitely involved in these early tallies.

But already by 1958 André Leroi-Gourhan had discounted the then current error that such tallies were hunting tallies. In an English summary of his earlier work [7] Gourhan noted their "rhythmic arrangement with regular intervals" which he also observed was the start of the concepts of the ruled measuring rod *and the calendar*. And it was known since the 19th century that lunar calendars were more ancient than solar calendars—again surprising because the cyclically varying appearance of the moon must have been one of the most striking aspects of human experience no matter how early. Even cats and dogs notice the full moon and take it into account in their behavior. A primitive neolithic/paleolithic astronomy in terms of bone-markings was asserted by Marcel Baudoin as early as 1916, and the reader is referred to his seminal articles [6].

2.1 The Roots of Symbolization: Metaphor and Meaning

The Greek roots are revealing. *bolos* ($\beta \acute{o} \lambda o \sigma$) is a *throw*, a launching into trajectory. *sym* ($\sigma \acute{v} \mu$) is "along or together with." Thus *symbolon* is a throw in the desired direction, something that aids advancement toward the aim of the trajectory. In this way "symbolon" came to mean a password, a *passe-d'entrer*, something that helped one advance in one's course. Since a password is a *contracted* form of a certification of legitimacy or rightness, symbolon then came to signify a compression of meaning into a recognizable (decodable) image or depiction of some kind, whence the present signification of the word *symbol*.

Likewise *dia* ($\delta \iota \acute{a}$) means "against or across" and hence splitting asunder, and so *diabolon* means an obstructing trajectory or throw (*bolon*). Thus the old Semitic root "to oppose," *Shaitan*,[3] found in both Arabic and Hebrew, has its Indo-European, Greek cognate in *diabolos*, and both terms come to refer to a perverse being whose acts go against those of a benign agency, whence the present signification of "diabolical."

Let us examine the symbolization or symbol-making process more clearly. The idea is letting one thing stand for another. Such a process makes sense only if the substitute is more easily transportable than the original; or else if the original is a psychological reality, which is thus pointed to or recalled or re-invoked by the substitute object, which is sensorily perceived. The substitution makes sense also if the original is a motion or action and not a material object as such.

It is becoming clearer that the symbolization process culminates in language, where the substitutes are still sensorily perceivable, but reduced to the easiest and smallest compress—mere marks made in some medium. Let us now go back to the three categories that are candidates for symbolic substitution: 1) sensorily perceivable objects; 2) types of motion or activity; 3) inner experiences.

It is clear that once we begin to embark on a program for easily communicable substitutes describing such categories, we then soon find that we need also to find ways of denoting relationships both between and within the categories and their various members.

Thus a complete symbolization program, accurate enough to convey to one person something experienced by another, speedily leads to *syntactical* language, since *relationships* must be included. That is, the vocabulary of actions and objects in any symbol system must be supplemented by a vocabulary for relationships of position, causality (and motivation), similarity (e.g. of shape or kind), and extent (in space or time); i.e. place and orientation (in space and time), contingencies, shape, size, and duration.

Trying to make an adequate symbol system that would function practically would automatically demand becoming consciously aware of these categories of relation. So the development of syntactical language and that of insight cannot be separated. There is no such thing as a "formal development" of a symbol system without meaning. *Meaning* is the foundation and underpinning of all symbolic systems, and even the most abstract differentiations rest finally on some meaning, however puerile or trivial.

In chapter 3, Section 3.2, we shall see how this primordial word and syntax-forming process had to be painstakingly repeated by the human race when we had come to the point where we could build machines capable of recording ways of thinking and acting on them in terms of data newly presented to them. That they can so record (past) ways of thinking and then execute those ways in the future on new data is why we have called computers Kronos machines. A computer is a way-of-thinking recorder, and thus the most subtle of all our recording devices.

We can even build into it ways of modifying the prior ways of thinking it recorded, but of course those ways of modifying are also limited by the definition of recording, and hence such machines could never exceed the resourcefulness of the human mind, though they could far exceed the human mind in their speed of data processing or the size of their accessible memory and association banks. But there is no contest otherwise. Who would want to be a steam shovel just because it can lift more than the human arm, or an electric typewriter because it can write faster than we!

Talk of computers being "beyond" humans is just as misguided and, when pushed to its extreme, just as psychopathological as would be our inappropriate awe or idolatry of any other humanly constructed device. And in the all-important realm of feelings, the computer is deader than the dodo, for mere verbalization built in by humans means nothing but electronic make-believe.

So *syntactic language* is the characteristically human trait of the human mind as distinct from its nearest mammalian counterparts. It has now been amply demonstrated that while certain animals, motivated by food and affection, can indeed conscientiously *imitate* a human symbol system, they cannot create new sentences in it, nor form a syntactical language of their own. It is impossible to express to even an intelligent animal that you are going on a trip, say, tomorrow or in ten days.

So we are back to *relationships*—between sensory objects, motions, intentions, memories, and feelings—as the heart of syntax; and Language = vocabulary + syntax is the basic equation.

We also have noted two processes in the *intentional* use of language: the *symbolic* (in the technical sense before discussed) or reinforcing use; the *diabolic* or opposing or at least diverting use. But now we see that we also have the *parabolic* or the side-by-side or parallel throw: that is, something that proceeds in the same direction, but on another track or level or with respect to another context.

With this third category, the possibility of the basic language-forming process begins: that of *metaphor* or "that which carries beyond," i.e., from the level or context of its apparent reality to that of its intended reality. Thus with metaphor we have the higher octave of *symbolization itself*. This insight into the fact that *metaphor is the semantic octave of symbol*, which we have now gained, will stand us in good stead in all future thinking along those lines by virtue of its power of clarification.

The essence of metaphor is animistic personification, e.g. "the mighty arm of the storm" or one thing being compared to another to the point of alternative identity as, for example, "the sun, that eye of the day." In all instances there is a transfer of *meaning* from one thing to another, as the perspicacious Abū Bakr 'Abdalqahīr al-Jurjānī noted already in the eleventh century [13].

The metaphor-creating process takes place *not* on the verbal level but on the level of *meaning*. The imaginative story writer Robert Sheckley rightly wrote (*Omni* magazine, April 1981, p. 96): "We understand the world by means of metaphor. It is the basic transformation." Philip Wheelwright, in his chapter in A. Tate's *Language of Poetry* (Princeton, 1942, p. 38), well regards metaphorical insight as "a dimension of experience cutting across the empirical dimension as an independent variable." Algebra itself ("let x be so-and-so") may be considered as a vast and precise metaphorical system; and Max Blackwell remarked in his *Models and Metaphors* (Cornell Univ. Press, 1962, p. 242) that "perhaps without metaphor there never would have been any algebra." There is no "perhaps" about it.

Metaphorical and typological thinking are essential to language, thought, and scientific theory and expression. One of the aims of this book is to bring this profound, powerful, and pervasive fact into more precise focus within the context of time and system theory.

2.2 The Impossibility of Pure Abstraction

No symbols, clearly, can be vacuous or without context or reference, despite the unsupported and irresponsible assertions one finds on occasion. No matter how abstract, their very syntax or laws of operation and interaction serve to reveal the delimitations (and hence literally, definitions) of their referential meaning—certainly as to the kinds or classes of objects susceptible of such rules. Thus something susceptible of a square root and something susceptible of an affective quality are not the same kind of entity. In fact, there can be no "pure abstraction." That very term holds a self-contradiction (hence is illegitimate usage) because the term abstraction itself is not a pure abstraction, since it contains an essential semantic image on which it is based: the image of drawing something (*tractio*) away from (*ab*) something else,[5] i.e., drawing out only those chosen elements which simplify the object for clear consideration in view of those of its properties by which one has chosen to represent the whole of the entity in the context being considered.

Moreover, the word *pure* has its Greek root in fire (*pyr*), that which freed from dross or cloying elements in ancient metallurgy; hence purifying is literally "fire-ifying" or fire-refining: *Fire* and *pure* are the same words. So a "pure abstraction" is simply, then, a drastic screening-out of almost all the traits of an object, which considered in its totality would be too complicated to deal with for the abstractor. George Klir well sensed this: "There is a general trend to formalize [or to abstract—*C.M.*] so as to diminish confusion. As a rule, however, the process of formalization narrows the original meaning of the entities concerned." [3, p. 31]

We couldn't agree more. Indeed, in 1978, but before having read Klir's interesting book, we wrote:

> In a report published in 1962 I stressed the context as inherent to language and programming. . . . I specified these concepts further at the Third International Congress of Cybernetics and Systems at Bucharest in 1975. . . . In sum, it is a fallacious approach to employ methods based on the *deprivation* of meaning and content to solve problems which inherently depend on context and meaning-related processes for their solutions. Context and form are inherently and inextricably interdependent in both natural and computer linguistics [14].

Since such choice may be felicitous, enlightened and insightful or insensitive, stupid and omissive, abstraction is an art; and some of its practitioners are talented, others mediocre, dull and even gravely misguided. In any event, symbols, however, "abstract," can never be semantically vacuous.

So an abstraction is by the very nature of things an oversimplification, useful or empty as the case may be. And "abstract thought" has *of itself* no particular virtue at all, contrary to what some ororverbalized educational systems erroneously preach. Any good poet knows this—because creative people know that metaphor is the very heart of language: the soul, *anima*, or livingness, of mind.

2.3 Semantic Resonance[6] and the Nonarbitrary Symbol

We can now set up a little table of primary correspondences:

resonant	↔	Symbolic	(reinforcing meaning and/or adding harmonizing nuance)
antiresonant	↔	Diabolic	(opposing or diverting meaning)
unison	↔	Parabolic	(metaphoric: re-emphasizing of sameness or identity of intent from another place or level)

The reader will note that we have, in the discussion of language, avoided any formalization that is too tight, and we have had good reasons: too premature a formalization would lose the reality, the veridical flavor, and the living phenomenology of the subject. The art of understanding is to seek to preserve these essentials by gently scanning the field (not destructively re-structuring or deforming it). Then the naturally inherent structure will ineluctably come to light and serve as the basis for a nonarbitrary and natural formalism, as the biological skeleton serves the rest of the body, though (be aware!) is no substitute for the rest.

This consideration now leads us to the important concept of the optimally *nonarbitrary* or inherently natural symbol or symbol system for any given set of phenomena. Let us become more precise. *A symbol is inherently natural or nonarbitrary to the extent that symbol and signatum* are homeomorphic two-way transforms. (We are here using the Latin *signum* as connoting more than mere "sign" or "mark.") That is, operations on a portion of the *signum* or symbol themselves accurately portray (symbolically) corresponding operations on corresponding portions of the *signatum* or thing symbolized. The extent that this subsymbolization program can be carried out in greater and greater detail measures the nonarbitrariness of the symbol.

On the other hand, the more arbitrary a symbol becomes, the more it becomes a mere sign or mark. Indeed, the office of a secret code or cipher is to mask as much as possible the sign's connection with its meaning, and hence a *codon* in such a code is the polar opposite of a nonarbitrary symbol, i.e. as arbitrary and meaning-reduced a symbol as possible. But such deliberate reduction or masking of meaning is a diverting or diabolizing process, and is used only between enemy groups one of which does not wish to enlighten the other.

A military intelligence *codon* is then, quite technically, a *diabolon*. A less exalted vision of the same thing is thieves' talk.

A similar pathological diabolizing process is largely behind the jargons of most specialties, in which the meaning is often desired to be masked from nonmembers of the guild or clique, not so much for fear that outsiders may use it in defense or counterattack (the fear behind the military and criminal diabolons) as for fear that what is really not that deep should appear more profound than it is. The very greatest persons in any field could always explain the key ideas without the crutch, or rather the impediment, of jargon.

A third example of the diabolizing process, this time motivated solely by the desire to *exclude* outsiders, by a microxenophobia if you will, is seen in the formation of special words and phrases among adolescents and post-adolescents. Such argots are principally xenophobic in motivation, whereas argot as such is not, but is based on original and colorful images and metaphors arising among the non-book-learned speakers of a language.

There is a general theorem lurking in all this. Anyone or any group driven to cultivate diabolization process is in some sense insecure. Whether the insecurity is that of military or criminal uncertainty, or status uncertainty of some sort, makes no difference to the establishing of a network of diabolons which, rightly or wrongly, are then perceived as protective and necessary.

The theory of analysis into symbolon and diabolon components is a powerful one in assessing the enduring value of what is being conveyed by the language: the more diabolizing and jargonistic, the more trivial, and/or the less capable of continued progress the field will be. Thus one is afforded a criterion of prediction of sociological stability of a given group of ideas based on the proportion of symbolon/diabolon components of the language chosen by the exponent groups of those ideas in a given society. Remember that more lack of understanding of a set of symbols does not render them diabolons. *But what does is the deliberate degree of arbitrariness built into them by their characteristic users.* Thus the rich and very meaningful system of ancient Egyptian hieroglyphs happens to be one of the least diabolizing languages in history, even though it lay uncomprehended for over a millenium and even when it was understood, only the educated could read it. But it was not arbitrary in its symbolism and that is the point.

There is another nuance of viewpoint regarding the foregoing and important concepts, the foundation stones of this chapter. A *sign* is a signal or codon denoting some act or change that either has occurred, is to be executed by the recipient of the signal, or that will occur, according to some pre-arrangement. A *symbol*, per contra, refers not to an act or change but to a state or a meaning.

Thus a sign or signal leads out of itself, while a symbol leads into itself; and the more so, the less arbitrary a symbol is. The more the form of the symbol approaches that of the *signatum* or that which is signified, the more nonarbitrary, the more homeomorphic, a symbol is. The most profound symbols are the most apt, i.e., the least arbitrary.

A symbol is, then, a more inclusive entity than a sign or codon, and a symbolic system may contain codons as well. But a code as such never contains symbols, but only signs. It is also now clear that an allegory is merely a very shallow symbol with little profundity and great arbitrariness, consummated in human beings marching about with signs of what they represent hanging around their necks—little more than abstract names on stilted legs.

On the contrary, the most profound symbols are *evocatory*, involving in their beholders the realities they connote and well-nigh incarnate, in all the richness of nuance and vibrancy of living texture. Symbols are creative and magical in this sense. And indeed Jacob Boehme and Paracelsus linked the two words *magia* or magic and *imaginatio* or creative evocatory imagination. That there is verily a magic in the latter every great poet has known and proved. There is the imaginal (*not* imaginary!) realm of the deepest Shī 'ite philosophers, so well described by Henry Corbin, and perceived independently by the Platonic-Buddhistic thinker, Douglas Fawcett. (See his posthumous philosophical poem* "Light of the Universe.") It is the realm of *theurgy* discussed by Iamblichus and Porphyry, of which the Byzantine philosopher Georgios Gemistheos, called Plethon, was also aware of when he brought the Chaldean Oracles and the Hermetic Books to the attention of Cosimo de'Medici. Together in Florence, where the East-West Church Council of Ferrara was reconvened, they chose the youthful Marsilio Ficino to found their Platonic Academy, one of the intellectual jewels of Renaissance Florence.[7]

It now remains only to assemble some of the key concepts suggested by the foregoing discussion. First we have a basic division of vocabulary into (1) object-denoting and (2) activity-denoting, and finally the inclusion of the syntax factor in vocabulary by (3) relationship-denoting. There is, it will be noted, a gradation of increasing abstraction as we proceed from objects, to activities, to relationships.

For categories (1) and (2) in human language entire words were used, but in category (3), what were originally words may be contracted into prefixes, suffixes, or even infixes or internal phoneme shifts. Thus were developed most of the endings found in the Indo-European language family, as well as the prefixes of the Semitic languages, or the internal vowel changes in, say, German or Arabic, denoting plurality.

The subcategories of category (3) are interesting, and our investigations show that they include: position (place and/or direction) in time and space, or process, including words that can relate two different such positions. It is not the place now to develop this last sentence in ramified detail, which would require at least another book. Suffice it to say here that in all this, time, whether as duration or change (process), dominates; and it must be

---

*Kindly made available to me through his niece (daughter of Col. Percy Fawcett, the Amazonian explorer), Joan Fawcett de Montet.

understood that all of space itself is comprehended in any given moment of time. Mathematically put, if $kt^1 = kt$ denotes k units of duration, then $kt^0 = k1$ denotes k units of space. And space is seen as the zeroth dimension of time. Thus all of physical space, of however high dimensionality, is included in but a point (moment) of time.

The talented writer Italo Calvino in his story *Ti con zero* ("*t* with zero subscript") grasped this fact poetically when he wrote that what must be simultaneously considered is the totality of points contained in the universe in that moment t_0, not excluding a single one. And he adds that it's best to put the film-frame image right out of your head because it only confuses things. In other words, the Bergsonian cinematic image of time is not yet unarbitrary enough, and Calvino rightly sensed this.

2.4 The Time Line

We have but one further theme to touch on before closing this chapter. Language, like time, proceeds in a multidimensional, multicontextual line, infinitely greater and richer than the line of space. (In a Supplement we shall discuss more fully the fact that the space line is the simplest of extensions, the first (positive) dimension, which is included in all higher spatial dimensions; whereas the time "line" is the first *nega*dimension, which like a fundamental tone in relation to its infinity of self-generated harmonics, itself includes the whole infinity of negadimensions. Mathematically, -1 is greater than any other negative integer. See first note of epilogue.)

Yet despite that richness, we still feel a kind of linear constraint, more keenly sensed in verbal exposition than in music, imposed by the necessarily sequential nature of occurrence, even though occurrence itself includes a whole gamut of changing recurrences or cyclicities, and a helically axial factor of *development* through recurrences of phase (e.g., the seasons), together with irreversible axial movement.[8] In that sense we are all screwed by time, and pessimists would interpret that sentiment in the sombre terms of "cheated," as the colorful argot indicates. But all we mean here is a quite factual and unfigurative screwing which may eventuate for good or ill as the choices of the turns may be.

2.5 Radial *Versus* Linear Language, A Key to Nonlineal Causation

Our languages and our music, then, reflect the basic linear sequential context of occurrence. Yet, as we already preliminarily adumbrated, the poets managed to break those fetters. By metaphors, the higher nature of symbols, yes, but even more: a whole radiant feu-d'artifice, a fireworks of related metaphors—centers of *radiative* context, rather than merely sequential or even hierarchical (that simply graduated form of sequence). Thus, we have language used to generate meaning-clusters that radiate multidimensionally through different contexts and override slow sequence to the point of generating ecstasy of the mind and feelings as do in some measure all successful poems that are not simply cerebral and clever, that is, translations of trivia into merely more disguised forms of trivia.

True poetry ennobles by uplifting, literally lifting one's awareness out of the time line into a blossoming, paradisical time in which strict law and sequence need no longer be imposed. By a more sublime power of affinity, each thing joys in its appropriate place for its current stage of development, yet all still growing. Not at all the static "eternity" of imaginationless and sterile dogmas, theological or philosophical, but a *developmental* context evolved beyond the straightjacket of sequence because able to self-generate harmonious appropriateness so naturally and abundantly that there is no longer need for order to be imposed from without by any stern destiny, which is but the image of the future implications of our own prior errors of choice and value. The message is that it is reachable, that land of all the rest, the best: the place where the numbers are at rest.

In this manner would the poet defend radiant or radiative language. But there is a scientific interest in the search for better, fuller, *wholer* communication—with consequently less chance of misunderstandings between even the sincere, or the deliberate obfuscations of the insincere who obstract inquiry either in order to exercise disproportionate powers (or else to retain them in the face of threat). The scientific side of the matter is that there is a complementary language to word-language per se which is built upon the emphasis on meaning rather than on syntax—an emphasis on the radiative rather than the sequential. After a study of generalized syntax in chapter 3, section 3.2, we shall meet such a radial language (psyglyphs) in chapter 4. A few preliminary words must suffice here.

Radial language may at first seem less than linear language in the sense that a point (the center of the radiation) seems less than a line. Yet actually a line is but a representation of one vibrational ray from a radiating point. Areas, of course, can represent shapes. Lines no longer can, but can represent only lengths, even though the lengths may be curved in one or more dimensions and thus tacitly express effects of higher dimensions. Here, in the line, shape or angle becomes ratio or number, since all rational numbers may be regarded as proportions between two integers, e.g. $3 = 3 : 1$, $\frac{1}{2} = 1 : 2$, etc.; and there are even irrational proportions such as $\sqrt{2} : \sqrt{3}$, or $\pi : 2$, this last representing the ratio of the length of a semicircular arc to a diameter (a semicircular chord) in a circle of unit radius. But in the point, number as length vanishes. Yet a point could change color or frequency, imagining it now as the projection of a vibrational axis, vibrating longitudinally, or as an infinitesimal sphere vibrating at finite frequency though with infinitesimal amplitude.

But if the point were the end-point of a longitudinally vibrating line, perpendicular to all the dimensions of the observable space, all that would appear in that space would be a point, but now vibrating with both finite frequency and finite amplitude. So let it be with radiative language, except that now, a bundle of supra-dimensional lines must be conceived, all intersecting in the common observable point, the center of all their severally radiating meanings (see figure 2–1) in innumerable nuances of contextual levels, related through angle or orientation of meaning—phase difference if you will.

The Center-of-Meaning may be a key image/idea or the basic notion contained in some word root, when the radiative method is applied in etymology. Thus radiative language, rather than linear, is the kind of language that is intimately connected with (re-evoked by or in turn evoking)

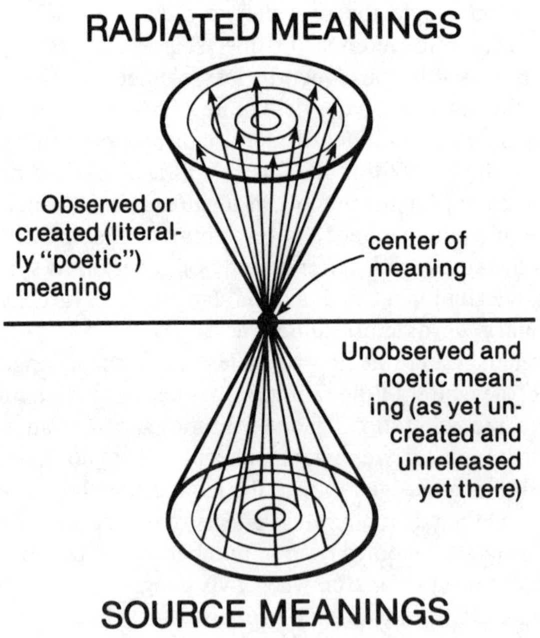

RADIATED MEANINGS

Observed or created (literally "poetic") meaning

center of meaning

Unobserved and noetic meaning (as yet uncreated and unreleased yet there)

SOURCE MEANINGS

Figure 2-1. Simple Diagram of Radial or Radiant Language

TIME-FORMED,
Blossomed, or
Radiated Meanings

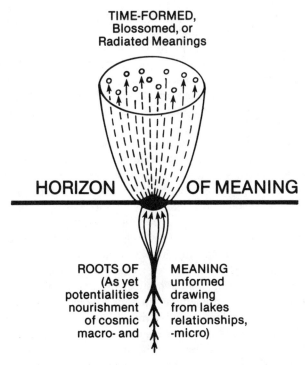

HORIZON OF MEANING

ROOTS OF MEANING
(As yet unformed
potentialities drawing
nourishment from lakes
of cosmic relationships,
macro- and -micro)

Figure 2-2. The Radiative Etymological Process Shown Diagrammatically in the Form of Lotus Root and Blossom (→ seed pod)

those states called "enlightenment" or "illumination" (note the nonarbitrary symbols in these word roots)—phenomena which always happen suddenly ("I saw it in a flash") and connect at once a great many disparate elements, as from a center of radiant meaning. This then is *radical* language, the root language by the processes of which all linear language was formed, and which accounts for the exceptionally rich system of continually reverberating associations in it that defy any linear analysis. All roots are rays, each radix a radius (figure 2–2). Such meanings are *intentional*, and thus directly related to time through negadimensionality (dimensions *ex*tend while negadimensions *in*-tend: cf. first note of epilogue) we see that Time, like Meaning, is a radial power and both share profound interrelations. "Source meanings" or roots of potential (figures 2–1 and 2–2) refer to the future; and, out of the central radiant point of the present, the past is then formed (radiated) by the interweaving rays of actions.

Every dictionary then becomes an arcane book leading to a veritable *themis mundi*, a shining and universal treasure-house of word roots. Let us remember that word roots are the most primordial human possessions and artefacts of all, older than the oldest known remnants dug up by archaeologists, for those ancient ones *spoke* to each other before the dates of their oldest extent vestiges. In archaeology, at least, in the beginning is the *word*, and the merely physical anthropologists, like misled beagles, are barking up the wrong tree.

Linguistic expression, which, well prior to writing, is first of all *speaking*, must take place in time, and hence reflect fundamental traits of time; for language provides a very nonarbitrary mapping of temporal process. So this consideration of language in the broader sense of all possible syntactic symbol systems—systems of symbols with modes and patterns of interconnection—is deeply called for as prerequisite to the consideration of time itself. Language and time interflow when language is expressed, for *expression* of even radial language invokes time. Then we have a succession of interrelated meanings, qualities, referrings and nuances, the relationships of which are quite nonlinear though super-linearly manifested in the time "line." We shall see in a supplement* that the first *nega*dimension (D_{-1}) has some bearing on this fantastically rich "line," which is more like a fundamental note that holds within itself an infinity of resonant harmonics since -1 is larger than all other negative numbers.

In this connection, it is well here to note that the rather shallow and misleading (and really meaningless) term "acausal" is too often used to refer to phenomena that are in fact "non-lineally causal," that empty word—the use of which (as in "an acausal connection") involves a basic error in the handling of language and thought—will not be used in this book. Radiative causation would then be "acausal" in that superficial sense, even though non-lineal or resonant causality is a profound, though no less efficacious way of producing effects. We need not throw the baby out with the bathwater like too superficial and zealot converts, just because the elementary fact has dawned that lineal causality is insufficient. The deeper and constructive truth is that resonance is simply a higher causal dimension. When that is clearly seen, the confusion vanishes.

We shall see in chapter 4 that psyglyphs are a radiative or two-dimensionally expressive language, which like painting, does not depend essentially for its communicated meaning on the order in which the symbols or brush strokes are made; whereas linear languages, including word-writing

*See first footnote of epilogue, p. 185.

and music, do so depend. Complex symbols (e.g. such as developed in India in yantras and maṇḍalas) are like paintings, while Chinese ideograms and Egyptian hieroglyphs are a fascinating mixture of the two kinds of language, since they represent meaningful sequences of readiative components.

When nonlinear, radiative symbols like psyglyphs or word root-images principles govern etymology. Starting from the Arabic word *tašbīh* "likeness, resemblance, allegory" (literally "similarity"), we arrive at the root *šibh* string or bell radiantly and nonlinearly seeks out its kindred frequency in any object in any direction within reach of its vibrations, so a radiative symbol seeks out and sympathetically energizes its semantic resonances in other symbols, calling them forth from unawareness. Thus the technique of resonant causation is evocatory. And so poetry has all through the ages been linked with incantation, that very word meaning a chanted poem of semantically resonant power.

Let us just look at one of countless examples of how radiative language principles govern etymology. Starting from the Arabic word *tašbīh* "likeness, resemblance, allegory" (literally "similarity"), we arrive at the root *šibh* "similar, analogous." We are at once reminded[9] of the Latin root *sib* "clan" or group of similar ancestry, whence *sib*ling, in one of those rare but not infrequent roots that transcend even great language families. The same image is mirrored in the ancient Germanic poetic-linguistic thinking process whereby the word *ähnlichkeit* "similarity" literally means "like its ancestors," "ancestral," the word for ancestor being *ahne*. Thus the two trains of images—the Arabic/Latin and the German—teach that similarities share ancestral common roots. This is but one illustration of how radiative language dominates and underlies etymology. The poetic, not the grammatical mind essentially generates language. The grammer is ancillary, and all endings were originally whole words, as agglutinative languages like Hungarian or its ancient forebear Sumerian, still show clearly.

There is an illuminating image for radiant or radiative language. In mathematics we can have a curve coiling more and more closely about a point but never reaching it no matter how far or long we trace along the curve. Such "centers at infinity" are called *asymptotic points* and they may be said to be a symbol of the transcendent with respect to the curve itself. They are thus like the ultimate meaning and reality of a symbol[10] which can never be wholly grasped by any simply linear logical analysis. Indeed there is a hypernumber (called Ω [16]) whose real powers form a spiral of Cornu and which shows two such asymptotic points (at $\pm\,\Omega$). As we wind around such an asymptotic center of meaning we approach it more and more closely at each turn of deeper understanding (semantic levels). But no matter how close we come, it still needs a *radial* jump to surmount the countless remaining, though smaller, turns and reach the jewel of meaning at the center—a jump literally across an infinity of (curvi) linearity. Thus there are mathematical representations of such symbolic ineffability.

Let us now, from the radiating point of timeless meaning, return to time and the manifesting or expressing process. But just a word on those often too empty things called "paradoxes" and how they may be resolved by improved thinking about thought processes and time.

2.6 A Note on Paradoxes, Logic, and Language

In this drawing away from, there can be many a slip in the mind twixt the draw and the maw. To take an example, the very property of being able "to belong to" or "be a maker of" some set or ensemble means there is some criterion of selection, some property or attribute(s) shared or held in common by all such "members." The word *class*, even more than *set* or *assemblage* or *ensemble*, denotes such selection or *classification* on the basis of some shared attribute(s). Once this fundamental fact is clearly grasped, the patent fallacy of lexicographical illegitimacy—employing the same term in two mutually exclusive ways—becomes apparent. Bertrand Russell, always too pleased with the specious superficialities of the mere word-juggling, tongue-is-faster-than-the-mind type of thing, never saw that his class-of-all classes "paradox" was an elementary example of lexicographical illegitimacy. The second appearance of the word class in the phrase "class of all classes" is quite correct, denoting a grouping by selection of some properties. But the first appearance is thoroughly discreditable: there can be no class or selection of "all classes" since then by the very nature of the case there would be no distinguishing mark or marks by which any selection could be made or a class formed. The concept of "all classes" simply means "everything without distinction" and is not a class at all anymore.

Similarly, "the male village barber who shaves all men in the village who do not shave themselves" is another example of inaccurate use of words, leading to, first, confusion and then paradox (that symptom of insufficient thinking) apparent in the question, Well does that barber shave himself? The linguistic misuse here is the imprecision of "all men in the village who do not shave themselves" in this sentence. When that fatally vague and flawed phrase is clarified to read "all men in the village who do not shave other men as a barber does a client," now the answer is clear. Of course the barber shaves himself, but as a self-shaving man and not as a barber with a client. Thus imprecision of expression and thought is the root of all paradoxes, and their only justification is to stimulate better thinking resulting in their dissolution.

Our third example goes deeper for its resolution. Consider the premiss "*A* always lies." Then is *A* telling the truth when he says, "I am lying"? The usual treatment of this paradox is an ignominious and servile salaming before utter confusion. Indeed, whole fatuous theories of "self-oscillating propositions" (i.e., that oscillate between truth and falsehood) have been erected as monuments to the failure to grasp the imprecision involved.

Admittedly the imprecision now involved is harder to spot. It is the opposite of the foregoing failure of logical continuity through a micro-hiatus of essential data. But the imprecision, per contra, is so huge that no one tends to notice it. The omission is nothing less than the *meaning* of the sentence. "I am lying" has no meaning, and cannot be adjuged true or false until its reference is supplied. The point would become evident in actual conversation. Someone (our "*A*" for example) comes up to you and says, "I am telling the truth" or "I am lying." And another says, "Yes, he is." The one spoken to then must ask, "He is lying (or truthtelling) when he says *what*? I haven't heard anything yet."

Then, when the omitted meaning is supplied, we are told: "*A* says that he lies when he says so-and-so (e.g., *x* is green)"; since *A* always lies, we now know *x* is green. Or if we are informed, "*A* says he tells the truth when he says *x* is green," we know *x* is not green. "To lie" is a form of "to say"; that *something* must be said is elementary but basic.

Curiously, the considerable number of analysts who have considered this old problem have consistently (due mainly to their following *fads of "thinking"* instead of *thinking*) lacked the really basic perspicuity of realizing that a sentence in any language may be grammatically complete yet semantically incomplete, as "He is lying" or "What they are saying is true." The truth-value of such semantically omissive statements cannot be evaluated unless the missing semantic reference is supplied. Syntax in this sense goes deeper than mere grammer. For full syntax demands that all pronominal-type references be supplied, i.e., that all indicated semantic linkages be given. Thus "so-and-so speaks truly (or falsely)" is semantically incomplete. We need the answer to the question, "When so-and-so says what?" The verb in such sentences acts like a pronoun and a modifier: pointing to an unspecified action and commenting on its nature.[11]

Thus the classic paradox of the liar, most clearly put by: "the statement I am now in the process of making is false"—said to have been invented by Eubylides—is actually vapid. The "statement" is merely the announcement of a statement not furnished, and its truth or falsity therefore cannot be ascertained until what is announced is in fact told. The nature of such content-announcing statements was overlooked, and they were then disastrously taken seriously by logicians, who succeeded only in having their collective leg pulled through the centuries. It is a careful time-analysis that discloses the fallacy.

The nature of time can help us here. Often converting such empty phrases to the past tense, which by nature refers to a more defined state than present or future, will help show up the existence of such semantic lacunae. Thus "All Cretans lie, and this Cretan says, 'I am lying,' " is to be converted into: " . . . and this Cretan says 'I was lying,' " whereupon one would immediately then see to ask, "But on what occasion does he say he *was* lying? He was lying when he said what?"—and the paradox is revealed for the farce it is. Indeed, its history has been a parade of Cretans being considered by cretins. It is high time we all enjoyed normal levels of intellectual thyroxin in such matters and stopped wasting victimized taxpayers' hard-earned money in teaching such stuff in publicly supported courses on logic.

"Paradoxes" are thus *au fond* misunderstandings through misinterpretation, insufficient knowledge, or both, as a pencil if believed to be truly bent when seen half immersed in water. Paradoxes are thus intellectual illusions, disappearing with greater insight, as when we know the light rays—not the pencil—are bent by the water, and the eye is seeing exactly what it should. The actual unbent state of the pencil is given at once by the alternative modality of the sense of touch, which, unlike vision, is free from errors introduced by a signal-transmitting medium (the water, in this instance, when the sense of vision is used).

All illusions and paradoxes are thus satisfactorily and fully resolvable, given enough data and insight. To *believe* firmly in them as if they were in fact what they but seem (e.g., to assert "the pencil really bends when half immersed in water") is to go beyond illusion into delusion. A similar delusory situation arises when people really believe lengths as measured from one moving object to another, change simply because their measuring signals of finite speed are of course then distorted.[12] Once we are aware of the origin of such error, however, we can avoid the misinterpretation that is so plausibly suggested in the illusory situation. We know then that the mirage city is not real but a phenomenon reflecting the nature of light, not of a city.

There is a rather simple test for fallacies as opposed to true statements or understandings. A truth pushed to the limit still yields a truth; for example, Mr. G's forty million dollar fortune is worth to him exactly zero if its availability for his use is continually postponed until G's demise. But push a fallacy to the limits of its implications, and it becomes an absurdity or an impossiblity. One might term this the test of implicational magnification.

Much the same principle holds for nonarbitrary symbols as opposed to more arbitrary ones. The latter, when one desires to extend the homeomorphism into further and further detail, finally breaks down and yield only erroneous nonsimilarity, whereas the nonarbitrary symbol can, under implicational magnification, still faithfully represent even the fine structure of the signatum.

2.7 A Parable on Logic

Logic itself is not the basic thing it is often misstated to be. It is not ontologically prior to mathematics, and their misguided belief in that priority was the prime error[13] of Bertrand Russell and his adherents; rather, logic is itself an outcropping of topology. Let us turn to a little story I wrote some years ago for a conference on artificial intelligence held in Locarno. It concerns a conversation between one logician (A) and a better logician (B):

B: Would you agree that a valid conclusion is implicated in its premisses?

A: Of course, that is its very definition and the basis of the logical process.

B: Then the apparatus of that process you speak of, the details of the logical demonstration, are in order to make explicit the fact that the conclusion was actually implied in the premisses.

A (a bit impatient): Of course, that is what we already said.

B: Then logic, as the subject matter of such demonstrations, exists only for the sake of those too insufficiently perceptive to have been able to see what was there in the first place.

A: Now my entire world is collapsed and burst as a bubble. What is there left, then, of Logic?

B: Ah, the best: the ways of finding the deepest and most far-reaching premisses.

A: But that involves acts of creative insight.

B: Exactly: the art and science of discovery itself—the executive key to all the rest of the mind, which is but administrative to this.

A: When might I know more about this?

B: We shall meet again. *Au revoir.*

What significantly emerges here is that the essence of logical implication and validity is *topological*, of the nature of connectivity.[14] Logic is thus a symbolic rendition or re-writing of the structure, that is, the self-connectivity of some reality. The better logician reminds the poorer one that the point is to perceive that reality in its wholeness and not become pettifogged in the ancillary enterprise of its re-writing.

Symbols point to their meanings. They are revolving doors, if you will, leading from a less to a more insightful stage. But entire intellectual movements (some lesser Jungians and some lesser mathematicians, for example) have become lost in the revolving door of symbols, forgetting that the purpose was to use that door to walk *through* into a far better place than the merely symbolic: that reality to which the symbols were only fingers pointing.

Notes

1. If this cognomen does mix Greek and Latin well, so did old Romans, as their abundances of Greek loan-words show.

2. Including a "no moon" or dark-of-the-moon phase, much more significant than "new moon," as we shall see in chapter 5.

3. Preserved in the Sàtníl of the Druses of Lebanon [12,13] and of course the current *Satan*. The Arabic *šaitān* is also linked with the root *šait* connoting a destructive burning as in burned food or, figuratively, in furious rage: e.g., the German word *wutentbrannt*. Here and throughout, overlined vowels in Arabic or other Semitic words indicate vowels that are fully written out as letters. Vowels without such overlining are implicit only, not appearing as full-fledged letters in the indigenous spelling.

4. Died *ca.* 1080. We transliterate the Arabic letter *ğim* as a "j" in English for convenience, even though the Arabic letter is cognate with the Phoenician/Hebrew *gimel*, and the "j" both alphabetically and phonologically belongs with "i" as present German usage still shows. For these reasons the Arabic "r grasséyé," the letter *ghain*, is transliterated as "gh." The seventh Arabic letter, pronouncas the "ch" in the Scottish *loch*, is likewise transliterated as "kh."

5. See *Paradoxes, Logic, and Language*, section 2.6, p. 24.

6. See section 4.3 also, p. 97f.

7. P. Kristeller's too pedestrian and uninsightful work on Ficino, with an undertone so apologistic as to almost be dogmatic Church propaganda, gives no hint of the Academy's basic dedication to the *non*-Church pursuits of the more occult philosophies of theurgy, magic, astrology, and that key doctrine of hidden yet cosmically pervasive sympathies and antipathies that was a principal concern of the Academy.

Giordano Bruno was of the same bent of mind as Ficino, and that other unaware apologist for the Inquisition, the late Frances Yates, though much more brilliant than Kristeller, also shows her prejudice when she (shades of the paranoid and sadistic inquisition) calls Bruno's heroic refusal to recant "obstinacy," implying it was perfectly moral for the ecclesiastics to have had him burned to death on February 16, 1600, a day of shame in the history of Europe.

Kristeller and his school—without in the least denying his usefulness as a bibliographer even if not a profound thinker—have understandably (given their biases), never wished to acknowledge two basic facts about the Renaissance. Namely that it was—certainly as far as "humanism" or the pursuit of the Graeco-Roman literay legacy went—nothing new, and had been going on since the thirteenth century, and before that in Islam. Second, its spiritual impetus came directly from Byzantium with the exodus of scholars thence after the Turkish conquest, although it blossomed and was financed in Italy. The only thing new in the sixteenth century was experimental method in the physical sciences, a tradition that had lapsed since the Roman and then Christian conquests of Alexandria, blighting all thinking outside of ex cathedra dogmas—a blight that very nearly silenced Galileo himself.

In the case of a great interpretative scholar, there is some reason for overlooking, even sympathizing with, natural human errors made in the white heat of a solid creative achievement. But in the case of someone whose sole claim to fame is bibliographical minutiae, like Kristeller's, there is no such room; for errors then tend to show up merely as such, unrelieved by a background of creative breadth, insight, or penetration. Raymond Klibansky, a too little publicized but towering (because so rare) *interpretative* figure in twentieth century scholarship, combined bibliographic virtuosity and interpretive genius. As to the former, he pointed out [15] five instances of error in one bibliographical work of Kristeller published in 1937, the correction of those errors having existed in works dating from 1896 all the way to 1929. On the interpretative side, Klibansky rightly stresses a thesis directly counter to Kristeller's entire limited and stultified approach to the Italian Renaissance of classical learning; namely, that it did not begin in the fifteenth century Florence, but in ninth century Baghdad, and that the very idea of the Florentine Academy was inspired by the Byzantine sage and magus, Giorgios Gemistheos, called Plethon—the guru of Cosimo de' Medici. It was also Plethon who directed Cosimo to choose Marsilio Ficino to head the newborn Academy.

8. In our first writings on chronotopology [10] we symbolized occurrence, recurrence, and development as the first, second, and third dimensions, respectively, of time.

9. Note that also unpointed Hebrew does not distinguish the s and $š$ pronuniations of the letter *Shīn*.

10. *Not* a mere *sign*, where the denotation is quite prosaic and placeable.

11. We shall discuss such generalized pronouns, which can be very useful when rightly used, in chapter 3, section 3.2, p. 72f.

12. This was shown as early as 1937–38 in two impeccably clear articles on "Relativity, Clocks, and Cameras" by E. Colthurst in *The Mathematical Gazette*. The use of retarded potentials in Maxwellian theory at once yields the Lorentz transformation, just as their use in Newtonian gravtitational perturbation theory (treating such perturbations as propagated at finite speed c) yields the perihelion shifts of general relativity (announced in 1915), whereas that little publicized genius, the physicist Paul Gerber, using Maxwellian-Newtonian perturbation theory with retarded potentials, had arrived at the identical perihelion-shift equations in 1898 in a stunning historical priority (*Zeitschrift f. Math. u. Physik*, vol. 43, p. 93), and giving further details in 1902, three years before even the first publication on special relativity, let alone general. The renowned German physicist Ernst Mach, one of Einstein's intellectual heroes, whom the latter carefully studied, had specifically cited Gerber's work on p. 201 of the 5th edition of Mach's greatest work, *Die Mechanik in Ihrer Entwicklung*. Gerber was also the first who proved that gravitational waves must travel at a finite speed.

13. Their second error was a naive credulity that axiomatic assertions created mathematical reality rather than the other way around: all axiomatic statements must not only be self-consistent but must conform to the whole pre-existing body of mathematical reality without contradiction. Humans discover and come upon mathematical truth; they do not invent it. The Fibonacci series was inscribed in the hearts of daisies and sunflowers long before Leonardo of Pisa's North African teachers themselves had learned of it. Real mathematicians like Hardy and

Riemann knew this. It is significant that Bertrand Russell discovered not a single new mathematical theorem.

14. As Venn-Euler diagrams and the programmable digitalization of them in my EXORcist form of Boolean algebra (see Musès in *Proceedings* of the Society for General Systems Research, San Francisco, 1979) make visually clear. See also section 3.3, p. 84.

3 *CHRONOS* AS A SYSTEM OF QUALITATIVE RESONANCES: CHRONOSYMBIOSIS

O Parvati: days, months and years are no more time than rulers are what they measure.

—from the Śiva-Tantra

Chronosymbiosis can be taken to mean the resonantly, mutually supportive interactions of two trajectories, careers, or destinies in time. There can also be counter-symbiotic or predatory interactions, reflecting in wave terms as damping factors, anti-resonances, power subsidence trends, et al. But in all these, however varied, there is a common denominator of qualitative as well as quantitative resonances and anti-resonances. Some situations are colored or nuanced so as to blend harmoniously in mutual furtherance; others less so; and still others, not at all. It is the chronotopological challenge to system analysis to come to grips with these key factors and their triggering timings closely enough so as to be able to deal with them in anticipatory guidance and control scenarios.

3.1 *La Forza Del Destino*: Time Waves; Phenomenology of Time

Complex timing phenomena began to be observed in the sun in the 1970s. One of the primary discoverers in the field, C.L. Wolff, speaking of solar pulsation theory in 1980, voices a principle and an insight that bode well for the development of all of chronotopology and not merely that small but important portion concerned with nonlinear solar periodicity:

> Today theory cannot make definitive prediction because of major unknowns. Therefore it is especially dangerous to ignore inconvenient observations (p. 270 in *Nonradial and Nonlinear Stellar Pulsation*, Hill, H. et al., eds., Springer, New York, 1980).

The example is instructive. As late as 1978, despite the clear results obtained in 1975 by F.L. Deubner [17] on the five-minute solar pulsation, the sun was pre-judged by conventional majority scientific opinion *not* to be a pulsator. All the more so, it was held, since conventional methods often did not corroborate analyses done by Fast Fourier Transform methods, such as the excellent work of Timothy Brown, R.T. Stebbins, and Henry A. Hill in 1978 [18], which was greeted with skepticism.

But before long the evidence was overwhelming that Deubner had indeed demonstrated our sun to be a pulsating star. The illogical sneers of "instrumental, granule or atmospheric artefacts" were silenced, and another scientific breakthrough, albeit against obdurate unwillingness to investigate anew, had been made.

The sun is now known to be an immensely complex and ramified oscillator with a time spectrum of stable periodicities ranging from minutes to hundreds of years [19]. Seismological investigation of the solar interior, by means of these wave signatures, is now but a matter of time—not far off.

The fundamental cause of these oscillations common to many if not all stars, as we are now beginning to see, is that of our vast ignorance. As one of the experts on Cepheid variables, M.L. Aizenman of the U.S. National Science Foundation, honestly and succinctly put it: "We don't know why they vary." We are suggesting fundamental causes in the nature and structure of the time dimension itself, and hence in the spatio-temporal release of all energy, already experimentally known to be quantized or pulsed. Indeed one of the implications of the revolutionary concept of universally quantized energy first enunciated by Max Planck at the opening of the twentieth century is nothing less than the operational existence of time waves or chronotopological oscillations.

This may be the signal for necessary changes in many viewpoints. Even the breakthrough on the sun as a pulsator had far-reaching effects, aptly summarized by the editors of the Tucson 1979 workshop proceedings [20]:

> Standard stellar evolution theory when applied to the sun at its present age fails to reproduce its [observed] radius, photon intensity and neutrino luminosity.

Therefore the standard theory of stellar evolution has to be modified.

We indeed have much to learn—and re-learn—about the world in which we find ourselves; and the fundamental science is more and more coming to be seen as the science of resonances and of time pulsations. We now know that the solar corona is basically associated with an entire spectrum of pulsations, certain frequencies being more causally active than others. Figure 3–1a) shows the solar corona as made visible to us by a solar eclipse. And—in Figure 3–1(b)—the startling likeness of that radiation pattern to that of the sound radiated by a violin at 1,000 Hz[1], from observations by acoustical engineer and physicist H.F. Olson [21].

Figure 3–1(c) carries the pulsator paradigm down to the very basis of the so-called material world, although what we term *matter* has been shown to be stunningly light-like. The figure shows the characteristic resonant pulsation patterns of a light wave—but they represent a material particle, the electron, as it passes through a thin plate of metal, as first reported in 1927 by Clinton Davisson and Lester Germer [22]. This epoch-making observation of the wave-like character of matter has been since verified many times over. We live, in fact, in a universe of resonances that maintain the standing waves which constitute the foundation of all natural forms, and—since artificial forms must of necessity be constructed out of natural constituents—of all objects whatsoever. This basic relation between standing waves and forms we noted some years ago [23]; and Ralph Abraham, following the work of Hans Jenny and Theodor Schwenk in the early 1960s,[2] developed the same concept later [24] in useful detail.

Pulsators of very high frequency may have important implications for time science. The discovery in the early 1980s of a pulsar in the Crab Nebula with a period of only 0.03 second [25] began an observational approach to the limit of 0.002 second stipulated by mathematician Frank Tipler of the University of Texas in the 1970s [26]. He had calculated that a cylinder of about 62½ miles long and 12½ miles in diameter, with the superdensity of a neutron star, would, if rotating with a period of 0.0005 second, distort space-time enough to facilitate observational jumps or "travel" in time. The incredible rotational speed of Tipler's envisaged cylinder may be visualized when it is realized that if our sun shrank in diameter to that of the cylinder, it would rotate with a period of only 0.001 second—only half as fast as necessary for the time effect even though the sun would then be rotating more than 2½ million times as fast as it does now. The experimental verification of Tipler's limit would, of course, have to be astronomical, and quite possibly through some space observatory like the Hipparchus satellite designed and planned in Europe in the 1980s.

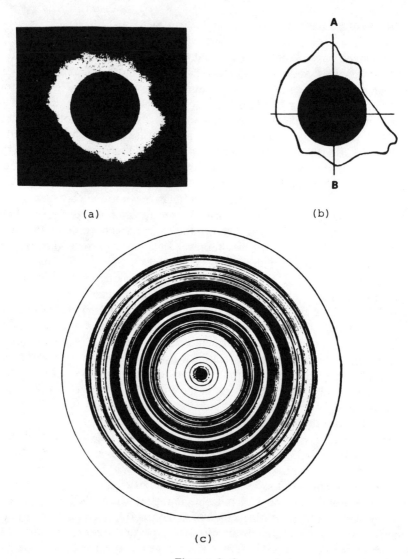

(a)   (b)

(c)

Figure 3-1.

Another straw in the wind was the scheduling of a conference on "Timing and Time Perception" by the New York Academy of Sciences for May 1983, and a later one in Florence at the Palazzo dei Congressi, on life-threatening arrhythmias. Eventually, most pathology will be able to be defined in terms of non-resonances or arrhythmias: the breaking of a wave transmitting phased energy. The Pythagoreans, voicing more ancient sources, said—not too differently—that health was "harmony."

On the chronobiological front similar evidence was accumulating in the work of Professor Frank A. Brown at Northwestern University [27,28] to show that many (and probably all) living organisms were bio-pulsators and have internal oscillators rendering them biological clocks—but clocks that respond also to pervasive external influences. Thus these bio-clocks are accurately attuned to lunar phases in many cases of sea animals, e.g., the grunion spawning times on the California coast and the palolo worm off Fiji and Samoa. In the case of the grunion the phenomenon is so exact, the following report is worth citing *in extenso*:

> The spawning season extends from March to August and during these months the female ripens a batch of eggs at two-week intervals. Thus spawning occurs only every two weeks and the time required to mature a batch of eggs is so mysteriously adjusted that the fish are ready to spawn only on the three or four nights when occur the exceptionally high tides (springs) accompanying the full and dark of the moon.
>
> These spawning runs take place only at night and only on those nights when each succeeding tide is lower than on the preceding night. On any given night, the run occurs just at or somewhat after the turn of the tide and lasts for about one hour. The grunion are washed up on to the beach with the larger waves, the female quickly digs, tail first into the sand for about half the depth of her body, then extrudes her eggs which are fertilized by the male as he lies arched around her.
>
> The whole process of laying takes only about half a minute. The eggs lying buried close to the high water level are buried deeper in the sand as the beach is built up by later but lower tides, and lie in the warm moist sand. A fortnight later the spring tides erode the beach, free the eggs, which immediately hatch the baby grunion, these being washed out into their natural element.
>
> Thus an extremely delicate adjustment between fish and tidal phenomena assures the perpetuation of a fish unique in its spawning behaviour. If the eggs did not ripen at intervals corresponding to the occurrence of the highest tides the grunion might spawn on a series of tides which increases in magnitude each tide. This would result in the eggs being dug out and washed back to the sea before hatching time had arrived. For the same reason, if the grunion spawned on any given night before the turn of the tide the eggs might also be washed out to sea. This mishap is avoided because the fish do not run up on the beach until the tide is on the ebb [29].

The timing of the runs graphs as a perfect luni-solar tidal wave pattern of annual recurrence, each spawning run occurring at about 9 p.m. on the evening high tide of the Californian coast, at both new and full moons between April and August, each run beginning about 15 minutes after the time of highest tide. There is clearly a luni-solar attunement, a chronotopological, chronosystemic connection here between the tides and *Leuresthes tenuis*, the remarkable grunion which, like the palolo worm, only responds more obviously to the effects of the pervasive influences of periodicities affecting all things on earth in subtler ways.

As Professor Frank Brown observed, "The evidence at hand compels us to conclude that the solunar clocks of life are either dually timed—i.e., by internal timers and pervasive, subtle external ones—or simply by external ones alone" [27]. Brown also observed metabolism cycles of monthly and annual periods. He also found that the metabolic rate of fiddler crabs lessened if cosmic radiation from outer space increased; and rose if the intensity of cosmic rays fell. As Professor Karl Hamner, who chaired the meeting devoted to photoperiodic time measurement during the 1969 Biochronometry Symposium sponsored jointly by the U.S. National Academy of Sciences, National Research Council, and National Aeronautics and Space Administration, remarked after the conference: "You know, our understanding of rhythms really stands where gravitation stood before Isaac Newton" [30]. Previous experiments of Hamner and his team [31] showed that changes in the earth's centrifugal force (e.g. the greatly lessened force near the South Pole) or magnetic field did not affect the diurnal rhythms of living things. As to what does cause them, Hamner is candid enough to admit he does not know.

Carl Linn (better known as Linnaeus, *fl.* 1750) was one of the earliest observers in chronobiology, and actually devised a "flower chart" based on the fact that (within 20 minutes or so) the spotted cat's ear opens at 6 a.m.; the African marigold, at 7 a.m.; the hawkweed at 8; the star of Bethlehem at 11; and the passion flower at noon; whereas the childing pink closes at 1 p.m.; the scarlet pimpernel at 2; the hawkbit at 3; the bindweed at 4; the white water lily at 5; and the evening primrose at 6 p.m.; the two gaps, at 9 a.m. and 10 a.m., are filled by the sow thistle and nipple wort, which respectively close their petals at those times.

A generation later, Augustin de Candolle of Geneva, found that plant clocks run faster when deprived of clues as to the time of day (e.g. when continuously lighted). This observation has been since amply confirmed, showing that such clocks are at least set, if not run, by influences from the external environment. De Candolle also found that some plants would not reverse their cycles even though he artificially lit them by night and darkened them by day [32]. He rightly concluded that different species require different light intensities to affect them.

The genius of Svante Arrhenius was adjudged by his alma mater (University of Uppsala, Sweden) to be "ummeriting of extraordinary praise," yet Arrhenius had announced nothing less than the theory of dissociation of molecules in water subjected to an electric current. He later won a Nobel prize in 1903. At the turn of the last century he collected data showing a cycle of some 25.9 days[3] in the periodicities of births, deaths, bronchitis, and epilepsy attacks, and of electrical variations in the earth's atmosphere. (It was not yet known that these were ionospherically correlated also.) Arrhenius prophetically wrote [33] that "the physiological influence of atmospheric electricity, long known in plants, may widely influence all of living nature. . . . This would affect the reproductive cycle of palolo worms and other animals . . . as well as markedly influence nervous disorders."

Arrhenius' last acute remark has been since elaborated by fire chiefs and asylum heads who respectively report an observed synchrony between full moon, on the one hand, and arson and psychotic outbreaks on the other. Hamlet's insight that there are more things in heaven and earth than are dreamt of in ordinary philosophy proved more and more true as human experience unfolded in the twentieth century.

His remarks on the palolo worm were substantiated for centuries by Fiji Islanders, and report first appeared by European observers around 1890 [34]. The palolo is a benign segmented (polychaete) sea worm related to the pathological tape-worm. In the last lunar quarter during the sun's annual passage through celestial longitude 210°–239° inclusive (i.e. the zodiacal sector called Scorpio), the sea worm separates from its head—which remains alive in the coral reef—and sends its more than a foot long, segmented body, filled with both ova and sperm, wriggling up to the surface just at dawn. As the sun rises further, the worms' segments separate and then dissolve, freeing the gametes which mutually fertilize, each pair forming a zygote, that in turn descends into the reefs as a new palolo worm head that in turn grows a body, while the old heads re-grow theirs.

3.11 A Case of Bio-Resonance

That bio-resonance extends to the cellular level is further illustrated by an example of molecular wave resonance in physiology that will take us from segmented sea worms to segmented caterpillars. This report concerns the writer's chronobiological systemic theory of cellular reverberation in terms of bio-microfields in auto-immune and allergic reactions. In July 1982 and again in early March 1983 I received strong confirmation of the theory conceived some time before in connection with the action of allergic symptoms.

At the time first mentioned, a close acquaintance in France noticed a characteristic procession in single file of black-banded pine-needle-eating tent caterpillars. Wanting to see if they would be able to close up their line with one link removed, he knelt down and picked up one, replacing it to one side of the line. The experiment showed that the catepillars could not regain their formation—a prime example of the fallacy of purely linear thinking.

It should be mentioned that my friend had had previous attacks of allergies through ivy and poison oak in North America, and also had been allergically sensitized to mosquito bites in Central America, and was allergic to bee pollen even in very small doses. Within five minutes after handling the caterpillars he broke out in one of the worst skin allergies he had ever suffered, with huge itching red welts on the neck and some in the chest, back, and abdominal regions.

However, since he had, just before the caterpillar episode, tried a new kind of home-brewed yogurt, he thought the outbreak was due to the type of yogurt ferment used. Soon after the episode he left France on a trip and found he had now become, since the attack in July, extremely allergically sensitized to vitamins of the B-complex, and could no longer tolerate them, even those prepared from rice. All this made him continue to connect the outbreak with the yogurt.

But on Saturday, March 5, 1983, the same person observed a nest of the same pine-needle-eating tent caterpillars in one of his trees, removed it with a stick and disposed of it in a plastic bag, in the process handling the nest and one of the creatures, but only with the tips of a thumb and forefinger of the right hand. Within minutes, huge red welts arose on the sides and back of his neck (more on the left), and on his hands, much worse on the right hand.

This attack was far more painful and lasting than the one the year before, and now he could connect it definitely with the caterpillars.[4] His allergic seizure climaxed for three whole days, beginning to subside from March 9th to 13th. It probably would have lasted even longer had he not remembered a very efficacious ointment, available only in Europe, and based on a form of ammoniated bitumen in a hydrophilic, skin-penetrating base.[5] He had discovered its virtues during a painful attack of *herpes zoster* (shingles) virus which terribly inflames the nerves, often around the shoulders and near the underarm.

That preparation helped now, too. But as each site of itching and burning was assuaged, another place on the skin was felt more, as though a signal had been transferred, as sometimes the new, badly itching place had not been bothersome, red, or even noticed before the application of the soothing pomade on *another* area.

Moreover, as the attack developed, the *exact worse places* of his *prior* ivy/ oak inflammations again broke out and even blistered, particularly between the second, third, and fourth fingers—sites that had not even touched the caterpillars or their nest. And there is no poison ivy or oak in France. Finally, he reported that the old *herpes zoster* site also—though more weakly—"began to be very bothersome" again; as though dormantly reverberating echoes were being resonantly magnified, in accordance with the theory of neural systemic resonance. And it was not until March 27, 1983, that the resonant outbreak began to disappear after a full three weeks of sympathetic reactivation of the old allergic sites of shingles and poison oak. The former still annoyingly reverberated through the first week of April.

In brief, we now know that complex protein molecules like enzymes, allergens, and antibodies interact through submolecular micro-electromagnetic fields of characteristic vibration sustained by hybrid and resonant bonding. Somehow, these electromagnetic wave patterns are transmitted along nerve fibers and may keep resonating in the nervous system for long periods of time even in greatly diminished amplitude. A strong new electromagnetic stimulus can then be transmitted, for example, by even the few molecules that touched my friend from the potent substance emitted by the tent caterpillars. Thus, then, huge resonance effects are aroused in all the *previously* (and still to small extent) vibratory molecules of neurons and immune-system bodies of an allergically sensitized person, giving rise to the phenomena described, with apparent recrudescense of old and long-since-gone symptoms.

The bitumenized pomade was so efficacious because it acted as a wave damper, thus preventing further resonance and diminishing the amplitude of existing waves. Molecules, like those of vitamin B-1 in this case, that are sympathetically resonant to the symptom-causing, molecular micro-waves, can then also initiate resonant allergic reactions. That is, the immune system functions bio-resonantly;[6] and in some way the effects of previously encountered antigens can be re-evoked by *different* antigens of a certain type.

In connection with this observed inter-neuron system resonance, a major supporting fact was known as far back as 1944 when A. Leao [36] discovered that stimulating one hemisphere of a rabbit's brain caused an answering resonant stimulation to occur at the corresponding spot in the other hemisphere. The pathway is not so important as the fact of the wave from the stimulated point seeking out its resonating anti-hemispherical counterpart. There is no reason to believe that the human brain behaves differently in this respect, and the facts of epilepsy only serve to confirm this conclusion. See also the writer's paper on quantum-triggering and resonant effects in biological causation [38].

3.12 The Resonant Universe

Returning to the matter of an all-embracing super-system of resonances guiding the cosmos, the theoretical breakthroughs and experimental confirmations of quantum physics put the concept of a *resonant universe* on a new, firm, and ubiquitous basis.

Werner Heisenberg had first introduced resonance in the mid-1920s when he showed, in a pair of brilliant papers [39], that two stationary (stable) states of the helium atom could continually interchange, by the outer electron of one state becoming the inner electron of the other and vice versa. This was the first illustration of a dynamic, recurrently maintained stability, the two states behaving like a harmonic oscillator. It is interesting that this phenomenon perforce shows that two electrons can be individually distinguished phenomenologically even if not observably—a fact often later forgotten by too statistical-minded writers on the subject.

When Heisenberg thus introduced this quantum-mechanical resonance (his term, standardly adopted since), the deep concept of zero-point energy was also introduced; because even with the principal quantum numbers of the two helium orbitals at zero, there is still observable energy. This phenomenon was soon found to apply also to the physical vacuum. That is, even in the total absence of matter or radiation, so-called "empty space" (clearly not so empty as before imagined) possesses inherent vibratory energy.

The old Samkhya doctrine of India, founded by the half-legendary Kapila, whose roots very probably go back to ancient traditions in the Near East, posited a universal vibratory οντσια or substance termed *akasha*, which was conceived as a collection of innumerable nodes of vibration, thus quantizing space in an at least three-dimensional lattice of micro-stationary states.[7] The ontology of the yoga philosophy, expressed so succintly in Patanjali's *Aphorisms* (*ca.* 300 B.C.), carried the idea one step further into a theory of qualitative time, based on the three *gunas* of the Samkhya tradition.[8]

In particular sūtras 12, 13, and 14 of Book (*Pāda*) 4 are of extraordinary interest and couched in a Sanskrit more compressed and laconic than even Latin can be. We give the English translations in order:

> 4, 12: The past, the future, according to their several natures depend on the paths (or modes) of existence (or becoming) as differentiated by their phase difference or self-characteristic properties (*dharmānām*).

These modes of becoming are the three *gunas*: the *sattvo-*, *rajo-*, and *tamo-guna*.[9] We now continue with

4, 13: They (i.e. these phase differences) are manifest or subtle (not manifest) according as they pertain to the past/present or to the future.

4, 14: The external manifestation of any object (out of alternate possibilities) occurs when the transformations (of its *guṇas* or modes of becoming) are in the same phase (literally "are in oneness," i.e., unison).[10]

This is easily applied to situations, that is, to the states of a chronosystem: manifestation of any particular aspect occurs with the chronotopological modalities (time waves, if you will) if the situations are in either the same phase or in harmonically related phases that permit resonance. These phase angles that can relate driving forces in a chronotopological context will turn up again in chapter 4, where the radial symbol system of psyglyphics is discussed. In its chronotopological deployment, that symbolic language provides the interface between psychology and physics—those two great polarities of science that Eugene Wigner [40] with much seminal insight suggested might be joined to make a carbon-arc lamp intensity of illumined understanding. And the philosophical novelist Marcel Proust had presciently proposed the juxtaposition of a *psychology* of time with a geometry (including physics) of space, thus connecting time more intimately with consciousness than space.

3.13 Cosmo-Ecological Balances

The need for a more precisely *qualitative* prediction scheme than provided by conventional mathematical systems theory is pointed up by T.P.T. Williams' perceptive review [41] of Douglas Hofstadter's and Daniel Dennett's *The Mind's I*:

> Unfortunately, in the nature of things the more closely a mathematical model mirrors reality, the more difficult it becomes to proceed from the equations implicitly describing a system, to an explicit scheme for predicting the behaviour of the system in any desired context.

Again, an analytic method not limited to mathematics is indicated. In this connection let us consider what may be called the Four Fundamental Cosmo-Ecological Balances.

The most important nuclear reaction for the human race is comparatively little realized by people at large or, indeed, by many scientists. It is the pion (π) exchange reaction between the protons (p) and neutrons (n) in atomic nuclei larger than ordinary hydrogen. Already deuterium or heavy hydrogen, with a nucleus consisting of a proton and a neutron, is governed by that primordial reaction (actually life-ensuring, as we shall see) which may be written so:

$$p_1 + n_1 \rightleftharpoons (n_2 + \pi^+) + n_1 \rightleftharpoons n_2 + (\pi^+ + n_1) \rightleftharpoons n_2 + p_2$$

the two subscripts here indicating two distinct particles in each case.[11] As the basic reaction we have, of course: $p_1 \rightarrow n_2 + \pi^+$ and $\pi^+ + n_1 \rightarrow p_2$.

Now in the nucleus the $p-n$ attraction is stronger than either $n-n$ or $p-p$ attractions, although it exceeds the $p-p$ attraction by only about $1/10\%$ or one part in a thousand. It is this very delicate balance that ensures the manifestation of the entire physical world; for without that tiny extra leverage binding together the neutrons and protons that are in an atomic nucleus, no other atomic species save hydrogen could exist; and the other three essentials for life—carbon, oxygen, and nitrogen—would not be here.

A similar delicate proportion of mass and distance between earth and sun ensures the maintenance of viable temperatures on earth; and still a third very delicate biochemical arrangement in living cells assures that neither their acidity nor alkalinity passes very far from absolute neutral. Finally the supply of oxygen, essential to mammalian and human life, is ensured by another delicate ecological surplus of rain forest and chlorophyll-bearing diatoms. If unwisely destructive technologies destroy enough of those forests and diatoms, we would be forced, using atomic fission power, to release oxygen from rocks or water in order to survive; and in the long term that bids fair to be an ecologically hazardous as well as doubtful enterprise.

The balance all told, ecologically speaking, for the maintenance of life is exquisitely sensitive, and the biosphere is an extremely delicate organism, not to be so crudely tampered with by greed as the human race thus far has dangerously done. It is symbiosis (direct or ecologically indirect), and *not* predation, that in the last analysis upholds the world.

It is interesting that there are just four of these ecologically cosmos-upholding balances. Then the universal mapping scheme outlined in section 4.3 should apply. The basic four-group there, we recall, consisted symbolically of $\triangle \; \triangledown \; \triangle \; \triangledown$, which on one level correspond respectively to the four states of matter: the plasma ("fiery"), liquid ("watery"), gaseous ("airy"), and solid ("earthy") states, in a vast "Correspondence Principle," which quantum pioneer Niels Bohr only dimly yet with sovereign intuitive insight stipulated as a principal foundation-stone in any scientific grasp of the cosmos. We here have a clear correspondence of the four primal life-sustaining balances as follows: (1) $\triangle$: the nuclear proton-neutron exchange reaction; (2) $\triangledown$: the acid-alkaline (pH) balance established in cellular fluids, lymph, and blood; (3) $\triangle$: the oxygen balance; and (4) $\triangledown$: the gravitational balance between the massive globes of matter, earth and sun. It should be noted that all these great balancing systems are *dynamic* and are cyclically timed in their functioning. That is, we have not simply symbiosis but *chronosymbiosis* as one of the essential factors for life itself.

3.14 Cosmo-Ecological Systematics as Chronosymbiosis

An important role in such chronosymbiosis is played by the tides, which are unmistakably correlated with astronomical or, more precisely stated, cosmobiological invariants that make themselves manifest through cycles that both determine changes and persist throughout them. Table 3–1 exhibits some of this complex time-interweaving.

It was probably some such perception of accumulated evidence that led to Max Born's "bright idea"[12] that the ultimately true equations of physics should be invariant under certain Fourier transformations. That would mean that the laws they expressed would be equally applicable in either the frequency (phase) or time domain, which I afterwards realized could be considered as the cyclical and non-recurrent, or axial projections of a process, to use a helicoidal metaphor. Whether it is the Fourier transform or, more likely, some more nonlinear analogue of it that will play such a commanding role in the expression of natural laws, it is clear from the data that various observable natural cycles are based on a set of invariants inherent in nature itself, in natural law and structure.[13]

The tides are probably one of the most ubiquitous of chronosymbiotic phenomena, providing as they do, both by their ebb and flow on all the world's beaches, the very means of life for many different kinds of creatures. In an interesting and authoritative study of ocean tides [42] Russell and Macmillan relevantly point out that

> ... scientific research has vindicated what used to be regarded as the naive conviction of the ancients of the eastern Mediterranean, that the tides and lunar phases determined the size of the sea urchins and their periods of reproduction. This tradition is today perpetuated by the fishmongers of Suez. . . . Research has confirmed that sea urchins (*Centrechinus Diodema sectosus*) are subject to a periodic reproduction cycle which is correlated with the lunar month.

We recall the palolo sea worm and the grunion already discussed.

We can add here that the two chronobiologists, Frank A. Brown, Jr. and H. Margaret Webb [44], found an exact solar 24-hour rhythm of color change, and later a lunar rhythm of 24 hours, 50 minutes (the lunar synodic

Table 3-1. Tidal Effects and Astronomical Cycles (after Russell and MacMillan, *Waves and Tides*)

Tidal Effects	Related Astronomical cycle	Period	Cause
Twice daily or semi-diurnal (varying with the moon's phases)	Interval between moon's upper and lower transits. Dominantly lunar.	12.4 hours	Rotation of the earth and resultant of sun and moon's tractive forces causing high water on both sides of the earth.
Once daily or diurnal (varying with declination)	Interval between succeeding upper or lower transits of sun and/or moon.	24.8 hours	Declination of sun and/or moon and rotation of the earth.
Fortnightly interval between spring tides	Half revolution of moon's orbit	14.76 days (Mean)	From conjunction with sun to opposition or opposition to conjunction (interval between syzygies).
Fortnightly interval between maximum diurnal effects at upper and lower moon's transits alternately	Maximum south to maximum north. Declination or vice versa.	13.6 days	Varying declination and rotation of the earth. Apices of tidal ellipsoid maintained on line of centres on both sides of the ideal earth on varying latitudes.
Monthly	Anomalistic or perigee to perigee.	27.5 days	Variation of tractive forces due to changes in the moon's distance.

Name	Description	Period	Cause/Relation
Half-yearly	Half revolution of earth in orbit giving cycle of sun's declination from zero through extreme north or south and back to zero.	182.62 days	Orbital movement of earth.
Yearly	Variation of sun's distance.	365.24 days	Movement of earth in elliptical orbit.
Long period. Lunar apsides cycle	Rotation of axis of moon's orbit.	8.8 years	Gravitational.
Nodal cycle	Revolution or regression of moon's nodes.	18.61 years	Solunar cycle relating planes of orbits.
Metonic cycle	Metonic cycle of recurrence of lunar phases in relation to solar calendar.	19 years	Solunar cycle relating synodic period.
Saros cycle	Saros cycle, or recurrence of eclipses, that is, coincidence of line of centres of earth, sun, and moon.	18.03 years	Solunar cycle relating nodes and periods.
Perigee/Perihelion Syzygy cycle	Recurrence of positions with earth in perihelion and moon in perigee at syzygies. (Conjunction or opposition).	1,600 years	Orbital cycles, harmonizing synodic anomalistic and nodal cycles.

day) for their food-gathering activities. He also showed [45] that oysters transported from Connecticut to Illinois had reset their bio-clocks within two weeks to correspond to the new zenith and nadir transit times for the moon at the Illinois longitude.

The tides also are one of the everyday expressions of one of the mightiest and essential of all forces, universal gravitation, which a past relativistic physics is seeing as far different in origin and nature from other forces differently producing the same acceleration. Indeed, simply because various kinds of forces all produce a given acceleration on a given mass gives no logical warrant whatsoever for the in fact erroneous belief that all those forces possess the same physical structure and character. That F implies A does not mean A implies F, for there may be G, H, and a host of other agents all of which result in A. That all forces may be made to produce identical accelerations was known since Newton, and there is clearly no reason they should not by the fundamental equation $a = F/m$ where a is the produced acceleration, F the force, and m the mass on which the force operates.

The tides are perhaps the most notable ecological example of kinetic effects due to gravity, and they are, as Table 3–1 shows, astronomically guided—a case of astrocybernetics, so to speak. Thus the Queen Mary ocean liner loses about 18 pounds in weight every time the moon is overhead. The sun's action on tides is only 0.46 that of the lunar effect because its greater distance more than counterbalances its greater mass. Planetary effects would be smaller still, through quite existent.

Standing waves are always resonantly produced—that is, by flows in phase, e.g. a fountain's form. And an authority on tidal phenomena notes [46] that "in the case of the great oceans and seas, the kinetic energy is generated by the astronomical tractive forces. To quote the *Admiralty Manual* 'the width of the Atlantic Ocean is quite large enough for [astronomically caused] resonance to occur.' "

Within the complexity of the cycle repertoire of Table 3–1 there is room for many nuances and emphases characteristic of a special geographical location. Thus in the remarkable high and low standing-wave tides in the Bay of Fundy and the Hudson Straits, the apogee-perigee lunar cycle wholly dominates the lunar phase and declination cycles, and is thus practically the sole cause of the phenomenon of those remarkable tides.

The interplay of two cycles can produce a perfectly modulated wave, wherein the cycle of higher frequency acts as the carrier wave. Figure 3–2(A) shows the modulated wave formed by the tides at Avonmouth, England, as governed by the lunar wave of approximately 12-hour period modulated by the longer lunar wave of 14-day period. Figure 3-2(B,C,D) shows the identical type of wave as produced in the transmission of electromagnetic waves carrying informational signals; and figure 3–2(E) shows that the same process is the basis of the wave packets that constitute the so-called elementary particles of the physical world, as the caption explains. Thus matter is not at all the "material" substance we thought. In fact, as a distinguished expositor of quantum physics, Bernard d'Espagnat, pointedly noted in 1976:

> The use of the expression "scientific materialism" should nowadays be tolerated only with reference to a set of methods or to an attitude of the mind. With reference to a general conception of the world, it has become a meaningless association of words.

But it should by no means be assumed that even the easily observable phenomenon of the tides is completely understood. Oceanologists tell us [47] that "tidal knowledge has not yet achieved such finality as to enable the tides to be explained without reference to observed values. . . . Tidal models are still matters of strong controversy." In other words, even ocean tides are still largely an empirical science—but no person of sound mind would attempt to say that they did not exist or that simply because we could explain exactly how, it was silly to say that the celestial bodies had anything to do with the tides.

In the case of much more subtle and complex chronobiological and chronopsychological phenomena (e.g., arson and other psychotic phenomena increasing at full moon), it would be even more foolhardy to attempt to deny the fact on the absurd grounds of lack of a theory. In deed, in all our sciences, technologists of various kinds are constantly working with, using, and developing further applications of natural effects whose fundamental basis remains quite poorly understood or else completely unknown. If we wanted to understand digestion and assimilation before we ventured to eat, we would all long since have been starved. So the argument that a phenomenon can not be accepted until understood is totally without merit, and indeed constitutes a deliberate obfuscation of inquiry.

3.141 Generalized Causality.   The problem is clearly one of our encounter with a less accustomed kind of causality: *resonant causality* rather than causation by gross impact. When the resonant wave medium becomes time itself, then we are faced with a complete task of re-thinking, and we must resist the tendency (due to our habitual acquaintance with grosser types of causality) to falsely call perfectly efficacious resonant causation "acausal." There is nothing acausal about it, and the more we study quantum physics the more it is beginning to appear quite the contrary: namely, that all the other cruder appearances of causal processes are ultimately reducible to

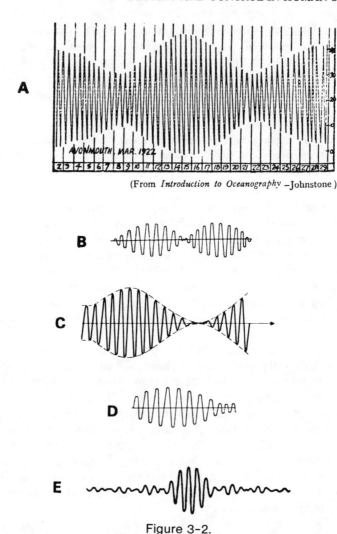

A

AVONMOUTH MAR. 1922

(From *Introduction to Oceanography* —Johnstone)

B

C

D

E

Figure 3-2.

resonances and anti-resonances, i.e., to harmonious or dissonant patterns of phases.[14]

It is clear that again an underlying unfamiliarity with the fundamental concept of qualitative time has caused many to falter and stumble, as did Carl Jung when he miscalled resonant causation "acausal" [48], undoubtedly being influenced by the defeatist posture of many quantum physicists following Niels Bohr who similarly failed to distinguish between not being able to ascertain the cause of a phenomenon and the nonexistence of the cause, much as though a mere agnostic were suddenly to announce dogmatically that he thereby had "proved" atheism. (The pertinent question here is, of course, How on earth did you ever find out?)

Jung criticizes Schopenhauer and Paul Kammerer quite drastically, yet explains the same phenomenon of synchronous connections no better than they, offering only an unnecessary neologism, "synchronicity," which he insisted (without demonstration as to how) was more meaningful than the common descriptive term "synchronous," which actually can be made as meaningful as necessary, without the clutter of the needless polysyllables. Thus when suddenly an accurately attuned television receiver then projects a sequence of actions on the screen, no one of course would claim that the TV set is the *cause* of the action depicted. But it *is* the cause of the *appearance* of that scene at that moment, by proper resonant tuning. And all similarly tuned receivers will simultaneously show it. If several harmonics vibrate in resonant sympathy to their fundamental note, there is no direct causal connection by impact from one string to another—but there *is resonant causality* by which several physically separated and highly selected areas may simultaneously be affected because of a shared and underlying wave phenomenon in some medium. Just as the usual sort of impact causality works principally in matter and space, so *resonant* causality works principally in energy and time.

Jung's word synchronicity simply *describes* without explaining, while his term *acausal* actually misrepresents what is going on. We may say of him, what he himself said of Schopenhauer [49], that "nonetheless it is to his credit that he saw the problem."

It was somewhat different with the original thinker Henry Corbin who, though he participated in many of the Eranos meetings, quite forthrightly proclaimed in a rare biographical interview[15] rather shortly before his death, "I am not a Jungian." Through his Shīʿite researches, Corbin learned something of qualitative time from the old traditions, and in particular the Ṭayyibītī-Yemenite branch of the Western Ismāʿīlīs;[6] for he writes that

> ... the only "historical" causality is the relations of will between acting subjects. "Facts" are on each occasion a new creation; there is discontinuity between them. ... To perceive a causality in "facts" by detaching them from persons is ... to affirm dogmatically the [merely] rational meaning of history on which our contemporaries have built up a whole mythology. But it is likewise to reduce real time to ... the essentially quantitative time which is that of the objectivity of mundane calendars, from which the signs that gave a sacred *qualification* to every present have disappeared [50].

Thus Corbin had a much clearer notion of meaningful synchrony than Jung because he realized that behind and between it lay the reality of qualitative time, and the necessity of approaching the problem in that manner.

We have already abundantly seen how qualitative time is in turn bound up with *resonant causation*. The precision of this term, which we arrived at only after much distilling of many facts and implications down to their essentials, was by no means easily evident as shown in the history of attempts to reach it.

First, out of the piecemeal (technically) incoherent theories of causation that governed modern science from its inception in Galilean-Newtonian, and later in Maxwellian-Gibbsian mechanics, another viewpoint slowly emerged, principally since the time of Jan Smuts and Ludwig van Bertalanffy (though Arthur Schopenhauer had adumbrated it). This viewpoint regarded things *interactively* in the light of a global theory of causation which could still do justice to observed specificities. It steadily gained headway until, as championed by generalists and organizers, it bids well to dominate applied science in the twenty-first century, as well as to furnish valuable insights for both theoretical science and aesthetics, thus bringing these disciplines together; and it is one of the attractive features of this approach to have specifically included the aesthetic component, which is so essential in all human systems and which *eo ipso* demands highly qualitative treatment.

Now to regard individual phenomena thus: not as isolated but as all deeply interrelated was also the point of view that reigned supreme in the scientific thought of Alexandria at the time when it was the center of the profound transcultural synthesis epitomized in the Great Library there. The immeasurable loss to us of this library dates from its destruction by fanatical mobs of the same brand as those who cruelly murdered with oyster shells that pinnacle of feminine preeminence in philosophy and culture, Hypatia, at the instigation of the infamous Cyril. He had gained for himself the position and title of bishop of Alexandria before proceeding so thoroughly to betray it and the ethics of his titular master, Jesus of Nazareth, whose bigoted adherents, paradoxically, accounted historically for more massacring of dissidents than did the non-Christian emperors of Rome, as Gibbon well notes in his history.

The crown jewel of Alexandrian thought was the doctrine of the *ordered interrelatedness* of all things by the power of what was then termed *sympátheia (συμπάθεια)* for want of a more technical terminology. To render this far-reaching thought into our analytic, scientific terms requires the sophisticated concept of holistic systems governed principally by the affinities (or antipathies) generated by resonances (or anti-resonances) in waves of some sort, i.e. in time periodicities, together with their cognate space periodicities. That this technical identification of the *sympátheia* doctrine with the theory of wave resonance was not hitherto made, points up one of the failures of too narrow specialization at the expense of a surer grasp of interdisciplinary interrelations: our mathematics and philosophy become too separated—a phenomenon preventing penetrating, interrelating insights.[17] It is only in the later twentieth century that we have been able to reclaim our intellectual heritage.

In résumé, then, system theory inherently involves cycles of some sort as a regulatory mechanism. Indeed it is very clear phenomenologically, even without the mathematical analysis, that what is termed negative feedback control must function *cyclically*, such control being implemented through changes that are effected periodically, as in each systemic cycle a given standard is compared with what was actually produced, changing course accordingly, much as a navigator keeps checking the stars and then re-steering to stay on course. Measurement itself is very often also a cyclic process, as anyone quickly learns who uses a rod of some unit length to measure a large room. Indeed, such measurement, with regard to the accurate re-placement and re-orientation of the rod, is also an example of a negative feedback control process.

But it has not yet been clearly enough realized that quantum physics is actually based on another and even subtler aspect of cycles—resonances—as its distinctive concept. Waves are fundamental in quantum theory since particles are analyzable into wave packets, a fact which emerged at about the same time in radio engineering as the concept of a *modulated carrier wave*, the amplitude of a wave of comparatively high frequency being modulated at much lower frequency, shown diagrammatically in figure 3–2.

All this is what makes possible what we have called chronosymbiosis: one entity's low phase is another's high, and vice versa. It is the very essence of resonant causation to arrange such resonant-feedback situations. The ordinary use of the time variable t is nothing but a linearly degenerate notion of time. We must do better than that to have a science adequate to the richness of experience. We must begin to think in terms of qualitative time, a time with inherent and shifting possibilities of change within its extension of duration, irrespective of the use or non-use we make of those possibilities. This view opens up a systemic approach to problems otherwise insoluble with a contentless and merely quantitative "t." Such notions, of course, lead to nonlinearity in mathematics. But, as we shall see in section 4.2, much more radical enlargements of method shall be needed to resolve the problems posed by chronosystems.

The late Erich Jantsch in his last definitive publication [51] was very much aware of the tremendous importance of the *timing* factor in complex systems.

He observes that "multilevel structures require the *synchronization* of many levels of self-organization dynamics. The ubiquitous fact of such a synchronization may be deduced from the systemic connectedness not only of structures, but, above all, of their homologous dynamics" (emphasis ours). In other words, the time waves have to be in resonance. And many other advanced system theorists are groping toward this clarification.

Plato in two important dialogues [52] voices much the same viewpoint, that of a chronosymbiotic, cosmo-ecologically resonant universe. Thus he writes in the *Republic* that "not only for plants that grow in the earth, but for animals that live on it, there are seasons of fertility and infertility of *both mind and body*, seasons which come when their periodic motions reach full circle." We have emphasized certain words to show how clearly Plato included the all-important psychic factors in his concept of time process and resonant causation. He also adds quite specifically [53] that if resonantly wrong conception times are chosen "then children will be begotten amiss" or else be "neither gifted nor fortunate." And in his *Timaeus* [54] Plato says that astronomical cycles strike fear into those devoid of the science of how to interpret them, for such are at the mercy of their ignorance, not having the means to prepare themselves against foreseeable future trends. There is no question that the Pythagoreans, devoted as they were to the cosmic meaning of numbers, frequencies, and periods of vibration, would not have showed or, more exactly, foreshadowed Plato's views here. Let us not forget that he opened his famous Academy in 386 B.C.E., just after his return from a year's stay with the leaders of the Pythagorean community in southern Italy. The perception of qualitative time died out with the rise of billiard-ball mechanics in the seventeenth century, and did not arise again until two hundred years later with the advent of quantum theory. It is now here to stay. We have regained the lost ground with interest.

All of which brings us back to those ever-attesting proofs of astronomical cyclical influence on earth through resonant causation: the tides. Tides are, in fact, primarily occasioned and synchronized by waves of gravitational intensity, thus released—as we know since Max Planck that all energy is— through quantized time "windows" or crested moments. So all energy is not only quantized but time-controlled. It is energies, acting through their material sheaths (which in turn are actually wave packets—see figure 3–2(D)) that cause all changes in the physical world. But it is time that enables those energies so to cause, by releasing them through its own inherent rhythmic structures. Thus we may say that chronotopological modes underly all the resonant energy-releases that form the standing waves that in turn manifest all material forms. Here indeed are tides—the very tides of cause.

In everyday life it is interesting to see how the pressure of time, in relation to desired ends, can cause oscillation to arise in very natural ways, given the constraints of a necessarily given duration interval and of a given purpose. Consider that, like a wave generated by some impact in an elastic medium, *time-pressure forces oscillation if the impact of its deadline is to be dealt with.* This very general theorem needs an example to be understood clearly. Let us suppose some pages need to be first photostated from a book before it is sent as a registered parcel, also required to be mailed by closing time of the post office on that day. Other letters by ordinary mail had also to be weighed that day at the post office before they could be mailed; and one letter had to be weighed before its enclosures could be inserted, because they had to be photostated first from the book. Hence the only way to do this was to use an oscillating system involving two persons taking the following steps:

1. *A* goes to the post office and weighs and posts all letters that could be posted. *A* also weighs, with dummy enclosures of same weight, the letter requiring the enclosures of photostats.
2. Meantme *B* photostats the necessary pages from the book to be mailed. But *B* has no time to photostat the enclosures for the letter because the deadline for registered mail is one hour earlier than the deadline for ordinary mail, and the photocopy shop doesn't close until the latter deadline.
3. Hence *B* photostats only the pages for the to-be-registered book, and then immediately wraps up the book and brings it to the post office and give it to *A* who gets it in under the deadline.
4. At that time *A* gives *B* the weighed and stamped letter. *B* removes the dummy enclosures, takes the letter back to the photoshop, and starts copying the enclosures.
5. Meanwhile *A* returns from the post office to get the letter and its enclosures from *B*, and then takes it back to mail it before the deadline for ordinary mail. This is easily done since the copying of the enclosures and the transit time both ways from post office to photoshop require well less time than the one hour available.
6. While *A* does that, *B* collates the other copies of the material, then rejoins *A* enroute from the post office and they both go home rejoicing.

Oscillatory programming has been victorious over time-pressure. There are many related examples of such a mode of optimization.

Cosmo-ecological thinking in twentieth century scientific circles began at least in 1911 when Arthur Shuster published a path-breaking paper [55] voicing the view that planetary effects were embedded in solar phe-nomena.

The next landmark came in 1923 with Ellsworth Huntington's thought-provoking book on the ecological relations between sun and earth [56], in which some important work by Henry Clayton was included that in turn supported Shuster's views. In the following year, Louis Bauer [57] published independent data correlating solar activity and terrestrial electricity, and showing double annual maxima for such correlations.

Then in 1940, William Luby [58] also observed planetary factors in sunspot frequency, pointing out that precessional or *turning* effects of the planets on the sun appeared to be more important than direct radial-tidal effects. Luby noted the same principle was at work in the movements of the Gulf Stream that were undeniably associated with extreme declinations of the moon (i.e. maximal distances above or below the earth's equatorial plane)—an oceanological phenomenon already noted by J.E. Pillsbury in the *U.S. Coast and Geodesic Survey Report* of 1983, though without Luby's sophisticated explanation.

Then in 1941 Clayton [59] who really devoted his entire life to cosmo-ecology, confirmed the observations of both Bauer and Luby. He advanced the subject still further by calling to attention the two crests of sunspot-number increase, pronouncedly associated with the orbital periods of Venus, Earth, and Saturn at maximum heliocentric declination—their greatest distance above (or below) the plane of the solar equator.

There was so little response to cosmo-ecological and chronotopological findings in their time that the interesting suggestions and data amassed by Bauer, Clayton, Huntington, Luby, and Shuster in this regard were practically totally neglected until the present book—so much stronger is fashion that fact in the history of the acceptance of scientific ideas. This book, providentially enough, rides a new wave, and there is reason to believe that this tide, like all others, is now starting to turn. The laws of chronotopology thus override even straightforward "factual" demonstra-tions: for even the latter are subject to cycles of acceptance; and changes of general opinion do not arise except in accordance with their own governing cyclicities of resonances.

What is worse, however, than the subjection to fluctuation of scientific fashion, is the attitude of deliberate denigration of the past—an attitude unfortunately that has increased because of its convenience in the face of the twentieth century publication (not information!) explosion, the sheer physical quantity of which in time discourages cross-referenced research. Such forced forgetfulness of the past is the antithesis of humanity's unique continuance of cultural memory, the loss of which would eventually be lethal to any civilization or society. And the origin of the word "lethal" is *Lethe* or the oblivion of forgetfulness.

The present writer has found a rich source of cosmo-ecological/ chronotopological data in the reports on ionospheric and geo-solar conditions published by the Central Radio Propagation Laboratory (CRPL of the U.S. National Bureau of Standards) at Washington, D.C., and then at Boulder, Colorado, from 1946 to the present: specifically the CRPL reports, "Ionospheric Data" and "Solar-Geophysical Data," and the valuable summary of North Atlantic radio propagation disturbances from October 1943 through October 1945. Analysis of these and of the CRPL "Daily North Atlantic Propagation Quality Figures" tables led the writer to an unquestionable shift in electromagnetic wave propagation quality whenever the sun's celestial longitude (λ) was a whole multiple of 30 degrees, as measured from the vernal equinox; that is, when $\lambda = 30n$ where $n = 0,1,2, \ldots 11$. We also found periodicities in propagation quality that were synchronous with the lunar longitude being $30m$, where $m = 0,3,6,$ and 9.

And the electrical engineer J.H. Nelson, who was employed by RCA Communications, Inc., long before the advent of radio astronomy, had found, since the 1940s, that the angles ($0°, 90°, 120°,$ and $180°$) formed between the planets, particularly the major planets, sun, and the earth were so accurately correlated with radio propagation quality that Nelson was able to use such configurations as the basis of verified *predictions of quality*—the commercially important bit—throughout his professional career. That is, he found[18] that planetary positions relative to the earth were correlated with the earth's experienced fluctuations of solar activity as mediated through the ionosphere; and topological dynamicist Ralph Abraham worked out a dynamical model capable of containing such effects and noting [60] that phenomena like planetary influence on terrestrial events "have a 'normal' explanation in this scheme."

Another more psychophysiological facet was added to the chronotopological systems data bank when two well-known practising London psychiatrists, Hans Eysenck and D. Nias [61], confirmed the work of the research psychologists Michel and Françoise Gauquelin, who had summarized their results in their work *Cosmic Clocks*. The Gauquelins had found that a rising or zenith position of Saturn (as viewed from earth at the time of birth) figured statistically far above chance among babies who later became professional scientists and physicians; and the same for professional athletes in the case of the planet Mars.

Eysenck and Nias concluded that there was no valid criticism to be made of either the Gauquelins' data or methods, and that cosmobiology "compares favorably with the best that has been done in ... any of the social sciences."

They concluded further that a human being still in the womb "tends to initiate its own birth processes in response to a particular planetary configuration. ... Some kind of signal emanating from the planets may somehow interact with the fetus in the womb, stimulating it to a struggle into birth at a certain [resonant] time." How such chrono-resonances may be understood in terms of quantum physics will be explored in a Supplement (v. first note of epilogue) and specifically, how an originally micro-shift in probability can change potential energies and hence entire outcomes.

The well-known topologist and expositor of theoretical mechanics, Ralph Abraham of the University of California at Santa Cruz, has, in kindred fashion, conceived that "the neural network functions mainly as a metabolic energizer for the maintenance of biochemical oscillation, and as a coupling device to other vibrators in the organism, such as the muscles and organs of perception. ... I propose that perception is a resonance phenomenon between the brain and external vibrators" [62] Abraham relevantly cites the work of Volkers and Candib [63] on high-frequency electromagnetic signals from muscular tissue, as well as Arthur Winfree's research on spiral types of chemical reaction waves [64], which appeared a decade before Winfree's interesting compilation on biological time [65]; and Abraham repeatedly refers to cosmobiology in his later publications.

Other latter twentieth century scientific investigators were on the same trail. As an article in *Time* noted [66]: "Dr. Ralph Metzner, a psychologist with Stanford University's counselling and testing center, uses astrology in a quarter of his cases in the same way Jung did. He thinks that it will soon be 'an adjunct to psychology and psychiatry' ... because it is 'much more complex and sophisticated than present psychological ways or systems.'" Metzner explained his views in greater detail in a later published paper [67].

The *London Times* reviewer of the work just discussed of Eysenck and Nias thoughtfully noted that "perhaps it is not the moment of birth that selects the future, but rather the future that selects the moment of birth." Such a time-reversed causation, as it were, is one of the prime characteristics of a chronosystem, as given in our first chapter, and we are now ready to give it more attention and turn to *la forza del destino* proper: the influence of the future, as well as of the past, on the present.

3.15 Future Feedback

There is always this bodiless half
This illumination, this elevation, this future.

—Wallace Stevens (stanza xxiii,
An Ordinary Evening in New Haven)

One of the most accessible illustrations of such future feedback is found again in those so subtle, complex, and instructive phenomena, the ocean tides. We have not yet mentioned what is called by seafarers "the age of the tide"—that is, the amount of lag behind the time of the generating gravitational impulse. Thus the lunar phases semi-diurnal tides of the North Atlantic have an average "age" or lag of one and a half days behind the time that their causing astronomical forces are exerted on the earth. It could be called a resonance response time to a periodic perturbing force. In some localities the lag reaches as long as a week.

Similar lags are shown interestingly in what is called the Barkhausen-Kurz effect. The technical definition is not at issue in the point here being made; suffice it to say, it is an oscillation produced in grid tubes of ultra-short radio wave circuitry. As Hannes Alfvèn's investigations of ultra-short waves made clear, the Barkhausen-Kurz oscillation is not an exact resonance effect since the negative resistances that occasion such oscillations never arise at the first calculated resonance point, and ordinarily never exactly at any resonance point of higher order.[19] That is, we must *in principle* not look for too exact timing agreements between effects and calculated causes in many resonance-response phenomena. Something like quantum indeterminacy seems to occur, but on a more macro-level and scale. The systematic lags in tide-peaks indicate that such phenomena have to do with nonlinear feedback relationships; and that when the lag involved is *negative*, with future-feedback or the future's interaction with the present.

Returning to the ocean's resonances, in some places there is the surprising phenomenon of a *negative age of the tide*, a negative lag, i.e., an *anticipation* of the forces. In such localities the maximal high or low tide now *precedes* the time of the external astronomical forces [68].

This notion was really dimly seen and adumbrated in the idea of "feedback causality . . . a flow of cause and effect in two directions [69,70]. And Michael Weir [71] has realized that goal-directed (i.e. directed by the perceived future) behavior is a part of the *entelecheia*—the concept of an in-held and self-directing aim—far and away Aristotle's most seminal concept.

It may well have come to him through Iranian sources devolving on the *fravashi* (more properly *fravarti*) notion: the in-dwelling, higher-end-shaping, guardian-awareness dwelling individually in all things.

At any rate, Weir's is one of the few twentieth century papers to have grasped that the present can be future-directed, one of the distinguishing features of chronotopological systems, as we have seen. What Weir finally ends with is a probabilistic trajectory-space of states instead of a state-determined system. He calls this a path-determined system, but he skirts the issue of future-directedness because that would require a richer notion of time than he has axiomatized and would lead directly into chronotopology. But he is very much on the right track, and his thought that it is the existence of several goals rather than instability as such that causes bifurcation is a more fruitful approach than catastrophe theory because it takes the nature of time more into account.

Already quite some time ago I pointed out [72] that adaptive and anticipatory control mean proper current timing *in continual* (i.e., periodic sampling) *feedback relation to the future* (potentials, aims, expectations, etc.). I also noted later the importance of feedback systems in which the control *standard* undergoes (r)evolutionary changes via a (dis)continuous guidance variable. It is relevant here to note, too, that the interconnectedness and mutuality so characteristic of chronotopological[20] systems is also characteristic of nonlinearity, and thus precludes any adequate treatment by methods of superposition, so useful in linear-wave phenomena and often, as a means of approximation, in some nonlinear situations as well. Linearity thus means the possibility of viable superposition or dissectability; whereas nonlinearity means that we are dealing with a nondissectable, holistic type of situation or system, with great interdependence of subsystems.

Time's topology is necessarily and essentially of this character and hence all natural phenomena are, since they are all embedded in the nature of Time. We mean here far more than the comparatively superficial phenomenon of the distortion of time *measurements* due to employing measuring signals of finite speed between a moving measurer and a moving object—that measurer thus forced into observing so awkwardly and with such built-in distortion. We really should not be surprised at nature's abundant nonlinearity, when merely finding the surface of relatively simple objects (e.g. an ellipsoid) unavoidably involves nonlinear differential equations. An egg is considerably more difficult! In fact, it is a problem not yet solved and, we suspect, may involve at least the first Painlevé transcendent as well, which requires more than elliptic functions for its determination, as Harold Davis' excellent text (far better than most later ones on nonlinear differential equations) makes clear [73].

One of John Casti's central conclusions in a paper on mathematical modeling [74] is perspicuous and has far-reaching implications. The conclusion to which we refer appears at the end of his section II and the beginning and end of Section III:

> What is needed are results which enable us to assert that a particular observed output pattern is stable (persists) over some range of local interaction hypotheses. . . . [We need] to construct models in which the observed macro-pattern imposes a class of local dynamics. . . . Whitney's theorem [which provides micro- from macro-dynamics] is another illustration of the point . . . that the global pattern actually induces a microdynamic that is unique, up to a coordinate change.

If we substitute macrocosmic for global or macrodynamic and microcosm or individual for microdynamic we see that Whitney's and related theorems, which Casti has so astutely grouped together conceptually, are actually an example of a general chronotopological principle that relates the inter-weaving of environmental patterns of periodicity with individualized event-occurrences and reaction-patterns: cosmo-ecology thus emerges, as a science combining climatology, orbital and secular variational astronomy, solar pulsation theory, chronobiology including chronopsychophysiology and chronopharmacology—all fields experiencing rapid development in the later twentieth century.

3.151 Nonlinear Waves and Future Feedback. In almost all mathematical treatises on waves, the basic paradigm employed is the so-called sine wavem whose varying height follows the projection or shadow of a revolving unit radius on the horizontal diameter of its circle. Thus the height of the wave, denoted in the language of nonarbitrary mathematical symbols as $y = \sin x$, varies between 0 and 1 as the wave rises and subsides (see figure 3–3).

Though the Chinese artists, and then their Japanese cultural inheritors, first featured such waves as shown in Figure 3–4, nature had them long before on every ocean beach. As a wave nears the land its crest bends over toward the land more and more until it breaks. Mathematically, its form assumes more and more the nonlinear profile of that figure.

We note in passing that the probability waves of quantum mechanics would be subject to the same law as they approached the beach of actualization, i.e. as the probability approached "1" or certainty of occurrence. Some years ago we adumbrated this concept less precisely and wrote that "the quantized appearance of energy is necessitated by the wave-nature of time. The waves of time breaking on the beach of occurrence, so to

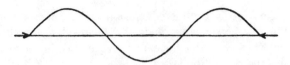

Figure 3-3. Ordinary Linear Sine-Type Wave (The above wave is actually an elastica curve, formed when a uniformly flexible yet stiff strip is pressed at both ends, as the small arrowheads indicate.)

speak, in releasing their energy create the effect of discrete particles or quanta of energy, while actually the source of the continuity of the phenomena lies in the wave itself. The celebrated wave-particle paradox of the nature of energy remains a paradox only so long as the chronotopological phases of the phenomena are left unrealized in the analysis" [75].

Since the ancient discovery that the frequency of a given vibrating string depended on its length, and the later one that the frequency, other things equal, depended on the square root of the tension in the string, people have dimly realized that waves and numbers are intimately linked. Then, as if the anciently known sea and lunar tides were not enough, our telescopes and other instruments made us aware of the great electromagnetic tides in the solar plasma, and before that, by the spectroscope, we knew that sunlight deluged us with a sea of vibrations that we perceive as colors.

Waves are like breathing—they are undulations, now convex, now concave, as shown in figure 3-3. Yet we have seen the profile of a sea-wave rolling ashore, and that is more like the illustration in figures 3-4 and 3-5. There is a profound distinction between the two kinds of profile shown in figures 3-3 and 3-4. In the first, a vertical line drawn anywhere will intersect the wave at only 1 point; but in the second, the vertical line may intersect in one, two, or three points as in *a, b,* or *c*. This second type is called a nonlinear curve, and its mathematics is far more demanding because its phenomena are subtler and more ramified. It is the basis of what is called

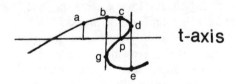

Figure 3-4. Basic Nonlinear Wave Form Showing Future Feedback into Present (from *d* to *p*) If Direction of Future Is Taken as the Positive Time Axis (as usually though inaccurately done—see text following figure 3-5)

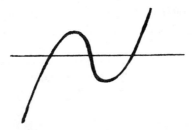

Figure 3-5.   Ordinary Cubic Function (not to scale) Seen as Resembling a 90° Rotation of the Nonlinear Wave Form of figure 3-4

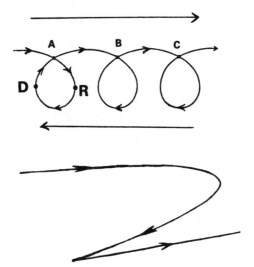

Figure 3-5 *bis*. *Above*: Loops Traced by Motions of Outer Planets. The figure is a stylized depiction of a three years' path for the planet Jupiter as it loops back into retrograde motion (direction of lower arrow) from direct motion (upper arrow). The letters D and R indicate the two stationary positions leading into direct and retrograde motion, respectively. Note similarity to figure 3-8.

Below: The Celestial Path of the Inner Planet Mercury as it Retrograded in 265 B.C.E. (after O. Neugebauer). Note similarity to figure 3-6 and 3-7.

---

*We pointed out before [76] the catastrophic quality of the nonlinear "Chinese"-type wave. Another interesting illustration of such a nonlinear wave is shown in figure 3–5 *bis* which depicts the path formed in the sky as seen from the earth when the planets Jupiter and Mercury turn retrograde and then direct.

elementary catastrophe theory, since such a "catastrophe" may occur on the line *d-e* where the amplitude suddenly drops from crest to trough as measured along the vertical.

Now let us turn figure 3–4 clockwise through 90° and we obtain the curve of figure 3–5 which is what is called a cubic equation (e.g. $x^3 + a_1 x + a_0 = 0$ where $a_{0,1}$ are constants) because the highest power of the unknown is a cube.

Hence we may conclude that a cubic is somehow essentially involved in nonlinear wave theory. More important for our purpose, let us consider the horizontal axis in figure 3–4 as the time axis, showing interval of duration proceeding, say, into the future from left to right. Then we at once see that if the point *p* is the present moment, then the movement *along the wave* proceeds *from future to present* from *d* to *p* and from present into past from *p* to *g*; while from *g* to *e* it proceeds normally from past to future. (On the allocation of the direction of becoming to the plus or minus direction, see discussion following figure 3–8.)

These observations confirm from another viewpoint our previous (chapter 2) definition of a chronosystem, part of that definition being nonlinearity. What if we have a *succession* of such nonordinary causal movements? We then obtain a wave some thing like this (figure 3–6). Now such a wave is actually obtainable as an "elastica curve" when a fairly stiff but vibrationally elastic rod is bent. The intrinsic equations of such curves require elliptic functions. However, we have found how they can be simulated by using a cubic modification of a circular (sine) function, for it will be noted that no vertical line passing through the wave-curve shown in figure 3–6 can intersect it in more than three points. The intrinsic equation is

$$d^2\psi/ds^2 = -\sin\psi \qquad (1)$$

where *s* is the arc length covered on the curve by a tangent line to it rotating through angle ψ. The relation between ψ and *s* can be expressed by means of

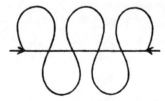

Figure 3-6.   Nonlinear Wave Train Shown by an Elastica Curve with $\theta = 55°$. Cf. figure 3 ($\theta = 30°$). Eq. (2) in the text is a useful approximation of this wave form derived by regarding the sine of a linear function of the independent variable as a cubic function of the dependent variable.

elliptic functions, and a parameter θ plays a fundamental role, whose sine (k in the usual notation) is the eccentricity of the ellipse involved. It is interesting that Equation (1) is exactly that for the motion of a simple pendulum where s replaces the time and ψ the initial angle from the vertical. Albert Eagle, in a too-little known but valuable work on elliptic functions [77], perceptively notes that "the inclination of elastica curves, as one goes along them, varies as the inclination of simple pendulum to the vertical varies with the time." The serpentine curve of figure 3–6 corresponds to a pendulum swinging with an amplitude of 110°, hence $k = \sin 55° = 0.819152. \ldots$

On a wall in the tomb of Seti I (19th Dynasty, Thebes, *ca.* 1300 B.C.E.) is shown the symbol of the power of all change and transformation (Khepera) being carried along by just such a future-interacting wave as shown in figure 3–6, stylized by the old cosmologist-priests in serpentine form. This highly nonlinear wave form reappears constantly in ancient Egyptian symbolizations of the wave-like, serpentine time-process.[21]

Showing more directly the link with that late twentieth century portion of bifurcation theory known as "catastrophe" (i.e. sudden change) theory, we can develop a curve very similar to the wave profile (cf. figure 3–4) of which Steve Smale well said [78] that the so-called "cusp catastrophe," which exhibits this profile in passing from a linear to a nonlinear wave (see figure 3–7) and which "is the most important example of a catastrophe." It develops directly, however, out of embedding a "Chinese wave" (called a bit too unperspicuously "the fold" in catastrophe theory) in the wave-front surface of a linear wave as figure 3–7 shows. We noted this dominating type of

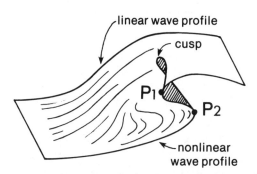

Figure 3-7.   How a Linear Wave Transforms into a Nonlinear Wave (P_1 and P_2 are points of discontinuous jumps, either up or down, depending on which direction along the profile is taken as the direction of becoming)

catastrophe in a 1962 lecture sponsored by the Theoretical Physics Department of the University of Naples, long before we heard of Thom's work. Our analysis was published in 1965 by the National Research Council of Italy [79] and we noted there, giving a figure showing the same type of profile as in figures 3-3 and 3-7:

> Systems whose differential equations are not linear ... are capable of discontinuous jumps in amplitude as either the frequency or amplitude of the driving force is continuously varied; and what is very important, they also can show generation of harmonics and subharmonics of the driving force, and hence the related phenomenon of frequency entrainment, wherein the oscillation frequency of the system itself is controlled by the driving force or frequency. Thus synchronization can result. Also, nonlinear equations and systems may have many equilibrium states, which may often be a guarantee of better stability, that is, one associated with a higher probability of endurance. It is not too much to say that, with sufficient unpredictability of environment (i.e., of perturbations) it is only the nonlinear systems which have any great survival probability at all. It is the reason which doubtless plays a fundamental part in the fact that the vast majority of systems we actually observe—and if we measure accurately enough, we can say all—in nature are nonlinear.
>
> Nonlinear systems are more lifelike too in that only they can react discontinuously to a continuous input. The equations of such systems are intimately related to a quite sophisticated feedback, as their coefficients are functions of the operating conditions or of the dependent variable. In linear systems the coefficients are constant, and in linear systems with variable parameter the coefficients are functions of the independent variable. Neither of these types is actually nonlinear, although the latter often may appear so.
>
> Another very important property of nonlinear waves (implied in what was said above on discontinuous jumps) is that a perpendicular to the direction of propagation, drawn to the wave profile, may cut the profile in more than one point. Such waves possess corpuscle-like as well as wave-like properties, and we must look to them for the solution of the wave-particle impass in modern physics, other than the defeatist 'solution,' which is none at all, of giving up all hope of successfully conceiving of what our equations, numbers, and observations refer to. Anything which behaves like both a corpuscle and a wave—as do both light waves and fundamental particles—must be associated with a deep-seated nonlinearity.

It will be noted that the idea of the excellent concept called "resilience" by C.S. Holling [80] as distinct from the more pedestrian (and precarious!) "stability" is here adumbrated. We will have more to say on resilience in chapter 6.

Returning to a new development of the wave profile under discussion, we note that the ordinary sine wave function $y = \sin (2\pi x/\lambda)$ shows y as the linear function of the sine of an angle x. It is clear from figures 3–4 and 3–5 that the wave profile has the shape of a cubic function, and we see that figure 3–7 shows a succession of such "cubic" profiles.[22] We then set up the wave form $f(y^3) = \sin x$ where now we have the sine as a cubic function of the dependent variable. We worked on this problem in November of 1982 and finally found a suitable function that would accomplish the needed nonlinear wave *succession*, like the elastica curve of figure 3–7, but expressed in the easier terms of a sine function, thus providing a simpler approach to applied problems involving the very commonly seen cusp catastrophe, and even envisaging systems where such catastrophes periodically occur, as in real life, as any insect ecologist, for example, knows.[23]

Continuing with our equation for a succession of nonlinear waves, we finally determined the following function as optimal for study, and as one that could be suitably parametrized to fit various situations:

$$y(3-y^2) = \sqrt{5} \sin \tfrac{1}{2}t \qquad (2)$$

or

$$t = 2 \text{ arc sin } y(3-y^2)/\sqrt{5} \qquad (3)$$

This equation has three real roots for all real values of t such that $|\sin\tfrac{1}{2}t| < 2/\sqrt{5}$; two real roots (actually three, with two coincident) for $|\sin\tfrac{1}{2}t| = 2/\sqrt{5}$; and one real for $2/\sqrt{5} < |\sin\tfrac{1}{2}t| \leq 1$. Moreover, y is extremal when $t = \pm(2n + 1)\pi$, $n = 0,1,2,3\ldots$; and if $y = 0$, then $t = \pm 4\pi n$. The functions of the type given in Equations (2) and (3) are interesting approximations to the elastica wave forms (figure 3.7) at about $\theta = 55°$; just as the ordinary sine wave itself approximates the nonlinear elastica wave with θ at about 30° (figure 3–3). These basic wave interrelations have not previously been noticed, though they cannot but aid the applied chronosystem analyst.

The interesting thing about these functions is that when the independent variable t is taken as time, we see that there is a continual periodic feedback from future into present, and from present into past, just as there should be. In the nature of time, experience—both in inner, felt (intensive) nega-space, and in outwardly perceived, extensive posi-space—moves along the *arc* of the wave form, dipping both into the future and the past as time (i.e. via the values on the t-axis) proceeds. The curves, of course, also show the more obvious portions of feedforward from present into future and past into present. Here is the fundamental time wave, in which the intensity of experience at any given point in time is measured by the degree of change (experienced in both inner and outer space) per unit of duration. Mathematically, that would be controlled by the slope of the tangents to the wave curve at $y = 0$.

If we want to take this phenomenon into account we must generalize the function and write instead of Equation (2), introducing as little alteration as possible,

$$y(3-y^2) = \sqrt{5} \sin (\tfrac{1}{2} \, t/s) \tag{4}$$

where the parameter s is associated to the intensity of experience. [Note that s here is not the s of Equation (1).] Then

$$\dot{y}_{t=0} = \sqrt{5}/6s \tag{5}$$

Thus as s increases, $\dot{y}$ decreases and there is more extended interaction with both future and past in almost every moment. Indeed, s is actually another function of t, and its fluctuations determine calmer or stormier seas of time as the case may be. We do not yet know enough chronotopology to determine that function, but there are methods to estimate it empirically; and outbreaks of hostilities, breakdowns in negotiations, etc., are much more likely to occur during periods characterized by high s than otherwise. With s on the increase, there are more intensive and extensive uprushings of normally buried memories into present and current contexts, as well as greater inpourings of anticipation and pulls of as yet unimplemented plans and visions: pulls of the future.

So the experimental profile of the wave front of a time wave is skewed with respect to both past and future. The arc-line or path of experience reflects and expresses the interrelations of change and duration; and the amount of change per unit of duration expresses the intensity of experience at a given point in time.

There is another form in which these various feedbacks can be depicted as in figure 3–8(A). It turns out to be another elastica curve, this time the analogue of a torsional pendulum, with θ about 150°. The (nonlinear) wave train is somewhat like the form of a trochoidal type of curve, formed by a point on a disc between its center and circumference as the disc is rolled along a straight overhead track. If the arc is imagined as being traced from left to right, then the sub-arcs can be described as follows: $a \to b$: feedforward into future; $b \to c$: future feedback into present; $c \to d$: feedback from present into past; and $d \to a$: feedforward from past into present. Note that there is no direct feedforward from past to future without passing through the present, and here again the model accords with our experience.

Memories can, of course, influence our hopes, visions, desires, and destinies; but that influence is filtered and cross-referenced through our current state of consciousness, whether we are aware of it as in the waking

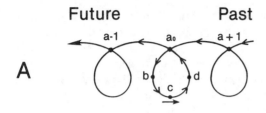

A

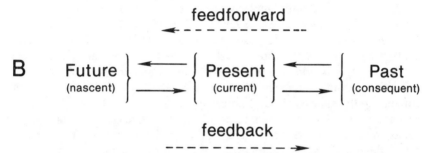

Figure 3-8. A. Trochoidal Form of Time Development. B. Characterization of the Loops of figure 3-8A

state, half-aware and quickly consciously forgetting as in the dream state, or not consciously aware of it at all, though it is still operative in that vast region of unconscious awareness that is too often inaccurately described as the "unconscious." Note, too, that similarly, the past can feed into the future only through the present, in a kind of overarching simultaneity.[24]

The "time line" consciously perceived without the subconsciously incessant workings of memory and desire is thus simply traversed on the arc passing through a_+, a_0, and a_-, etc., without any need to be consciously aware of the feedback and feedforward paths connecting past, present, and future states, those more hidden arcs being diagrammatized in figure 3–8(B). We do not ordinarily realize these feedback-and-forward turbulent "bubbles" in the (normally to us) laminar flow of time. Some poets and prophets in non-normal states of more powerful awareness have sensed them; and many more quotations to this effect might be adduced than the few given previously in the course of this book.

In figure 3–8(A) the present conscious moment is a_0, although the time loop associated to that moment dips into both past and future; a_{+1} is the past moment leading into its loop, and a_{-1} is the future moment poised at its loop. We have deliberately assigned positive numbers or accumulations to the past and negative numbers (which may be regarded as the molds or solid "negatives" of positive numbers) to the as-yet unformed future.

The theory of functions bears us out here for it is with negative arguments that active wave-like phenomena arise in the most basic of functions as Euler's Gamma function and the Euler-Riemann Zeta function; whereas their behavior on the positive side is accumulative and non-oscillatory. Continue the likewise basic Fibonacci series[25] into negative arguments and you will see the same phenomenon arise; the positive sequence of terms 0,1,1,2,3,5,8,13,21,55,89, and so on, whereas the negative sequence of terms is oscillatory: $\ldots -89,+55,-21,+13,-8,+5,-3,+2,-1,+1,0$. Even the powers of -1 itself oscillate, whereas those of $+1$ do not. Thus $(+1)^n = 1$ where n is any integer; yet $(-1)^n = +1$ if n is zero or even, and $(-1)^n = -1$ if n is odd. There are deep implications in these observations, giving the startling agreement between mathematics and the nature of the structure of the spatio-temporal universe.

Hence we see past moments as positive; and future ones, yet unmanifest moments, as negative or "not there." Zero itself, with its own mysteries, is thus to be associated with the current or present moment.

3.16 Fate and Free Choice Are Not Contraries

The only meaningful or precise interpretation of fate is that of a set of *consequences* from some act or commitment or structuralization already effected. The term "fate" is in fact so used in comparative embryology, to refer to the eventual organic structure that is to be associated with a particular site in the embryo; and molecular biology is fine-focussing such "fates" to specific genes, those tiny controllers of biological destiny.

Let us for a moment imagine a world *without* fate or laws of consequence. A world without an ordered effect-structure, a network of consequential implications, would be one in which it would be impossible to predict. Any actin at all would result in unforeseeable effects. We ordinarily do not realize how much in our movements and acts we are constantly depending upon the fact that the world in which we live possesses definite laws of consequence. In our imagined world, for instance, tossing away something might result in its coming back and striking one. Or what had been solid ground beneath one's feet could, at the next step, become hollow space.

It is clear that one would have no free choice whatsoever in such a world for the very good reason that one could not predict. To *plan* a new course, we must inevitably be able to count on certain factors remaining the same while the plan is being implemented. Prediction (i.e. some stability of consequence) is essential to free will.

Without laws of consequence, free choice would shrink to a microscopic mockery of itself, and we would be the slaves of an utterly capricious universe. Of course, there may arise situations in a consequence-endowed world where we—through either insufficient foresight or too-rapid changes— cannot avoid certain consequences. But that fact is part of the very realities that also guarantee our ability of free choice. To plan new alternatives requires a fundamental stability, as well as flexibility, in the structure of the universe. Luckily, we live in such a world.

The basic law then boils down to: "pay and take." That is, fulfill the required conditions of your planned or chosen consequences, and then they will be able to be implemented and eventuate. Realizing this principle, which is also deeply bound up with the nature of time, is what is basically meant by the phrase "to be realistic." Realism in this sense goes beyond either pessimism or optimism—both of which in too large doses lead to unrealism and hence inevitable setbacks; for the nature of any reality will persist and effect results whether human beings are aware of that reality or not.

In general, in chronosystems there is no unique future because of the existence of alternative choices and paths. Hence in such systems *desire-priorities* (sometimes more vaguely and less usefully called "values") become extremely important in prediction. Clarifying the nature and distribution of such priorities constitutes one of the principal contributions of the psyglyphic analysis discussed in chapter 4.

Desires all have a history (a past), constitute a current demand (present), and project a dénouement (future), all three factors being inextricably intertwined and mutually interactive, i.e., thoroughly nonlinear, mathematically speaking. Again, the words "past," "present," and "future" betray the deep-seated inadequacy and inapplicability of ordinary analytic, linearly sequential thinking with regard to Time.[26] In conventional state-space treatments of systems theory, to cite a typical standard text [83], one must from the outset "specifically rule out relations whose present outputs depend on *future* values of the inputs" (emphasis in original).

That is exactly what *cannot* be done in chronosystems. An example from biology comes conveniently to mind. In its 1983 Conference Proceedings Circular, the New York Academy of Sciences announced a conference on what is now a well-accepted part of electrophysiology: fluctuating electric potentials in the brain that are event-related and that characteristically occur *before* an action is performed (e.g. swinging a tennis racket to hit the ball). Here is a quite everyday category of instances of future-dependent input; and such phenomena, so characteristic of chronosystems, are fundamentally linked with that deep relation and interdependence of fate and free choice with which this discussion began. We need to know *more* than some linear past → present to predict properly. Conventional sunspot predictions based on past averages have been as much as 12½% wrong (e.g. in 1979 at the peaking of cycle 21) at times of unusual planetary clustering. On that occasion, in fact, a temporary decrease had been predicted for the time when in the outcome a maximal increase occurred [84].

True, the present is always there, making seeming illusion of past and future—yet they retain quite objective reality in their counterinvasion of the present as memory and anticipation, respectively. The dynamic nature of memory is too often overlooked. Under memory are subsumed habits and, in general, substructures and foundations already established, and skills formed through prior practice. Under the rubric of the present fall sensation, perceptions, and acts par excellence, for every perception or sensation is also an act; while the future is involved in hopes, expectations, and wishes—all forms of desire.

Indeed desire is in a bonafide sense the very "memory" of the future, and its persistence is the strength of that inverse memory that addresses a direction opposite to the memory of the past, which is a recall or summoning up of what was once achieved (in the present). Desire as the memory of the future is a retention of *intent*, a constant addressing—the word is exactly enough used here to serve in a desire-simulating computer program—of what is being directed towards an achievement not yet consummated in the present. To desire, then, is to "remember" the future.

Throughout all these processes runs imagination[27], too: one can imagine or represent inwardly to oneself how someone is doing *now*, or how they *were* at some time, or how one estimates they *will be* at some other time. Further, imagination can function even in the still more removed world of *might be*. One can imagine what might, may, or would be (depending on the strength of consciously or unawarely estimated probabilities) under various circumstances or conditions. When we are in a position to specify conditions, we have a *would be* . . . if, or the computer programmer's IF THEN, ELSE: e.g., if A, then B; else C. When less in command of knowing the variously determining conditions, then we have the less restricted and more imaginative *may be*, and with even less certainty, the *might be*.

So the roots of the past are always pushing back into and feeding from the present. The branched arms of the future are there, too, beckoning us along pathways of wish and desire which are potential and potentiation—the creating of the very wherewithal to be able to do something later. And the past, too, enters the future by way of (intellectually or emotionally) remembered elements, restructured in wish and imagination. Something of all this richly nonlinear interaction of future/present/past has already been indicated analytically, and we saw how the past and future interacted through present acts. Now we see that they may also interact through either conscious or unconscious imagination. These considerations can be of extreme practicality in explaining and predicting human behavior, and so cannot be neglected in any adequate discussion. When we add imagination to figure 3–8 we obtain an unequivocally nonlinear flow diagram (figure 3–9), in which we have placed appropriate number units. Since $(+i)^2 = (-i)^2 = -1$ in the model, imagination acting on itself either consciously or unconsciously is inherently future-directed.[28] In the future, the to-become, lie its natural development and application—which accords with experience and supports the model. But *unconscious* imagination interacting with conscious imagination refers to the *past*, to the experiences which launched those seeds of unaware images. Using the model, $(-i)(+i) = +1$ again confirms experience. Even if the model serves only as a convenient mnemonic device in thinking accurately about chronosystems, it justifies itself.

As figure 3–9 also shows, the future, both in terms of imagination and present act, can also interact with the past by reinterpreting memories and changing habits (for better or worse) in the interests of newly emerging aims

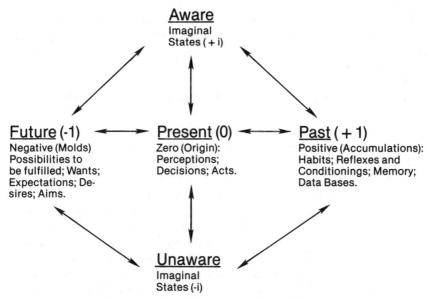

Figure 3-9. The Networking of Time

and strong desires. So, too, the past can help mold the future through delimiting of potential. The past, of course, directly influences the present and the present, the future; and these two modes have always been so obviously in evidence as to overshadow the other subtler, yet nonetheless effective interactions we have discussed.

The present also can act to alter the past, as when we change habits, generating new types of memories to supplant the former ones in importance. Similarly, but less understood or perceived, although universally operative, the future influences the present by *planning*, which is but the schematic specification of ways of implementing desires, hopes, and wishes. This means, among other things, that simplistic, linear notions of causality will have to give way to the deeper notion of resonant and future-involved causality. For the most part, we do not act solely in response to stimuli from present or past, but often more frequently in response to signals from the future, to straws in the winds of time. Such activity can take quite prosaic forms as becomes evident in observing the otherwise inexplicable actions of men in process of constructing a machine or boat or building, a feline stalking prey, or some other everyday occurrence of future-directed activity. The phenomenology of time demands that we traverse the arcs of experience and not simply an omissively idealized line of duration. We experience influences of both anticipations and habit-orientations—influences from the future and from the past on and in the present.

We thus have arrived full scale at our starting consideration: that rules for orderly consequence are part and parcel of what it means to exercise free choice.

3.2 The Computer as a Kronos Machine

Though few outside the field are aware of it, the *sine qua non* of the construction and functioning of any computer is a basic internal master-clock that generates a series of square waves in time (see figure 3–10). These mesh with other pulsed oscillations to provide time windows for the various essential transports of net electronic charges that in turn underlie the execution of any program whether serially or parallel processed. The program execution thus proceeds in a chain of wave-resonances and anti-resonances that together perform the complicated and intermeshing selection and gating operations that are the dynamic heart of the computer. No electronic computer can operate without a system of internal clock-pulses at precise regular intervals (of very short duration). All the computer's acts and

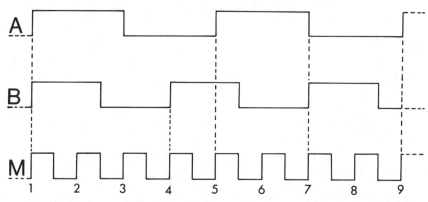

Figure 3-10. The Computer Is Controlled by Phase Resonances of Its Internal Clocks as They Time-Gate Its Functioning, All Clocks Being Governed by a Master-Control Clock

Wave A and B: Clock pulse for gating two functions, "A" and "B."

Wave M: Master-Control clock pulse (square waves or successive unit functions).

At master pulse 1, all three clocks are in phase.

At master pulses 1, 5, and 9, the M and A clocks are in phase and the "A" function can occur.

At master pulses 4 and 7, M and B are in phase and function "B" can occur.

functions depend on the synchrony patterns or syzygies of these clock-pulses at various key places in its circuitry. Internal computer time is quantized.

The phenomenon of software vying with and even on occasion eclipsing the importance of hardware in the crucible of the market-place, that melting pot of pooled experience, is now too well established to need further justification. That phenomenon entails, of course, a like importance of programming languages, and the desirability of some exit out of the current babel of them. Some guidelines to that end, in the direction of a universal assembler language (UAL) and a Syntactical Universal Programming Language (SUPL), were voiced by the writer as chairman of the artificial intelligence section of the Third World Congress of Cybernetics and General

Systems convened in 1975 at Bucharest, and published in the Proceedings [86]. The key idea behind SUPL is *typological* thinking as described in chapters 2 and 4 of the present book. That idea is, in turn, closely related to associative processes induced through *context*. As we wrote in 1978 [87]:

> The basic trouble is that *parsing* is *not* the way anyone learns, understands, or uses a language. But context or meaning *is*—as the main architects of all natural languages, the poets of every tongue, knew and still know well. Hence to base the specification or programming of natural languages on a confessedly "context-free" (hence parse-full) basis must be self-defeating. And so it has proved. Semantics, rather than grammar, is the key to language specification.
>
> A fundamental principle, not yet clearly enough realized, is that syntax is *contextual* rather than formal. Parsing just won't do the job, so neither will any context-free approach. The essence of a language is its idioms and they are invariably based on semantic realities rather than on grammatical artificialities.
>
> As early as 1960 (in a report published in 1962 [88] I stressed the context as inherent to language and programming, and *context-analysis* (rather than mere formal parsing gymnastics) as the key to language specification—each language differing in its mode of handling such analytics.

The basic idea of UAL is simple, though so fundamental that it is easily overlooked. The possibilities of all software have, as their lower constraint or limit, the possibilities inherent in the basic electronic hardware (and its architecture) built into the computer. The upper constraint on software is simply the limitation of any given software designer's creative imagination and ingenuity. The middle constraint consists, of course, in the several constraints imposed by the nature of the problem itself and/or the set of givens or initial conditions in a particular instance.

Having said that much, we can pursue the matter by noting that computers in general are capable of only a necessarily finite, and in practice fairly small, set of basic operations, irrespective of the proliferation of names by which they are called. Contents, whether consisting of data (operands) or program elements (operators), may be electronically moved from one place to another in the machine. That "place" may be a temporary or virtual buffer or bus area, dynamically shifting—perhaps by the nanosecond; or it may be a more stable and physically fixed location in the machine. If it is a shifting area or group of bits, the shifts may be governed by various conditions, or the whole area may shift in physical location constantly, following a set of evocatory associations—the calls and demands of some associative memory system.

Depending on the program motivation for those movements, all internal bit and bit-group transfers will fall under several clearly defined categories, the primary ones being: storage (momentary, temporary or archival); recall from some store; transfer from one store to another; transfer from a store to some operations area or bus (displayed or not); transfer from some store or buffer to some output.

3.21 Defining the Computer

There has been no serious attempt, despite the enormous publicity given to the subject, to define what a computer in essence is, rather than simply describe what it does and offer that description as a bonafide definition. Actually, that the computer is a very sophisticated type of recording and reactivation device has not been understood, largely because what is recorded was not perceived.

The computer is a servomechanism for both the writing and the implementation of *ways of thinking*, usually called "programs" when they are focused on the solutions of particular problems or kinds of problems. In brief, the computer is a thought recorder and reactivator. That is what makes it a far more sophisticated machine, on a much higher level than a television recording device, for example, which records and replays changes of form, color, motion, and sound. Unlike the sensation processes, however, one of the prime necessities of which is unexceptionable fidelity to the original, the process of thought possesses intrinsic and necessary tolerances, and an innate leeway allowing it to adjust to changing circumstances. That is, the process of thinking is unavoidably *conditional* in nature.

The computer, to record thought, must have the means to simulate it. It does this through switching circuits that are homeomorphisms or non-arbitrary analogues to logical primitives like AND (and/)OR, (either/)OR, and NOT. But a computer, to imitate thought successfully, must also be able in its behavior to simulate the act of *distinguishing* one datum or signal from another. To do this, it must be able to simulate by pre-built electronic means the psychic act of *comparing* or judging.

Soon after the basic circuits for the logical primitives became known, largely through the work of Claude Shannon, *comparator and selector* circuits were also worked out that could electronically "compare" and "select" binary-coded signals. The binary code or base-two number system was essential to use here, since a switch could only be on ($=$ YES or 1) or off ($=$ NO or 0).

Since the ancient Egyptians [89] it had been known that any number could be represented in this system, which uses only powers of two, namely 1,2,4,8,16, and so on, remembering that these are respectively, 2^0, 2^1, 2^2, 2^3, and 2^4. Indeed the ancient Egyptian system of multiplying or dividing two numbers depended entirely on a version of base-two arithmetic [90], which appeared later (*ca.* 1000 B.C.E.) in China under the guise of the *I-Jing* (Cantonese *Yi-King*) system of yang (—) and yin (— —), corresponding to the 1 and 0 of the base-two system. This fact was already known to Gottfried Leibniz's informant, the Jesuit missionary J. Bouvet writing to Leibniz from China in November 1701, in response to Leibniz's having sent Bouvet a write-out of the base-two numeral system [91].

What really produced the thought recorder was the "IF ... THEN; ELSE" circuit, which thus provided the essential elements of the thinking process in electronically simulated form: comparing, selecting, and then acting in one way on one outcome and in another, on another. It must be stressed that all this simulation is accomplished by pre-human thinking built into the clever homeomorphic circuitry[29] which per se is quite devoid of awareness, feeling, or any other psychic component. One can even simulate a more advanced computer with sharp enough use of a more primitive one in some instances, showing that no actual thinking at all is involved in the machine.

I still have the excellent little programmable calculator that was manufactured by Compucorp of Los Angeles in the early 1970s—their model *Scientist* 324G. It was a very simple machine—a mere 80 byte program memory—even though it had one of the first LSI (large scale integrated) silicon "chips" at its core. But it did have 10 scratchpad memories, programmably accessible, as well as an autostop on "error." One of the defined errors was the overflow induced by attempting to divide by zero, and another was induced by trying to obtain the square root of a negative number. (Arithmetically this little computer was only up to the seventeenth century.) It had, of course, no keys for jumping or for subroutines that would, when completed, return to the main program; neither did it have conditionals or DO loops.

Nonetheless it had a built-in precision to 13 decimal places—better than most personal computers on the market a decade later, which could provide only up to 10 decimal places. The point, however, is that one could program both DO loops and a conditional stop at a prescribed number. The loops were effected by using one of its ten storages as an operational cycle memory and including in the program a "subtract-one-unit" instruction that would apply to that cycle storage or counter. Then to stop the process at zero, say, all that was necessary was one more instruction to program at the appropriate phase in the cycle a division of, say, 1, by whatever number was in the cycle counter. When zero was attained in it, that division instruction would cause an automatic stop. Meantime, the needed results had been *programmably* collected and assembled in other designated storages.

One could also program it to recursively find the roots of given polynominals, real or complex, and to autostop at a predesignated accuracy of approximation. One got around the square root negative numbers by programmably designating a given storage as the repository of the imaginary part of the result and programmably arranging matters so that multiplication between any numbers so designated would be multiplied by -1. The recursive behavior was achieved by simply disregarding the solemn rule in the instruction manual never to omit a "STOP" command at the end when writing a program into the machine.

Of course, none of these capabilities was given in the user's manual: they all arose through "legally forbidden" ways to deploy the circuitry. Yet they were all implications of the hardware and could be discovered by anyone with sufficient imaginative interest. Obviously, this small device which was able to execute simple IF ... THEN; ELSE instructions no more "knew" what it was doing than the much larger machines with far more sophisticated conditional instructions implicit in their hardware. The electrons in either case are simply doing what comes naturally to them as they encounter the various constraints and pathways of the circuitry that was intelligently designed for expressly and literally ulterior motives by thinking humans, and then constructed either directly (by hand) or indirectly with the aid of automatic or even robot devices,[30] whose prototypes, of course, were also built by human hand. The moral of this entire story is a very basic *Theorem*: Every result a computer produces must be so produced by some implication of its circuitry, including built-in pseudo-randomizers.

The *Corollaries* are:

1. No program can be performed on a given computer unless the electronic consequences of each instruction of that program lie within the circuitry capabilities of the machine's hardware.

2. A computer can do nothing that is not an implication of its program.

Of course, a computer might well provide and act on implications not humanly foreseen (or even not normally foreseeable because of huge data mass or complexity). But such phenomena, far from demonstrating any psychic or bonafide psychological act on the part of a computer, merely demonstrate the well-known "magnification effect" embodied in many inventions, and even literally in, for instance, the electron microscope. The computer in handling such colossal masses and complexity of data and instructions, or in supplying unforeseen confirmations or implications, is producing a magnifying, electronic *simulation* of human thought processes, as on the mechanical level, a steam shovel magnifying simulates a muscular arm and hand. The computer thus serves as a very useful electronic homeomorph of the mind, allowing us to see more clearly the precise necessary and sufficient conditions of our various thought processes, but it no more thinks than an electric typewriter thinks to print the letter "A" when the appropriate key is struck.

The computer has, in brief, a determinate behavior. True, as we wrote some time ago, a computer could be made to simulate unpredictable moods, for example, by its designer interlocking combinations of long-term (longer than average human life span) and shorter term cycles, so that no pattern of its behavior would ever recur for, say, a hundred or even a hundred thousand years. But such prestidigitation (which is all most so-called "artificially intelligent" devices amount to) changes the ultimate determinism not a bit. Even if a built-in randomizer, like a radioactive substance, were introduced into the computer, we would then simply have meaningless randomness and not intelligently directed, much less creative unpredictability as in the best of human genius.

What the computer does teach well, however, is the lesson that after the initial creative human insight (always launched in humans by intense affective components: feelings, deep interests, intense motivations, and the like), the *rest* of the development of any idea is in comparison mechanical and is machine-simulable and -performable. That is, the greater part of our mental processes are deterministic routines, quite simulable by the electronic means we ourselves have now devised. But let it not be forgotten—as it too often seems to be by some schools of artificial intelligence theory—that such electronic circuits do not and could not have come into existence without the originally psychic process of living human thought.

This fact leads to another theorem, one of constructibility: If H can make C, but C cannot make H, then H is a greater entity than C. Thus humans can produce computers, but computers cannot produce human beings; and this distinction of differential constructibility is crucial. We can now appreciate the really logically inappropriateness of Marvin Minsky's remark [92] that "there is nothing more important than computers." He forgot that humans are, and immeasurably more so. But perhaps Minsky was speaking only rhetoric and what he really meant was that no field is more important than artificial intelligence, and hence the most important people in the world are artificial intelligence theorists and technicians. If this is what he actually meant, it is more understandable because it is more human: each human being wants to feel his or her own activity has prime significance.

But such distinctively human feelings are quite alien to the simply electronic nature of computers, and so the above remark comes with whatever sense it has, squarely back into the human fold. We do not single out this one spokesman whom we know and like personally; but only cite his attitude as one entertained misguidedly and in psychological naivety, and as one to be avoided if we want a viable human future. Computers, like all other machines, make good servants but very poor masters. The degree to which man cultivates computolatry is the extent to which he must gradually disinherit himself from his own natural intelligence. Thus near the end of the twentieth century, the human race came to be weighed in Time's balance both ecologically and technologically. We shall return to some aspects of these sociological implications of computers in chapter 6. Computers are to be *used*—not abused to enslave people or nations which, in politically paranoid or megalomaniac hands, they could well do.

The computer, then, is a device for recording and re-implementing human thought processes, and is only inappropriately turned into either an idol or a tyrant by humans so desiring to deploy it for various quite human motivations of their own. But such a thought-process recorder and re-implementer is in itself a benchmark achievement in terms of our handling of time: the computer can effectively displace consciousness or human awareness in time by means of an electronic counterpart that simulates the presence of intelligent behavior. The computer is a Kronos[31] machine, enabling previously impossible chronotopological connections to be made.

The computer can also be programmed to simulate very slow (e.g. geological) processes so accurately that we may learn in a few hours what we could not have known even after millennia of normal observation. The same applies to computations that would normally exceed a lifetime. Other types of programs could depict extremely rapid (e.g. intra-nuclear or intra-cellular) changes in much slower terms so that again we might observe otherwise unobservable processes and relationships. The computer is thus a time displacer, a time compressor, and a time expander.

3.22 The Computer's Functional Architecture

Now that we see clearly what the computer is (and is not) we can explore its functional architecture—the optimal categories in terms of which its necessary repertoire of functions may be understood, as well as its minimal vocabulary of commands, instructions, and effects. What we are saying is that there is a theory of functional architecture for the computer. It is, of course, directly related to hardware design, as we have already seen. Delineating it becomes principally a matter of paying attention to what is appropriate and natural.

The three categories that emerge are, first, the functional triple of Address, Instruction, Data (a content categorization); and next, the hardware-coordinated triple: Input, Throughput, Output. Next we have another triple, now concerned with internal functioning: Memory (Storage/Recall), Arithmetic/Logic String Processing, and Transduction systems. Finally, we have a fourth triple concerned with external functioning: Control, Servo, and Audio-Video outputs. Throughout any processing also runs a twofold role categorization of codons: Operand, Operator.

These considerations can provide a concise and topologically uniform mapping of both internal and external processes and capabilities of a computer in its most general form. See figure 3–11(*a*), (*b*), (*c*), and (*d*), the explanation for which follows.

(*a*) *Key Mapping of the Fundamental Functional Types of Electronic Codons, the Life-blood of the Computer*
　　C: electronic *C*odons, which may concern
　　　　A: *A*ddressing
　　　　I: *I*nstructions
　　　　D: *D*ata
　　P: the *P*rogram or controlling set of codons that coordinates generation, movement, and transformation of all other codons involved in the processing.

(*b*) *Topologically Similar Mapping of Basic Processing Stages and Levels (BASIC)*
　　STAY: *Stay*put i.e., basic codon-retention facility of a CPU (Central Processing Unit), without which none of the other functions are possible.
　　　　In: *In*put, including sensors
　　　　THRU: *Thru*ughput or actual processing of Input
　　　　OUT: *Out*put or the final transformation of the Input in the form called for by the Program
　　SCS: *S*upervising *C*ontrol *S*ystem, including security with its own stayput.

(*c*) *The Same Topology Maps the Typology of the Computer's Internal Functions*
　　P: 　the *P*rogram, from which emanate
　　M(=*S/R*): *M*emory (or *S*torage/*R*ecall) capability
　　ALU(=*SSP*): *A*rithmetic-*L*ogic *U*nit (or *S*yntactic *S*ymbolic *P*rocessing) including arithmatic/algebraic operations, binary string or bit operations, and general string operations, e.g. concatenation, comparing, and deconcatenation
　　T: 　*T*ransduction *G*enerating *S*ystem, or codes for converting program-generated output signals into codons alerting and instructing output devices
　　OS: *O*perating *S*ystem or processing supervision and housekeeping.

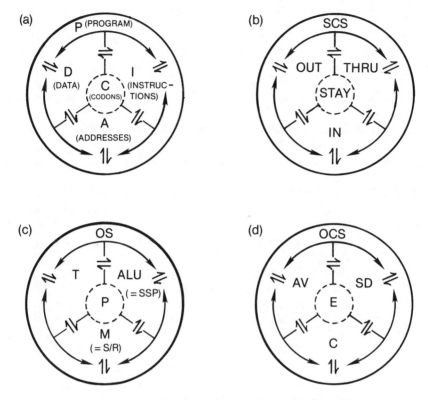

Figure 3–11. Typological Topology of a Computer
              Codon Types
              Processing Stages
              Internal Functions
              External Functions

(d) *Still the Same Mapping for the Computer's External Functions*
    E: *E*lectronic Output, i.e., the most general description of all output, which
        may include
    C: *C*ontrol Output, to control another CPU
    SD: *S*ervo-*D*irecting Output, enabling, instructing, or disabling various
        devices to implement program output, e.g., robotic devices, robot
        factories, military or security uses, etc.
    AV *A*udio-*V*ideo Output, providing suitable transducers furnishing auditory
        (timbre, pitch, duration, number of voices) and visual (form, color,
        motion) outputs.
    OCS: *O*utput *C*ontrol *S*ystem.

It is important to note that in the functional analysis of computer architecture, there is this category of *Address* in addition to Data and Instruction. Thus a given electronic code may represent data, instructions, or the addresses for either. The profound implications and importance of the *Address* category of codon have not been generally recognized, and one often sees in computer theory an alleged exhaustive dichotomy of *Data* and *Instructions*, without a hint that the concept of *Address*, on an equal footing with both of these, is needed to complete the picture.

It is in a sense quite natural to overlook the addressing function. Although in human thinking both data and instructions are conscious, addressing is largely an unconscious process. (Posthypnotic suggestions illustrate addressing in the human mind.) It is very often out of our direct control, as we notice when something becomes inaccessible to conscious memory and defeats willed efforts to recall it. The computer forces one to become consciously aware of addressing. Indeed, all the subtleties of pointer registers and indirect addressing (i.e. programmably operable addressing, without human intervention) prove that. The prime importance of addressing is illustrated in the following sentence: I've something of real value to give him and all the necessary instructions for what to do with it and how to use it— but I can't reach him! Addressing means accessibility—means negentropy.

There are also deep typological resonances between *Data/Instructions/ Addresses* and *Input/Throughput/Output-Stayput* respectively (cf. figure 3– 11). It is readily comprehended that data are principally *input*; that instructions concern primarily *throughput*; while addresses or destinations importantly relate to *output* and *stayput*. (Such destinations can of course be either delivery or pick-up points.) Speaking of *stayput*, it is also worthwhile to note here that *variables* in mathematics are storage *addresses* for a computer, whereas the assumble *values* of variables are storage *data* (contents). Also, *stayput* may be temporary (virtual) longer term, or completely archival.

The address, although usually an evoking operator, may also be an operand, as there could exist subtle processes of computer syntax which first manipulate and/or transform addresses (i.e. the addresses become operands) before deploying some thereby achieved address in its characteristic evocatory function. An address code, as far as its role is concerned, is rather amphibiously poised between an operator and an operand in any case, since it is the means whereby the actual operands receive operations, and also the means whereby the actual operators convey their operations.

There are thus nine functional modes for a code: I (instruction) operating on D (data), A (address) or I itself (e.g. "If so-and-so, then change instruction so-and-so thusly"); A operating on D, A, or I; and D operating on

D, A, or I. There is also a deep conceptual correspondence between corresponding portions of figure 3–11 (*a*), (*b*), (*c*), and (*d*). We can also characterize Memory (S/R) as **STAYPUT** and thus have the more succinct functional description of a computer:

$$\left.\begin{array}{l} \text{IN} \\ \text{THRU} \\ \text{OUT} \\ \text{STAY} \end{array}\right\} \quad \text{PUT}$$

As we have already noticed, the basic operating or indicative Instruction[32] is the *transfer* or *movement* (of either data or instructions) from one storage site to another or from one application or execution site to another—this fact serendipitously revealing another category pair: that of storage state (passive) and execution or performance state (active). Either data or instructions thus may be (1) operands or (2) operators, and, independently, may also be in either (1) storage state or (2) execution state, these last two possessing definite, nonarbitrary analogy with potential and kinetic energy respectively.

3.23 *Some Advanced Design Considerations*

Implicit in our analysis of computer architecture are matters of the context of machine interpretation and of the hierarchical level of an instruction. Citing Compucorp again (because it had a bright group of designers in the 1970s led by Dwight Jividen, who as of this writing lives near Santa Barbara, California), their Model *Scientist* 400 (which was also distributed by Monroe as the latter's Model 1800) contained a "symbol" key which if pressed or programmed would turn any following command (e.g., "square root") into a *symbol* for a thus designated storage, the contents of which could then be in turn programmably manipulated. Thus every instruction had two contexts: one its literal meaning, and the other its use as a name for the symbolic addressing of storage and recall commands.

But an even deeper concept of context was embodied in those remarkable machines: what were called "Group C" instructions. These were a whole set of different instructions, assigned to certain codes, than what they normally would do. Entry to and exit from the Group C level was done by a small programmable subroutine, after which all codes meant and did something else—providing a sort of extra and normally inaccessible level of machine "awareness" and capability, very suggestive of human non-normal states of different degrees of insight. Group C included also an overriding supervisor state that was designed, as part of the "firmware" of the machine, to handle such tasks as initialization, overflow or underflow, and error conditions.

Later computers had supervisor states (sometimes even more than one level, as in large IBM machines, for security control purposes—a fetish of IBM); but no later machine, despite the advances in technology, has attained that peak of humanly usable design which placed such states at the programmable behest of a user's creativity.

We have already alluded to the computer's indicative and imperative modes. Its conditional mode is instituted by IF . . . THEN; ELSE program sequences, plus DO loops for comparison-controlled executions. The subjunctive mode of the computer still awaits full implementation: we are only beginning to give our computers electronic *imaginations* as well as electronic memories. When that is adequately accomplished, we will be able to program in the subjunctive mode: imaginative recombinations and electronic fantasies, which some machines—not yet quite consciously designed to do so—can already begin to invoke. New vistas of humanly helpful, user-friendly, and psychologically healthy computer development are on the way.

We will next consider a special computer language application allowing the topological relations between various class-clusterings of properties to be programmed on the time line of computer operations. The means of doing that is a new approach enabling the translating Venn-Euler class-relation diagrams into binary strings by way of a set of primal binary matrices including the matrix for the theoretically vital though neglected "exclusive or" (EXOR) operator.[33] The fact that the topological underlies the logical (which we have before noted on another occasion [88, p. 141]) again becomes apparent.

3.3 EXORcist: Programming Self-Typing of Classes Through Resonances in Binary Strings

The theory of class relations was founded in chronological order by Leonhard Euler and George Boole in the eighteenth and nineteenth centuries. The two men were both trail-blazing mathematicians—minds distinctly not of the narrow-gauge conventionally grooved cast. To the end of their happily long lives they remained excited over still-to-be-explored possibilities.

To their fundamental contributions, later professional logicians added so-called quantifier theory, but one of their fairest spokesmen, Willard Quine in 1970 [93] almost wistfully though a bit convolutedly admitted the power of

Euler and Boole's class/system approach, so concretely different from the contentlessness of the quantification school:

> This exorbitant schema [now come two lines of extravagant notational jargon] is one among countless laws [of logic and set theory] that gain much in brevity and intuitiveness [read meaningfulness] by translation from the schematism of pure quantification . . . into the schematism of . . . classes and relations. Other examples are the familiar laws of Boolean algebra. . . . Down the centuries a major motive for assuming such objects as relations and classes . . . has been this kind of convenience.

We would add that clarity (non-obscurantism) and not mere "convenience" was the desideratum. We end up with a more compact and yet more pervasive set of axioms for Boolean algebra and class relations than was previously possible.

The crux of the matter as we before pointed out [94] is that logic and set theory are branches of topology: the science of inter- and intra-connectivity, and as such a necessary cornerstone in any theory of self-organizing systems. This basic ontological fact about logic and kindred set theory is most naturally and appropriately reflected in the Euler-Boole approach and its related algebra. It is the generalization of this approach in the direction of inherently self-organizing systems of interlocking classes, together with a very parsimonious treatment of their interactional possibilities, that forms the framework for EXORcist, a method of programming the self-typing of classes through resonances in binary strings.

An abridged form of it was presented at the 1979 San Francisco meeting of the Society for General Systems Research, and appears in those Proceedings, in the session on methodology, chaired by George Klir. EXORcist was first communicated in August 1978 to the American Mathematical Society *Abstracts*, and subsequently introduced during an invited graduate seminar on systems analysis given at the Trieste International Centre for Theoretical Physics, in three lectures presented November 1–3, 1978, at the invitation of John Casti. That version will not be repeated here, but an expanded version (omitted now for reasons of space) will appear separately (see footnote at start of the epilogue).

Suffice it to say here that prior attempts to extend George Boole's algebra lack a complete arithmetic—the core of any algebra—since the operations of division, as well as a satisfactory subtraction, are missing. Attempts to induce subtraction suffer not only from being too arbitrary and insusceptible of extension to the division operation but, relatedly, also contain incompatibilities with respect to what the most natural and appropriate Boolean subtractive operation should be: e.g., Halmos [95] (a normally good expositer who here only follows prior misguided tracks[34]) gives a very artificially "defined" version of what is really a form of Boolean subtraction, though rather perversely calling it "addition" and omitting to explain the deep relation to 'symmetric difference' which involves EXOR and hence true Boolean subtraction.[35] Elsewhere, Halmos has also repeated the common error that for a matrix A, $A^0 = 1$. This is true only if A is nonsingular, i.e. if $\det A \neq 0$. That $A^{-1} = 1/A$ suffers similar restrictions. Musès first noted and demonstrated this behavior in 1972 in a paper on topological fractional dimensions, and again in 1978 [96, pp. 51–54].

Mr. Tarik Peterson was my most able student at a series of two post-graduate seminars on hypernumbers I held at Berkeley and Santa Barbara, California, in the late 1970s. During the second seminar EXORcist was presented, as well as my indexed hypernumber representations for octonions [96] and for counteroctonians based on $\varepsilon_n^2 = 1 = \varepsilon_n$ and $\varepsilon_n \neq \pm 1$; and the connections of Boolean algebra with binary strings. Tarik noted that the indices for two octonions or counteroctonions could be treated as two binary strings which when EXORed with each other produced the binary string for the correct index of their product. Thus $i_3 \varepsilon_5 = \varepsilon_6$ where $3_{10} = 011_2$ and $5_{10} = 101_2$. Then, 011 EXOR 101 = 110 = 6_{10} which is the correct index for the product. It gives me great pleasure to mention Mr. Peterson's contribution here.

3.4 Some Extensions in Class Inter/Intra Dynamics

We have noted how classes can be objectively treated and their self-organizing interrelations (symbolized via binary string interactions) computerized by a fruitful generalization and application of Boolean algebra. Now let us briefly consider some feedbacks in that largest of all self-organizing classes: human society.

The current fate of primary societal buffers will now be considered.

The imperatives to acquire scientific knowledge that can help the human situation of the late twentieth century are considerable. The buffers that hitherto normally shielded human society from its own possible malignancies and worst manifestations were principally: (1) decentralized small communities in which increased ease of observation and contact engendered enough beneficent social pressures to stabilize behavior harmoniously to mutual benefit; (2) close-knit families with early fostered and deeply rooted ethical and behavioral norms; (3) widespread belief[36] in organized religions with a key tenet of each being the existence of an intelligent power or powers surpassing our own and thus helping to maintain human societal order; and (4) a steady-state or at least nonexponentiating population rate.

These stabilizing buffer factors have begun, especially since the mid-twentieth century, fast to erode and disappear, with appropriately deteriorating social stability and sharply increasing numbers of police states as results of self-exacerbating positive feedback loops. In consequence of such erosion, competition for any factors contributing to material security and social position and well-being have taken on a rapid rise, so that a stunning mixture of urban cunning and jungle savagery on all social and political levels is being more and more necessarily exposed and dominant, to the point where it tends to become perforce accepted simply as a fact of late twentieth century life.

3.5 Brief Prognosis in the Light of Time-Systems Theory

The imperatives outlined and analyzed in the preceding section are becoming steadily more defined and pronounced. It is not fatuous under the present circumstances of burgeoning sociopolitical instability to entertain the needed hope that the pursuit of increased knowledge of our own nature as reflected in the study of chronosystems can help bring the human enterprise through threatening waters. Society in any fruitful form, as well as science, is at stake; and the second can help the first—and in fact must learn to do so henceforth more than ever if both are to negotiate the rapids of a now swiftly closing century and era.

Notes

1. No other frequency matches the eclipse pattern.

2. Their springboard was the original work of Chladni and Lissajou in the nineteenth century, and we still speak of "Chladni figures" and "Lissajou figures."

3. Which he concluded was lunar, but which better fits the period of solar rotation, the sun's independent turning on its own axis. Arrhenius' introduction of cosmo-ecological rhythms into science continues to bear fruit. In a Russian technical review journal of 1979 Alexander Melixetyan noted that [35] "rhythms of cosmic processes have been found and corresponding rhythms of geological, physical and biological phenomena on the Earth.... The Russian scientist, A.L. Chizhevsky, who studied the sun's activity, as early as forty years ago predicted epidemics of influenza in 1957–1959 and in 1965.... Increasing solar radiation activates viruses and causes epidemics." The review goes on to note that recently it was found the phases of the moon are correlated to changes in atmospheric ionization and terrestial magnetism which also

influences human beings; and it was found that during magnetic storms, changes in the cerebral cortex occur and a person's reaction time is speeded up by a considerable factor.

4. We learned later that they contain a substance in their skin so virulent that a dog who ingested one by chance would soon die. But the strong allergic effect on certain humans, as the substance affects not the sites immediately touching it, but ones that can be far removed from the place of contact, was not realized prior to this report, nor was the month-long result of a few seconds of contact.

5. Ammonium sulfobituminosum (in a hydrophilic base): "ichthyol" first trademarked by Cordes, Hermanni & Co, Hamburg-Lokstedt, and then later improved by emulsification with a hydrophilic pomade.

6. Quantum biochemistry shows that bio-"recognition" between agent and receptor molecules depends upon their patterns of matching or resonant fields, in turn determined by the wave functions of their electrons and energy levels [37].

7. This point will be resumed in a mathematical context in the announced Supplement.

8. These are intimately conceptually connected to the trions of our chapter 4, section 4.3.

9. These correspond well to our circumferential, radial, and central trions, respectively, in chapter 4, section 4.3.

10. As an example of the enormous compression of meaning, the almost cryptic Sanskrit original of this *sūtra* consists of only three words (the first admittedly a compound): *pariṇāmaikatvād vastu tattvam.* Here *tattvam* means "manifestation" rather than "suchness."

11. This intranuclear resonance of deuterium, incidentally, shows that elementary particles can be distinguishable at least in phenomenological effect—in this case by the stability of the nucleus.

12. These are the words of a long-term colleague, the mathematician and physician Marco (M.P.) Schützenberger who interestingly recalled Born's statement when we were engaged in conversation along these lines in November 1982.

13. Actually this fact provides the foundation for a theory ancillary to the technique of forecasting which is called that of "embedded invariants" [43].

14. Which can often be conveniently represented as angles, then called "phase angles," which may also depict phase differences or "beats."

15. This was kindly brought to my notice during a conversation at the Corbin home in Paris with his widow Stella Corbin in September 1982. Madame Corbin very graciously also aided my researches by providing copies of other needed material.

16. This is not be be confused with the much more political and wordly minded Eastern Ismā'īlī sect headed by those astute business men, the Aga Khans. The clarity of Henry Corbin's wonderfully inspired exposition is regrettably diminished by his consistently misleading use of the term "Ismaili" without qualification. Indeed the present Bohras, heirs of the remarkable Yemenite tradition on time (that we will examine in chapter 5) are by no means the doctrinal friends of the Aga Khan's brand of Ismailism. Quite the contrary. That fact makes Corbin's and others' ambiguous use of "Ismaili" all the more historically and philosophically misleading.

17. Thus it became well-nigh forgotten in twentieth century scientific theory that Theon of Smyrna (*ca.* 130) had come so close to present notions as to use the term *sympátheia* in acouxtic theory to refer to two strings which resonantly or "sympathetically" vibrate, a scientific term and concept straight from the ancient thinkers.

18. See, for example, his *Propagation Handbook*, published by 73 Inc., Peterborough, New Hampshire, 1978.

19. It is interesting to note that maximal resonance is in the B.-K. effect associated with minimal resistance, thus naturally linking resonance with minima of the first time derivative of entropy, i.e., with minimal rates of entropy increase. We have already published [reference 11] the guiding principle here: time is so organized as to select probability chains that minimize entropy increase.

20. It should be borne in mind that topology in the time context is not at all the topology of the usual space context, and hence prevailing topological methods cannot be of too much avail. The topology of time is a highly dynamic one, governed by very interactive (nonlinear) resonances which are *qualitatively* released, maintained, and transformed. The only appearance of the quantitative aspect would be as ratios of intensity and, at the end of an analysis, as a set of predicted time spans for the occurrence of the kinds of events sought in the analysis; or else as sets of times to be used in chronavigation (chapter 6).

21. These concepts were deepened in ancient Egyptian and Iranian traditions (see chapter 5) into an entire doctrine of the nature and meaning of time, inextricably bound up with the way our present universe arose, now functions, and will turn out.

22. These considerations provide the deep morphological reason why cubics had to be the foundation stone of that portion of bifurcation methodology called catastrophe theory.

23. In this connection see the excellent work [81,82] of N. Gilbert and R.D. Hughes.

24. A correspondent, Margaret Long of Wraxall, interestingly bore this observation out in a synchronous communication in April 1983 that arrived the day after the above passage was written. From her journal of ideas she sent me the following relevant passage when learning I was doing the present book: "Time seems to be consecutive in its movement . . . but Time is simultaneous for it moves neither forward nor backwards but in all directions at once. . . . Time has a circumference and dimension which cannot be seen by Man [who comprehends] only his own vision of Time as a flat progression." The sense of the inadequacy of a simplistic past-present-future schema is here apparent, and another intuitive correspondent (Mary Woodlee in New Mexico) wrote that she perceives a whole "multi-tracked tape" playing through each moment, with inherent resonances to both past and future-projections on each "track" or level. Keenly aware persons (among whom may certainly be included the great Henri Poincaré) appear to sense innately that time is essentially nonlinear. As chapters 2 and 4 amplify, time is not intrinsically consecutive but rather of radial nature, manifesting through apparent cycles but actually radiating through the ever-present moment and recalling us ineluctably to re-contact our origins, in a prodigious and profound context of what memory means. Chapter 5 will further explore this last clause.

25. This series is so basic that it is found throughout the flowering plant kingdom as the numbers of spiral strands in the capitulum of a flower (e.g., daisy, sunflower); and also as the numbers of helical rows of seed pods in pine cones or heads of wheat. These flower-found numbers are always exact and come in pairs, since the spiral arrays in the capitulum or cone can be traced in two opposite senses. In zinnias one finds the pair (13, 13) and, in large enough sunflowers, (55, 89). No flower has less than (13, 13), the pairs (8, 13) and (5, 13) belonging to pine cones. The numbers of spirals traced by cacti spine-clusters are also Fibonaccian.

We found [Musès, C., "The Functional Basis of the Fibonacci and Related Series," Amer. Math. Soc. *Abstracts*, vol. 2, no. 4 (June 1981), p. 398] that the basis of the Fibonacci series is a Diophantine hyperbolic functional equation, in which certain hyperbolic functions are always integers. Where f_n is the nth Fibonacci number ($f_0 = 0$, $f_1 = f_2 = 1$, $f_3 = 2$, etc.), that equation is

$$1/2 f_n = k \left\{ \begin{array}{c} \sinh \\ \cosh \end{array} \right\} (n \text{ arc tanh } k) \left\{ \begin{array}{c} n \text{ even} \\ n \text{ odd} \end{array} \right.$$

where $k = 1/\sqrt{5}$ which is the hyperbolic tangent of the natural logarithm of the so-called "golden number" $\frac{1}{2}(1 + \sqrt{5})$, often written τ. But k is even more fundamental (and is also simpler). The co-Fibonacci series: 2,1,3,4,7, etc., sometimes called the Lucas series, is also easily expressible by means of k in terms of hyperbolic functions.

26. We shall use the initial capital letter on occasion to distinguish the subject in its wholeness rather than as a designated moment, period, or occasion—a specific time.

27. Including the non-illusory and archetypcal *imaginal* (in the sense of Henry Corbin and, before him, Douglas Fawcett [85], harking back to ancient contexts long pre-dating Plato.

28. Also note that $(\pm i)^2 = -1$ means that desire finds it origin in the imagining process, in the imaginal, which thus ultimately creates desire, that in turn creates all other manifestations (see also figure 3–9).

29. Also of human devising and origin!

30. The first robot factory was achieved in Japan in the early 1980s.

31. We use the name of the god here, which even in ancient times was identified with *Chronos* or Time.

32. Instructions as distinct from imperative *Commands* like CLEAR (e.g. filling with zeros or ones as need be), START, HALT, ENABLE, or DISABLE.

33. EXOR was unfortunately overlooked from the start by Bertrand Russell and Alfred Whitehead in their *Principia Mathematica*, the least profound of Whitehead's work.

34. Nothing personal is here conveyed, and Paul Halmos and I have invited each other to dinner at our homes, with mutual enjoyment.

35. The best that can be said for the other view is that while EXOR is definitely Boolean or logical subtraction, it may in some electrical circuits correspond to the sum of the probabilities of each exclusive alternative. Probability operations, however, are not always isomorphic to Boolean logic. Overlooking that fact is the error of the view here faulted.

36. In time as well as space. Whether such belief be yet factually proved or not is irrelevant in this context: the belief itself performs the important psychosociological function referred to in the text.

4 *ANIMA ET THEMIS MUNDI*: PSYGLYPHS, A MULTILEVEL LANGUAGE OF QUALITATIVE TIME

We think, and indeed remember also, basically only through and by means of *images*. Sometimes these are less consciously evident, sometimes more so, but they are *always* there. Without this fundamental substratum of images, the mind could neither reason nor remember, hence could not function. "Pure" abstraction, as we saw already in chapter 2, just doesn't exist.

Now behind all imagery, however, complex or ramified, there is a comparatively small set of *fundamental or root images* which stand in relation to all the rest, as an alphabet to its language.

This fundamental set is repeated in each human mind as the DNA in each human cell, with individual variations of course, but enough redundancy to make communication and mutual comprehension possible, by providing enough shared or common denominators, so to speak. Hence Jung's term "*collective* unconscious" was misleading.[1] It is rather a set of *individualized* but *shared* and sufficiently *redundant* unconscious contents that is involved; and not at all the undiscriminating and senseless mixing implied by the word *collective*. The only actual collectives are garbage cans and refuse piles, whose function it is to collect indiscriminately. State collectives are in that accurate sense "garbage governments" regardless of ideology.

The fundamental realities of the mind are quite otherwise, and we function by alphabets of basic images, Alphabets of Reality. The rendition of these

91

alphabets in symbolic form is denoted by the term *psyglyphs* representing the "nucleotide" basis of the DNA/RNA of the psyche, as it were. In this connection C.G. Jung recounts an interesting remark of the great quantum physicist Wolfgang Pauli [97, p. 133], noting that "there is some possibility of getting rid of the incommensurability between observed and the observer. The result in that case would have to be expressed in terms of a new conceptual language—a 'neutral language,' as W. Pauli once called it." Here was a dim recognition of the deep scientific need for psyglyphs—a language capable of appropriately, i.e. nonarbitrarily including both nature and psyche in its gamut of meaning.

An important moment in the development of humanity's understanding of the cosmos occurred on October 27, 1859. On that day Gustav Kirchhoff had announced to the Berlin Academy of Sciences and hence to the world (the epochal result being soon translated into English by the British physicist G. Stokes) his discovery, made in collaboration with Robert Bunsen of burner fame, that the sun was composed of the same kinds of chemical elements as those found on earth. That typologically small group of substances thus specified was then found, on April 1, 1872, to embrace the entire cosmos when Henry Draper showed, in his pioneering spectrum-photograph, that the same was true of the distant stars as Kirchhoff had found of the sun. Thus the Periodic Table, typologically classifying the chemical elements, was now applicable throughout the entire physical universe. It was a stunning victory for typological methods in systems theory.

The biological world, it was likewise realized (about a century later), is built up in a staggering variety of protein types which, however, are all derived from a very simple typological alphabet: the four nucleotide bases of desoxyribonucleic acid (DNA) and its related molecular variant RNA, which program in marvellously, amazingly ingenious fashion the 20 principal amino-acids from which all proteins are built. Another typological break-through.

Yet in the psychosocial world we have thus far been backward in realizing that here also the amazing observed variety of traits and behaviors requires a typological approach if its essential morphogenetic structure is to be grasped.

The objection that ancient astrological and alchemical doctrines would say this, too, is beside the point since such pseudo-objections do not reason or express any logical conclusions; and Jungian psychology was not too proud to borrow from the psychological treasures of those doctrines. As the science historian I. Grattan-Guiness trenchantly observed in the November 1982 *Bulletin* of the American Mathematical Society (2nd series, vol. 7, p. 642):

"Historiography cannot be swamped by a mere shower of sneers." Neither can phenomenologically and experientially verifiable typologies. The periodic table and the genetic code are here to stay and are but the tip of the iceberg, as we shall begin to see.

We seem to be in a position with regard to nature's universal languages somewhat similar to that expressed by one of the novelist Eric Knight's sturdy and common-sense Yorkshire characters speaking to his favorite dog: "You can understand some of man's language, Lassie, but man isn't yet bright enough to understand thine."

4.1 Languages and Their Levels

In this chapter we return to the question of language taken up in chapter 2, but now from a more particular viewpoint rooted in chronotopological concerns. In this computer age people are sufficiently aware of the significance of the *level* of a problem-solving language without our wasting time and space on copious preliminary explanation, otherwise easily available in any case. Suffice it to say that higher languages in this sense are designed to spare us the necessary but repetitive, boring and countless details of "housekeeping" operations, and are thus able to devote our attention to the essentials of the problems themselves rather than to the detailed methodology of our instrumentalities for solving them.

Thus the binary coded[2] "machine language"—which was the only computer language available in the electronically primitive 1950s—is the most clumsily extended one to use, although it is still the primary basis for any computer's switching circuits which simulate human intelligent activity and behavior by the astute way some human mind has arranged them.

The machine is thus like a group of morons who, however, can go through their collective elementary repertoire of abilities with extreme rapidity, thus arriving at results (when they are properly arranged and ultimately directed by human intelligence) well before their human designers and programmers.

But it was soon found that it was quite unnecessary to have to spend valuable human effort and energy on writing each small operational detail again and again in a binary coded program—*if* one could use an electronic code word that would be so wired into the machine that it would automatically unleash a whole lengthy and complicated functional unit of machine-coded or "micro-coded" instructions. An "artificially intelligent" machine generates such higher commands from built-in rules. It must be stressed that the primordial rules generating the eventual sophisticated, intelligence-simulating behavior *must* be built in to begin with by humans, and in that very direct sense the claim "machine intelligence" is charlatanism.

Thus macro-codes or "higher computer languages" came into being. The first is one still in use; FORTRAN, an acronym for "*for*mula *tran*slation." Now we are glutted with a competing babel of such higher languages, each with its group of devotees who claim it is "the best." Actually, the best one has not yet been found, although in chapter 3, section 3.2 we indicated the lines along which truly universal computer languages are to be sought. We called them UAL (pronounced "you all")—Universal Assembler Language—and SUPL (pronounced "supple")—Syntactic Universal Programming Language.

The point for us in the present chapter is that it is pointless folly to use a very low-level language to solve problems requiring highly evolved, high-level concepts. In such situations one seeks, or devices if need be, an appropriate high-level language. Let us look at an example of a situation like that.

When two persons walking down a street meet each other and begin to converse, we have, of course, physics operating in the situation: their walking is undeviatingly subject to the laws of gravity. We have also photochemistry, as complex photochemical processes in their retinas enable them to see each other; we have also still ill-understood acoustic-neuronal interactions enabling them to hear each other; and complex organic chemistry—down to the DNA/RNA level—is going on in each of their bodies in order to maintain them structurally and functionally, moment to moment.

But all this wondrous micro-level complexity simply serves to enable their brains, the neuronal transducers for their minds and memories, so that they might frame and express their thoughts to each other within the anatomical/physiological constraints of their bodies. All that even more wondrous complexity is in turn simply the underpinning for those two persons to implement their aims, desires, and interactions; let us suppose, for instance, that their conversation turned on a matter very important to both of them, and one that had to be decided then if it were to take place successfully.

Thus all the physics and chemistry support *the higher level of psychological reality*. These two people are also not functioning in a social vacuum, and hence each is embedded in a culture. (Let us further suppose that each grew up in a quite different culture with a different maternal language.) There is here a complete interplay of intercultural anthropology and sociology as well, since both are now functional while also being embedded in the matrix of a third culture that controls their current surroundings and habitat.

Novelists concentrate largely on the very top levels: the psychological and socio-anthropological. Only a few science fiction writers found it necessary or even literarily advisable to devote any great space to the physics and biochemistry underpinning the situations of their human (or alien) characters, and even then only in only few of their stories. The literary tours-de-force of Italo Calvino's stories "Mitosis" and "Meiosis" are rule-confirming exceptions. Most authors would have failed out of hand had they tried that.

4.2 When Mathematical Language May Be Inherently Inappropriate

What we are suggesting, then, is that while mathematics is the discussion language par excellence for physics, chemistry, and even ultimately physiology, it becomes increasingly inappropriate[3] as the level of the considered phenomenon rises. Finally, it is quite inadequate to do justice to psychological and socio-anthropological phenomena per se.

Systems analyst John Casti, writing with Stafford Beer in 1975 in a IIASA* Research Memorandum on preventing organizational disasters, well noted that scientific modelling in sociology and economics could defeat itself if it "slavishly . . . adhere to the modelling apparatus [mathematics] which has served so well in physics and engineering." And another colleague (we met in the 1960s), Heinz von Foerster, well remarked on this very point in 1971 before the New York Academy of Sciences (*Annals*, vol. 184, pp. 239–241), that mathematics "lacks the contextual richness originally perceived." Rather, he advised, we should "develop the algorithms that transform the descriptions of certain aspects of a system into paraphrases that uncover new semantic relations pertaining to the system as a whole." Clearly, new tools are being called for.

This limitation, as the prior quotations adumbrate, applies also to economics, the moment the latter emerges out of the mere logistics of goods and services and gets to the point of the driving forces for all economic activity: human aims and desires. To present "economic theory" without its master-controlling psychological factors is either to be very deceptive or self-deceptive and naive in any application, as all good politicians well know. In systems theory, we are beginning to learn to our chagrin, most of the

---

*International Institute for Advanced Systems Analysis.

important systems are human-dominated, and their crucial factors and critical points intimately and essentially involve human beings, with all the sociopsychological richness, complexity, and frustration that that implies.

Thus mathematics is too low a language level by which to approach the vast majority of system-theoretic problems we have. The quest for solutions is thus seen to devolve on the question of finding a higher level language for the problems of so-called "soft" or human-dominated systems. People like P.B. Checkland [98,99,100] and his co-workers have recognized this fact and have come to grips with it in pragmatic terms [101]. What they have actually done, unbeknownst to themselves, is to use a higher level language in their *thinking*, though they used it tacitly without making it explicit and hence available to others or even to themselves. That is why few have been able to replicate Checkland's successes. His approach is basically human therapy rather than inhuman expertise.

Let us now try to specify the needed higher level language for human-nominated systems which, as was shown in chapter 2, are chronosystems as well.

There is a useful negative lemma that can render service at the outset; namely, that what we do *not* need here is a computer language. Not to say that the appropriate high-level language we eventually specify will not be computer-programmable. It assuredly will. But rather, that we should first seek it in terms of the sociopsychological realities themselves, and not becloud the issue at the beginning with then irrelevant computer requirements. There will be ample opportunity later for computerization.

Another facet of the inappropriateness of an intransigently mathematical approach to psychosocial problems has been trenchently pointed out by one of the important mathematicians of the latter twentieth century, Stephen Smale, in the course of his criticism of René Thom's catastrophe theory (CT) and elementary catastrophe theory (ECT) as expounded by Thom and applied principally by Christopher Zeeman. Not mincing matters, Smale says: [102]:

> I feel that CT itself has limited substance, great pretension and that catastrophe theorists have created a false picture in the mathematical community and the public as to the power of CT to solve problems in the social and natural sciences.
>
> To my mind, when CT goes beyond ECT it loses pretty much any direct touch with mathematics. . . . Good mathematical models don't start with the mathematics, but with a deep study of certain natural phenomena. . . . On the other hand, around CT not only does mathematics come first but one sees a sort of mathematical egocentricity.

As we have previously seen, Smale's point has much larger significance than catastrophe theory. There is, in fact, indicated a shift or quantum leap in viewpoint that may well prove to be a key phenomenon of the movement of the late twentieth century thought; namely, the realization that that truly wonderful and nonarbitrary symbolic language, mathematics, nevertheless possesses an inherent inappropriateness in trying to deal with problems demanding *qualitative* richness and precision among interrelationships of also qualitative type between irreducibly and essentially qualitative factors—problems that are the very stuff of psychosocial systems.

The almost overwhelmingly topological trend of twentieth century mathematics can be viewed as a continued attempt to accommodate mathematics to qualitative milieus; and the trend did very well as far as it went. But by the very nature of the case, it could not go far enough for psychology,[4] and a symbolic language of essentially qualitative rather than quantitative power was thus urgently called for—with a vocabulary and syntax that were qualitatively appropriate, and a basically radial and radiant rather than linear structure.[5] In chapter 2 and in this one, I have sketched the outline of such a language, first broached in 1972 in a seminar on "Symbolic Insight" I was invited to present at the Maryland State Institute for Psychiatric Research.

4.3 Typology as a New Tool in Systems Science

There is a common tradition among almost all cultures and races that holds that people fall into psychological or personality types and subtypes, and hence appropriate social roles. The ancient Indo-Europeans, and not only India, recognized, for instance, savant, warrior, craftsman, and general service types, hardening this analysis into hereditary castes in India. This, of course, was a psychological error, obviously committed on the insistence of the ruling élites, the *nomenklatura* of their day, to use a modern Russian ironic argot so well applied to the actually governing élites of "people's republics." Yet there is great truth in the principle itself, as its widespread use in many stable cultures shows. A society simply must then provide means of psychological growth so as to allow for mobility, on demonstrated capability, between social roles.

To cite a notable example of such a psychological typology, the system of psychological typing, inherited from a complex mix in ancient Sumerian, Egyptian, and Magian sources, went much further than the three or four Indo-European types and resulted in an elaborate system of personality analysis intimately linked with a ramified religious and symbolic language. Alchemical traditions, also originating in Egypt,[6] applied the same principles.

The only attempt thus far to make use of this rich symbolic system as a modern language for psychology was on the part of the well-known psychotherapist Carl Gustav Jung, whose terms "extrovert" and "introvert" stem from the old day- and night-side personality types of "solar" and "lunar," respectively; and whose four types of "sensation," "thinking," "feeling" ("emotive" or "reactive"), and "intuition" (and conation) were based directly on the Hellenistic-Egyptian mapping of human personality into a classification of the "element" called "earth," "air," "water," and "fire," symbolizing, respectively, the four states of matter (solid, gaseous, liquid, plasma) and their psychosymbolic homologues, persisting in the respective Galenic "humours": melancholic, sanguine, phlegmatic, and choleric. Jung studied this system extensively, and his entire analysis is but a partial rewriting of the former rich psychological-archetypal language. The four can be respectively and conveniently symbolized as $\triangledown$, $\triangle$, $\triangledown$, and $\triangle$, which will be of use when writing in the language.

At the invitation of the Maryland State Psychiatric Institute, in February and March of 1972, the author conducted a seminar on Symbolic Insight, attended largely by psychiatrists and psychologists. The seminar was concerned with the modern necessity to deploy such a typological approach and language to psychological analyses and the writing of protocols—which at present are unstructured, confused, and largely conceptually unorganized except for the arbitrary imposition of Freudian terminology, now shown to be quite Procrustean, biased, and unrealistic.

The positive reception of that audience of professionals enabled me to see that people were ready for a high-level and sophisticated typological language that not only could do justice to the richness of human personality but that would be simple and straightforward to symbolize and manipulate expressively. The material and psychodynamic language presented during the course of that seminar will be re-given, updated, and enlarged here.

It is a radial, radiant or cluster language, as might be expected from the multidimensional needs it must fulfill, given human personality as its basic subject matter. The reader is here referred to the appropriate sections of chapter 2 for the introductory discussion of such nonlinear language. Let us now specify that language, the basic elements of which we will call *psyglyphs* as they refer principally to psychological realities.

Jungian psychology's four types are only the most meager beginning and must be first of all supplemented by three independent types whose nearest modern analogues lie in the Indian tradition (going back to Sankhya philosophy, and thence more ancient sources) of the three *gunas*: *tamas*, *rajas*, and *sattva*, imaged respectively as darkness (fuel), fire, and light. Jacob Boehme, sixteenth-seventeeth century pioneer depth-psychologist and heir to kindred Alexandrian and earlier traditions, uses such a triple symbolic basis throughout his writings [135]. Those three psychological roots also have symbolic affinities with the nature of center, radius, and circumference (radiant surface), respectively: the dark fuel, centered in the hot flame, that in turn emits the light.

In terms of personality[7] that time-honored trinity would in modern terms respectively refer to (1) source or focus (i.e. secondary source) of potentials;[8] (2) implementing or manifesting powers; and (3) expressive or communicating powers.

We may summarize this threefold basis as (1) centralized, focal *feeling* in the sense of deep and affectively charged and felt urgencies; (2) *acting* or manifesting; and (3) *perceiving*. We will symbolize these as (·), (|), and (○) respectively which in writing the language eventually will save much time and needless repetition of words. Let us call these three the basic *triple* or *trion*. We can now re-write the four elementary types, or the basic quadruple or *quadron* as 1) *initiation* (of which inspiration, intuition, and conation or willing are all exemplifying facets); 2) *formation* (of which Jung's "sensation" is but one specialized facet, that of perceived forms); 3) *relation* (of which thinking is one facet); and 4) *reaction* (of which emotion is a facet).

We now can combine the trion and quadron either supplementively by addition, or interactively by multiplication, arriving at $3 + 4 = 7$ distinctions in the first case and $3 \times 4 = 12$ distinctions in the second.

Let us first look at these 12, starting with "1,1," the first number denoting the number of the trion and the second, of the quadron.

1,2—focus or center of formation, source of forms; and with the interaction taken in reverse order, the formation of foci or the foundation of a center.

1,3—focussing on and of relationships, i.e., making them central; or, in the other permissible order of interaction, the relating of centers or foci.

1,4—focussing or centralizing reactions, i.e. making *them* central in concern or attention, first in priority; the other sequence being the interreaction of centers or foci on each other.

1,1—centralization of volition or initiation; or, the initiation of central or focussed organization.

2,1—activation or manifestation of initiating will, i.e. origin of all manifestation; or, the initiation of action, by reverse sequence of interaction.

2,2—activation and manifestation of form; also, formal manifestation or activity.

2,3—activation or manifestation of relationships; also the relating of activities.

2,4—activation or manifestation of perception; also by reverse interaction of the two components, the perceiving of activities or changes.

3,1—the perceiving of initiations, origins, and beginnings; or, the initiation of perceptions and imagination.

3,2—the perception of forms; or, the formation of perceptions.

3,3—the perception of relations; or, the relating of perceptions.

3,4—the perception of reactions and emotions; or, the reacting to perceptions by rendering them emotionally, i.e., supplying them with affective associations.

But our numbering can be improved, since the *manifestation* of something in the trion provides a natural "first,"[9] and so does the *initiation* phase of the quadron.

We have then these revised and more apt number assignments for the trion, realizing that circumference can follow center as its infinite expansion, begun by the manifesting radius. We then have 1, 2, and 3 assigned respectively to radial, central, and circumferential elements, thus: (1) acting or manifesting; (2) centralizing or focussing; (3) comprehending (literally "enclosing" something by the mind) or perceiving. And for the quadron we have, as before, the order of: 1) initiation; 2) formation; 3) relation; and 4) reaction.

Our twofold interactively generated typology now becomes the scheme shown in Table 4–1, and this will be the form in which psyglyphic language deploys this series, the second digits having now the revised meaning assignments just given, the new trion member being given first, followed by the quadron number, as before (Table 4–1).

But in this typological arithmetic, three times four is not the same as four times three (symbolically $3 \times 4 \neq 4 \times 3$). In more technical terms, this arithmetic is noncommutative. "Three times four" here refers to the threefold grouping of the four types based on their sharing the same trion number; whereas "four times three" refers to the quite different fourfold grouping of three types based on a shared quadron number. We thus have for the threefold grouping, using the 12 sequence numerals on the left in the preceding listing, the following three groups (Table 4–2). We also have the

Table 4-1.   The 12 Trion-Quadron Combinations

Sequence Number	*Psyglyphic Significance*
1 = 1,1	activation or manifestation of initiating will; or the initation of action.
2 = 2,2	focus or center of formation; or the formation of foci, the foundation of a center.
3 = 3,3	the perception of relations; or the relating or perceptions.
4 = 1,4	activation or manifestation of perceptions; or the perceiving of activities or changes.
5 = 2,1	centralizing of volition or initiation; or the initiation of central or focused organization.
6 = 3,2	the perception of forms; or the formation of perceptions.
7 = 1,3	activation or manifestation of relationships; also, the relating of activities.
8 = 2,4	focussing or centralizing reactions, i.e., making them central in concern and value; also, the inter-feedback between such centers or foci.
9 = 3,1	the perceiving of initiations and origins; also, the initiation and origin of perceptions.
10 = 1,2	activation and manifestation of form; also, formal manifestation or activity.
11 = 2,3	focussing on and of relationships, making them central; also, relating such centers or foci.
12 = 3,4	perceiving reactions and emotions; also, the reacting to perceptions—furnishing them with affective associations.

Table 4-2. The Three Trion Groups

Trion	Quadron Sybmols and Numbers
I (❘)	△, ▽, △, ▽ = 1, 4, 7, 10 (all characterized by their sharing trion number 1)
II (·)	△, ▽, △, ▽ = 2, 5, 8, 11 (all sharing trion number 2)
III (○)	△, ▽, △, ▽ = 3, 6, 9, 12 (all sharing trion number 3)

Table 4-2(a). The Four Quadron Groups

Quadron	Trion Symbols and Numbers
i △	(❘) (·) (○) = 1, 5, 9 (all sharing quadron number 1)
ii ▽	(❘) (·) (○) = 2, 6, 10 (all sharing quadron number 2)
iii △	(❘) (·) (○) = 3, 7, 11 (all sharing quadron number 3)
iv ▽	(❘) (·) (○) = 4, 8, 12 (all sharing quadron number 4)

following four groups, based on shared quadron numbers, as shown in the second part of the Table (Table 4–2(a)).

The significant point is that this typological symbology is nonarbitrary and those groupings also refer to psychological types, as the reader can verify from the basic definitions already given of the typological elements or alphabet. The additive group of 3 + 4 is different and in a way more subtle, referring, as we will see, to basic aims, ends or desires, rather than (as in the twelve-fold scheme already given) to the psychological channels or means of complementing the various desires of which they are the *strategies* so to speak.

We shall return to this point. Suffice it to say now that the basic psychodynamic ends are: (1) the maintenance of self-nature and individuality, desire to be oneself, to accord with one's own nature; (2) the reactive expression of it as reflected in personality structure; (3) the desire to release activity on a situation or task, to direct or focus energy; (4) the desire to reason and express implications of reasoning and to explore consequences; (5) the desire to imagine and express imaginative intuitions and projections; (6) the desire to express affection, harmony, and concord; (7) the accumulated desire-inertia which itself desires to deepen grooves of behavior to which it is already habituated. We should note that aggression originates in (3) when resistance is encountered; and that fear originates in (5) and (7) when what is undesired is believed in, or when an external situation overturns all expectations so as to threaten prior stability.

Now the old tradition of the typological approach interestingly averred that it was not to be considered as statically archetypal, but rather dynamic and momentary in nature; and that their time manifestation was periodic in nature, impulsions or typological energies being synchronized with temporal patterns related to other natural periodicities, the most accurate being those of the solar system, observable against the backdrop of the earth's orbital and equatorial planes, and the horizon and meridian circles at the particular terrestrial latitude and longitude of concern.

All this was comprised in the doctrine of $\sigma\upsilon\mu\pi\acute{\alpha}\theta\varepsilon\iota\alpha$ (*sympatheia*) related to the verb $\sigma\upsilon\mu\rho\alpha\rho\alpha\theta\acute{\varepsilon}\omega$ (*symparatheō*), meaning to "go together or run along with," i.e., to *resonate* with. The doctrine re-emerges in the twentieth century concepts of synchronicity[10] and non-locality, the latter concept entering quantum physics through the observations and papers of J.S. Bell, about which physics Nobelist Eugene Wigner has penetratingly commented.

It must not be thought that the viewpoint just described entails a naive concept of causation. It does not. Rather, the celestial bodies were looked on as the indicator needles of, say, an ammeter or voltmeter, which indicate but by no means cause the time fluctuations of forces and phenomena otherwise inaccessible to observation. We could today shoot one of these indicator needles (the moon, say) out of the sky with a great hydrogen bomb. But that would only prevent *us* from reading the meter as it were, and would in no wise change the realities or power of the circuit. There is here involved a logic of synchronicity that demands investigation and respect, especially when we see simpler causal models failing at the most fundamental levels of physical nature that have been investigated.

In addition to being periodic in time, these sources of typological dynamism were considered ubiquitous in space, *just as is each moment of time itself*; and able to manifest themselves with appropriate timing and circumstance. They were, indeed, *logoi spermatikoi*, seed-words of power— power to cause manifestations in time like a seed produces its appropriate plant.

Thus the seeds—the manifesting possibilities—of living intentions are complete in all of space always, as though the entire cosmos were a superhologram.[11] Those seeds are there, together with their means of manifestation, like zygote-seeds of living things. If someone knew enough, the seeds could accordingly be incited to manifest, embedded in a connected scheme of priorities. They then appear as an interlocked system of intentions with a priority scheme imposed on them. That, in turn, is the core of what constitutes intelligent behavior. And moreover, in each such seed-intention of the set are the microseeds of all the rest, there being no absolute separation. This is the meaning of what suddenly emerged into acute awareness when I was seventeen. I scribbled on a sheet of paper: "One cannot fully define anything without knowing everything."

But we humans, in our understandable efforts to comprehend, try to make crude barriers and partitions where in fact in nature none such exist. We try to separate the inseparable—a hopeless task; and even though it may be a temporary heuristic help, it should never harden into closed compartments. If this occurs within the personality, those deep and *irremovable* (as long as the attempt is persisted in) contradictions would then arise that could finally shake the personality apart into shattering neurosis and psychosis. We shall see this in greater detail in the next chapter, where certain aspects of psychopathological morphogenesis are discussed as a part of the implications of time's possibilities and the nature of time itself in our universe.

Such time-germination is the essence of the old Alexandrian word ἀποτέλεσμα (*apotélesma*), the full completion of an event or result through time-held and time-conveyed causes, the word connoting an accomplishment made manifest in observable effects. In the same sense, destiny is called by Euripides in his *Herakles* the "Completion-giver" who leads all time seeds to their appropriate ripening and maturity.

It is also interesting that this linking of psychodynamics and chrono-topology possesses the prime characteristic of a viable scientific theory: it provides a means of making predictions, which are then perfectly open to wide-scale and multiple testing by all who are competent to do so—as with any other scientific theory. Thus it deserves a test, and moreover cannot validly be denied without thorough testing, unless one would wish to descend to the level of arrogant ignorance of the pompous fools who, in hypocritical hauteur, refused to look through Galileo's telescope for fear they would see Jupiter's moons.

Returning to the chronotopological psychodynamics, we now can see that chronotopology also implies chronotypology, a typology of psychodynamic forces in time. We have already derived twelve basic modes of channeling or psycho-implementing desires. Let us now resume the derivation of the basic scheme of those desires themselves by means of our typological sum of the trion and quadron of psychodynamic elements already discussed, and which we have for convenience symbolized respectively as (|), (·), and (○); and as △, ▽, ◭, ▽, these four being easily remembered as relating to Solomon's seal thus: ⊕ → ✡, which can be seen as △ + ▽. We now need a contextual

symbolic differentiation to denote these symbols in the context of representing distinct desires or *ends* rather than their previous context of being the
combinatory elements for psychological *means*. We accordingly write
conveniently

$$(|) \rightarrow (1); (\cdot) \rightarrow (2); (\bigcirc) \rightarrow (3); \triangle \rightarrow (4); \triangledown \rightarrow (5); \triangle \rightarrow (6);$$
$$\triangledown \rightarrow (7);$$

denoting in this way the elements of the circuit of desire. Interestingly, there
is a correspondence with the known electrical circuit elements of resistance;
power-source or input (battery or generator); power expression (bulb or other
output device); power transfer and control (switches); power conduction and
filtering (wires, transistors, rectifiers); capacitance (electrical field storage);
inductance (magnetic field storage). A diagram will easily demonstrate this
(see figure 4–1). Note that inductance (e.g. a transformer) can empower

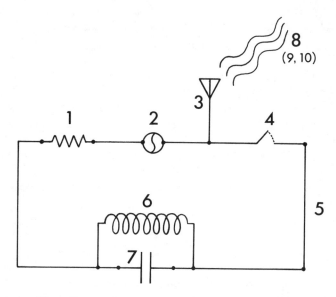

Figure 4–1. The Basic Set of Seven Oscillatory-Circuit Elements
Related to Psychodynamic Symbols (psyglyphs) in Chronotopological
Context. 1. Resistance; 2. Power Source; 3. Power Expression (antenna); 4. Switch (power direction and control); 5. Conductor; 6. Inductance; 7. Capacitance (suitably tuned to Inductance). The remaining
three numbers do not figure in the circuit, but enable it to be significant
in a wireless or wave-propagational context. They are: 8. Wave of
electromagnetic energy generated by the circuit; 9. Quantized field or
wave medium; 10. Dirac sea of negative energy supporting the field.

voltage expansion or amplification, whereas resistance causes a voltage drop or constriction.

Bearing out the universality of this scheme there is a stimulating confirmation of it in the "Root Definitions" and their elements given by Smythe and Checkland [108]. The Checkland scheme features the six essential elements in the basic (root) definition of any relevant system giving "catwoe" as the mnemonic for the following six: customer or client, the ultimate receiver and expressor of the systemic activity; actor(s) or agent(s) of the transformation or activities of the system; transformation or the basic relational changes and process effected through the system; weltanschauung, the attitude and concept framework validating the root definition; ownership, by which is meant control or sponsorship by a wider system, empowering the one discussed; environmental constraints, i.e. those of wider systems imposed on the one under consideration. Checking against figure 4–1 and its discussion above, we see that these six elements, empirically and independently arrived at, reflect six of the seven essential systemic components called heptons, above given. So CATWOE = heptons 3,4,5,6,2,1, respectively. It is thus seen that the Checkland scheme omits one essential element: a number 7, which is closely related to 6, their harmony making resonance possible. If 6 is the store of framework attitudes that creates a magnetic field of meaning, so to speak, for the activity; then 7 is a similar store of electrifying, fruitful, and stimulating ideas and plans related to those attitudes and concepts; that thus can motivate the entire system. Inserting an "S" at the end for attractive stimulation (hepton 7), we have the now complete mnemonic CATWOES. Without the seventh element there is no incentive— the fatal lack and flaw in totalitarian systems. This example shows how useful the psyglyphic underpinning can be to the merely empirical analysis of chronosystems.

In addition to the now well-known seven first given in figure 4–1, if the third circuit element (3) be an *antenna* instead of an ordinary output device, and elements 6) and (7) are resonantly tuned[12] then we see that there are necessitated at least two more elements: a transmitted *electromagnetic wave* (8) and an imperceptible but implied quantized field (9); then also from quantum physical considerations, we need the unmanifest Dirac-sea of negative energy (0), thus bringing our set of dynamic elements to ten, of which nine are manifest; and of these a set of seven is manifest in fixed form, a useful illustration of typological application.

There is a tradition with roots extending as far back as Sumero-Babylonian civilization, that assigned, on the basis of an observed concordance of synchronicity, the bodies of the solar system to the basic set of primal desires, corresponding to the fundamental seven circuit elements of figure

4–1. That correspondence, using the figure's assigned numbers and conventional astronomical symbols, run as follows, the basic typological septenary being 1: ♄ ; 2: ☉; 3: ☽ ; 4: ♂; 5: ☿; 6: ♃ ; 7: ♀. Now the ancient cyclical order of weekdays, still preserved in many modern European languages, is 1: Saturday (Saturn's day); the next two are self-explanatory, namely, 2: Sunday and 3: Monday or Moon (Luna) day (lunedi in Italian); 4: Tuesday,[13] Tiwas' or Mars' day (*mart*edi in Italian, *mar*di in French); 5: Wednesday, Wotan's or Mercury's day (the Italian *merc*oledi); 6: Thursday or Thor's or Jove's day (the French *jeu*di and Italian *giove*di; 7: Friday or Freya's or Venus' day (Italian *vener*di).

Noting that this sevenfold ever-repeating cycle can be generated by repeatedly traversing in order the verticles of a heptagram, we may write them as in figure 4–2(a). But a heptagram is capable of circumscribing two distinct stars, whose generation traverses the seven vertices in two still different orders. The first star, generated by drawing successive chords to every other vertex, is given in figure 4–2(b), yielding the order 1, 6, 4, 2, 7, 5, 3 or Saturn, Jupiter, Mars, Sun, Venus, Mercury, Moon, which is exactly the sequence of these celestial bodies as seen from the earth, in their order of decreasing period, Saturn traversing the phases of its rings once in about 29½ years, down to the Moon or Luna traversing its phases in about 29½ days.

But we generate a third heptagonal star by skipping two vertices at a time, generating a last[14] order, as shown in figure 4–2(c); namely, again using figure 4–2(a) as the reference point for numbering the vertices: 1, 5, 2, 6, 3, 7, 4 or, in symbols: ♄ , ☿, ☉, ♃ , ☽, ♀, ♂. But these are also ancient glyphs[15] for the metallic chemical elements that were an important basis of all ancient civilization: lead, assigned to the planet Saturn ♄ ; quicksilver, assigned to Mercury ☿ and still called "mercury"; gold, assigned to Sol ☉; tin, assigned to Jupiter ♃ ; silver, assigned to Luna ☽ ; copper, assigned to Venus ♀; and iron, assigned to Mars ♂.

Now let us write the modern chemical symbols and atomic numbers (numbers of protons in the nucleus) of these same key metals in the same (third) heptagonal sequence we have already derived that of figure 4–2(c). We then have: Pb 82, Hg 80, Au 79, Sn 50, Ag 47, Cu 29, and lastly Fe 26. We at once see that our third derived order is that of the numbers of protons in the respectively atomic nuclei—something that became known to the modern world only in the twentieth century.

This is a small but far-reaching illustration of the semantic cross-referencing power of typological methods: sequences of apparent orbital periods in the solar system and atomic structure are related in some symbolically deeply rooted fashion with each other and with the ancient order of weekdays going back to the mists of Chaldean antiquity; and *any of*

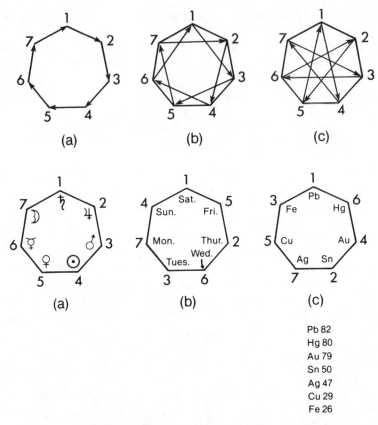

Figure 4-2. The Three Possible Hepton Cyclical Arrangements and Some Typological Correlations

the three sequences could here be used to derive the other two by means of a heptagonal mapping. So the other two must also anciently have been known. There is far more here than chance alone could possibily predict.

When it is realized that the same symbols can also reference basic colorings of states of consciousness in a system of typological depth psychology,[16] huge vistas of cross-referencing possibilities emerge. We begin to see at least the direction for realizing the otherwise vain hope of correlating and assimilating the ever-increasing mountains of information being amassed almost momentarily in every file and repository of our data-inundated century.

Some systems scientists are just beginning to sense the profound implications of typological and chronotopological thinking for systems theory. Crawford ("Buz") S. Holling, currently the Director of the International Institute for Advanced Systems Analysis (IIASA), provides an interesting example of this fact. He notes in IIASA's official journal [110] that "formally equivalent causal forces that are known to generate the ecological patterns in space and in time also occur in economic systems. Some are amplifying ... others are dampening. ... And the sets of inter-acting variables themselves act on different time and space scales—some fast and some slow; some local and some extended.

There is at least the potential, therefore, that macroeconomic systems can generate patterns of behavior in space and time that have the features of discontinuity and multiequilibria states that are found in biophysical systems. ... Long-term patterns such as the Kondriatieff cycles [of 50+ years] have been proposed ... [and such cycles] bear the seeds of their own change and renewal within them." My own invited lecture [9] at IIASA (October 21, 1982, on surprise and timing in systems theory), delivered before the preceding publication, independently underlined the same principles; and John Casti has patiently listened to me talking about my ideas of qualitative time in connection with timing, since 1975 when we first met at IIASA on the occasion of a talk on hypernumbers I gave there.

4.4 The Phosphene Prototypes

Another source of typological analysis in biosystems theory lies in the biological realities themselves. A fascinating illustration of this is the phenomenon known as "phosphenes," which are subjectively perceived light patterns arising after non-specific stimulation affecting the optical processing areas of the brain. The energy of the nonspecific stimulus (e.g., periodic electric or magnetic field pulses) is used to generate such images on being processed through the lateral geniculate bodies and the optical centers of the occipital cortex. The interesting point about these phosphene patterns of luminous forms is that first, they reflect aspects of the functional structuring of human vision; second, the patterns so formed reduce to a comparatively small number of independent types; and third, they can also be produced endogenously in either normal persons (e.g. airplane pilots), especially children [111], and also in abnormal states of epileptiform discharge.

When I analyzed the most specific and informative sources of phosphene observation back to 1959 [112, 113, 114] I found even more specifically

Rank Number	Occurrence Frequency (%)	Phosphene Form-Types (with variants)	Semantic Connotations
1	21.5		interfacing of two and more systems into a larger whole
2	16.6		ray radiation
3	15.4		wave-organization
4	13.0		basic structure and central support
5	9.6		wave-radiation from a center
6	8.8		ulitimate seeds or particles

#		Description
7		 completed, reciprocal balance
8		power release
9		pairing, reflection, fissioning
10		controllability and positioning (by coordinates)
11		released or freed unit or quantum form (triangle is minimal-edge enclosure)
12		rhythm and development by successive reaction (wave generation)

Figure 4-3. The Set of Human Phosphenes in Order of Decreasing Frequency

Table 4-3. The Twelve Prototypic Phosphenes and Their Psyglyphic Assignments.

Basic Sequence No. (see Table 4.1)	Quadron No.	Frequency-Rank No. (see Figure 4.3)	Observed Frequency (%)	Basic Phosphene Forms§	Copper Age Sign Numbers*
1	1	2	16.6	(cross)	66 89
2	2	4	13.0	(three parallel lines)	15
3	3	9	<3.5	(four-pointed star)	166–167 185
4	4	12	1.3	(horizontal spiral loops)	134
5	1	5	9.6	(concentric circles with center dot)	135–136
6	2	6	8.8	(rows of curved marks)	138

7	3	7	>3.5	(overlapping squares)	171
8	4	8	3.5	(spiral)	137
9	1	11	1.5	(triangle)	54–57 63
10	2	10	1.8	(grid)	106
11	3	3	15.4	(zigzag)	113
12	4	1	21.5	(waves)	131

*These numbers refer to the listing of signs on pp. 291–292 by Winn [109], where he shows the semiotic commonality of the very old (Copper Age) Cultures at sites like Vinča, Phylolopi, Troy, and pre-dynastic Egypt, ca. 5000 B.C.E.

§There are recognizable variants, e.g. (symbol) for 7, *et al.*

than above noted that they occur in a small group devolving upon only 12 elemental patterns (figure 4–3) of which all the rest are variants. They appear to be the principal morphogenetic alphabet used by the visual brain, the basic means used by the processing center to construct the outlines of all visual images. In this connection see also Greguss and Galin's interesting article [115] of 1971.

As figure 4–3 shows, the similarities to paleo- and neolithic petroglyphs are arresting, and evidently humans are early struck by these basic internal patterns which appear genetically inherited rather than environmentally learned, thus inherently embedded in biological reality.[17] We shall now undertake to classify these figures according to the 12-fold typology already adduced, using as a basis the summary of observations embodied in our figure 4–3.

On the basis of the fourth column (connotations) of figure 4–2 we have the following assignment (Table 4–3) to the twelve prototypes already adduced in Table 4–1.

It is now known, from the works of archaeologists in Old Europe (notably M. Gimbutas, B. Nikolov, M. Vasič, et al.) that the earliest extant human use of a corpus of script signs was in the middle of the sixth millennium before the current era, i.e. nearly 8000 years ago,[18] a set of such shared signs appearing in the early Vinča culture near the ancient gold and copper mines not far from Tordos in present Transylvania (now a Rumanian province); and also in the culture of Phylokopi, Troy, and pre-dynastic Egypt, showing an ancient Mediterranean glyphic system. The first (and still only) comparative study made of this material was done by Milton McChesney Winn, a former doctoral student of Professor Marija Gimbutas at the University of California, Los Angeles [117].

From the data and sign lists collected by Winn, who has given a useful set of reference numbers for each Vinča-type glyph, the striking similarity to the basic Phosphene glyphs is unmistakable, and in the last column of Table 4–3 we have indicated these ancient glyph numbers corresponding to the fundamental phosphene images.

There is a persistent relation between frequency and quadron number that becomes apparent when we group the frequencies under the same quadron number and list them in direct or reverse order of basic sequence numbers, thus:

Note that in the lower two divisions of Table 4–4, comprising quadron numbers 3 and 4, the pattern of decreasing frequency requires decreasing sequence numbers, whereas in the upper two divisions (quadron numbers 1 and 2) decreasing frequency goes with increasing sequence numbers. We can exhibit these characteristics in one simple and consistent arrangement,

Table 4-4. Phosphenes and Their Psyglyphs

Quadron Number	Phosphene Sequence Number	Observed Prototypic Phosphene Frequencies (%)
1	1	16.6
	5	9.6
	9	1.5
2	2	13.0
	6	8.8
	10	1.8
3	11	15.4
	7	>3.5
	3	<3.5
4	12	21.5
	8	3.5
	4	1.3

shown in Table 4–5. Moreover, if we add together the percent frequencies for the four quadron numbers (see table 4–4) we obtain (cf. also table 4-6): Thus the odd quadrom number frequency almost exactly equals the even quadron number frequency—a further substantiation that our psyglyphic

Table 4-5. The Close Relation Between Phosphene Frequency and Psyglyph Sequence

Quadron Number	The 12 Sequence Numbers (and their frequencies)			Quadron Symbol
	direction of frequency increase ←			△
1	1 (16.6)	5 (9.6)	9 (1.5)	
3	2 (13.0)	6 (8.8)	10 (1.8)	△
2	3 (<3.5)	7 (<3.5)	11 (15.4)	▽
4	4 (1.3)	8 (3.5)	12 (21.5)	
	→ direction of frequency increase			▽

Table 4-6.   Quadron Number and Frequency

Quadron Symbol	Quadron Number	Phosphene Frequency (%)	
△	1	27.7	⎫ odd Quadron number
△	3	22.4	⎭ total 50.1%
▽	2	23.6	⎫ even Quadron number
▽	4	26.3	⎭ total 49.9%

system is phenomenologically fundamental. We now have completed an introductory sketch of a vast radial and nonlinear language whose elements are psyglyphs.

4.4 Psyglyph Computerization

It remains to show that the typological scheme therein sketched is, as said at the start, readily computerizable. But proper programmability requires, first, all the essential elements of the picture, which in this instance we now briefly complete. Two prime factors have already been considered; that of psychological ends or aims, with their basic set of seven (4 + 3) psyglyphs; and channels (psychological modes of going about achieving a given aim) with their set of twelve (4 × 3) psyglyphs.

There is, then, one phenomenological aspect of the whole phenomenological reality still to supply—that of the *types of circumstances* or vicissitudes. These, suffice it to say here, also fall into a typal set of twelve, which can be specified as follows: I—Bodily and personal appearance and characteristic approach; II—Finances and possessions; III—Relationships with one's immediate environment in terms of nearby persons who figure in one's life in a familial or neighbor-like way; IV—The home life: one's life away from the more public world; V—Creative self-expression, whether emotionally as in love affairs, literally as in children, or still again, in works of more abstract creativity; VI—Matters of daily routine and habit: health (maintenance of proper body functions), hygiene, exercise, and daily occupation; VII—Formal associates and partnerships, including marriage;

VIII—Partner's finances and money, and in general possessions of others; inheritances; tolls and taxes; and the final toll exacted by nature: physical death; IX—Relationships with distant places; car voyages, dreams, visions; X—Public career, position, and reputation; XI—Aspirations, wishes, ideals, friendships; and XII—The part of oneself hidden from conscious awareness.

The reader as a psyglyphic exercise may trace the derivative relations from the latter to the former, connecting the set I–XII with the set 1–12. Thus, for instance, "2," the second psyglyphic channel, devolves upon the organization or centralization (attracting power) of formations, of formed things, i.e. of objects; and "II," the second psyglyphic circumstance-type, concenters on the acquisition of possessions and finances. Further, if, say, the basic desires to be affectionate (aim-type 7 as in the scheme given by figure 4–2) must work through this sector of circumstance, then we have affection and harmonization functioning through possessions and expressing itself thereby. If you like someone, give them some tangible gift—is the motto here. Such a psychosomatic combination could work toward confirming that "diamonds are a girl's best friend." If the same aim were also functioning through circumstance-type 6, we would have affectionate expression through nursing and support in daily routine; and so on.

The programmatic manipulation of psyglyphs is straightforward. We first note that, just as the basic set of seven aims or ends can be formed into an additive ring, modulo seven, so can the sets of means and circumstances[19] also be put into a ring-format, in turn mapped on a circle with each of the twelve being assigned thirty degrees. Incidentally, there is a deep connection between 7, 12, and 360 by way of what we called circular permutations or the patterns of circular arrangements of things. We shall call the patterns $abcd, a \ldots$ the same circular pattern as $adcb, a \ldots$ for the latter merely traverses the pattern in the opposite sense of rotation around the circle. Then, as we can readily derive (see any text in combinations and permutations), if the number of circular arrangements of n things is P_n^0 then $P_n^0 = \frac{1}{2}(n - 1)!$ where "$(n - 1)!$" denotes the product of all the integers from 1 through $n - 1$. Thus $P_7^0 = \frac{1}{2}(7 - 1)! = \frac{1}{2}(1 \times 2 \times 3 \times 4 \times 5 \times 6) = 360$. Similarly $P_6^0 = 60$ and $P_5^0 = 12$, thus deriving these ancient Egyptian and Chaldean basic numbers from the circular arrangements of 5, 6, or 7 things— operations that the old mathematician-priests could easily perform with the means at their disposal. The 360 degrees of a circle thus arose as the total number of distinct zodiacal (circular) patterns of arrangements of the seven classical celestial bodies.

The numbers 5, 6, 7 extend also deeply into the properties of *primes*: numbers that have no divisors other than themselves and 1. To see this,

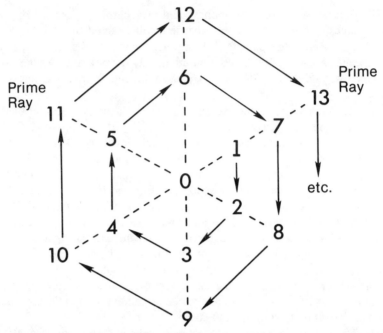

Figure 4–4. Hexagonal Spiral of the Integers Generating Two Rays of Primes. No higher number than 6 thus separates all the primes > 3 into two classes (the "5" class and the "7" class). No number lower than 6 does this with as great a density of primes on the two rays. The basic typology of a set of 7 (central disc plus 6 tangent discs) is again exemplified.

arrange the natural numbers in a flat spiral of period 6 (figure 4–4). It will now be noted that all the prime numbers (except the single even prime 2) will fall only on the two radii shown in dotted lines (along, of course, with other non-primes such as 25, 35, 49, etc.). But 6 is the largest integer number in terms of which any prime number (except 2) may be written as either $nk + 1$ or else $nk - 1$; in the case of maximal n, as $6k \pm 1$, where $k = 1,2,$ 3,4. . . . The minimal natural numbers for $6k \pm 1$ are $6(1) \pm 1$ or 7 and 5. So that 5, 6, 7—the basis of the anciently used numbers 12, 60, and 360, respectively—form a quite nonarbitrary set, reaching deep into the properties of numbers, all odd primes being of the form $5 + 6m$ or $7 + 6m$, where $m = 0,1,2,3, \ldots$, and thus $m = k - 1$.

So now we have in sum a threefold set of psyglyphic characters: a set of prime functional radiating centers of desires, aims, or ends; a set of psychological channels, modes, or means; and finally a set of circumstantial implementations, all of these sets being typological in character. Thus, say, "[7]2 X" can programmatically designate aim 7 working through channel 2 and implementation X, etc. It is clear that the psyglyphic approach makes possible cross-referencing and associative memory in programming very simply approachable and achievable, with a minimum of notation. The simplification of psychotherapeutic protocols therein suggested is considerable, and points a highly efficient way out of the current word-bogged morass of personality analysis, aptitude testing, and the like. We now have very succinct means of referring to personality and circumstantial traits.

There are always ways to indicate the *relationships* of one implemented (or circumstance-embedded) and psy-channeled aim to another. Such relationships denote ease or difficulty of co-functioning on the one hand, and the degree of self-involvement or other-involvement entailed. We can map them on a circle of self- and and otherness (figure 4–5) using the angular intervals (shown in degrees in the figure) to symbolize the crystal-like demarcations of the various types of relationships, each assigned a number (written in a circle in the figure). Computer-wise, there is no problem in programming such relationships. We thus could write 4:7, IV (6), 5:10, VII, meaning "the fourth type aim, working through channel 7 and implementation IV is in relationship 6 with aim-type 5 working through channel 10 with implementation VII." Notice the clarity and brevity of the psyglyphic as contrasted with the verbal notation. The programmed psyglyph approach will be of great use in the applications discussed in chapter 6.

Without such a typological approach, as is evident from various attempts, we are far from even being able to formulate a program for the computer recognition of handwritten letters or individual (i.e. non-robotized) speech. We should not wonder, then, in the slightest that, without such an approach, it would be immeasurably even more difficult to formulate the recognition and delineation of that enormously more complex entity, human personality. The psyglyphic transcription mode, however, makes it clear. We could, for example, have: Aim x_1 in one person working through mode x_2 and implementation x_3, in, say, relation z_1 with another person's similar aim (y_1) via channel y_2 and implementation y_3 Yet though psyglyphs thus solve the formulation problem, the limitation is in our ability to *interpret* the highly nonlinear interaction.

The situation is analogous to the problem of the *physical interpretation* of a mathematical equation that emerges out of the experimental frontiers of quantum physics. The pathway to the resolution of such problems is time-honored in science: observe and compare many cases, and continue doing so. Obtain as much feedback from reality as possible regarding necessarily

Number of sides n	2	3	4	5	6	7	8
Central Angle (1/n) 360°	180°	120°	90°	72°	60°	51³/₇°	45°
Polygon of n sides							
Name	Digon	Triangle	Square	Pentagon	Hexagon	Heptagon	Octagon
Face Angle (½-1/n) 360°	0°	60°	90°	108°	120°	128⁴/₇°	135°

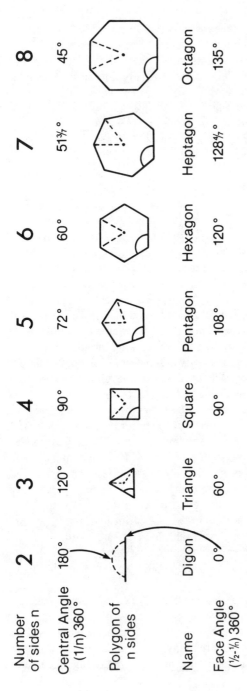

Figure 4-5. Relationship Angles of Psyglyphs. Central angles are typologically assignable to auto-involvement, relationships within oneself; face angles then denote allo-involvement: relationships and attitudes toward others. Also, the central or intra-relations belong with specialization and analytic traits, whereas the inter-relationships go more with generalization and synthesis. Note that 60°, 90°, and 120° appear in both groups. A natural limit is provided at $n = 8$, after which stellated or star-polygons no longer exist in a bonafide sense since the star points then become obtuse or blunted (at $n = 8$ the points are rectangular). Interestingly, at the far limit $n = \infty$ (which answers to a circle) we have the same kind of interchange of central and face angle shown between hexagon and triangle, the circle answering to the digon as the formulas $1/n$ and $\frac{1}{2}$-$1/n$ (or $n-2/2n$) clarify, since $n = \infty$ in the first yields the same result as $n = 2$ in the second, and vice-versa. These symbolic angles play interpretational roles in psyglyphics and help delineate relationships between radial types of syntax and semantic development. Even including $n = \infty$, a manageable set of 11 distinct relationship angles still results, the circle adding no new relationship angle.

tentative interpretations, refining them by that feedback. With that challenge, then, we close this chapter, having indicated a new language for the description of personality constitutions and interactions in time, as one person's inner configuration (concisely describable psyglyphically) interacts with another person's, or with those of a working group. Psychological outcomes now come within the province of systems theory, and we will return to this crucial point in chapter 6.

The viewpoint proposed in this chapter is beginning to seep into the more advanced twentieth century scholarship, and it is instructive to cite as a typical example of this movement the work of Luigi Aurigemma[20] done through the French National Centre for Scientific Research, School of Advanced Studies in the Social Sciences, who independently came close to our concept of nonarbitrary symbols,[21] a psyglyphic language capable of relating macrocosmic and microcosmic data, and the idea of inherent qualities in time itself. The emphases in the following passage are those of Aurigemma [119][22]:

> Est-il possible de considérer l'astrologie comme un *langage* exprimant d'une manière propre des observations sur les caractères et les modes de comportement humains? Et peut-on espérer de parvenir à déchiffrer ce langage . . . de parvenir à éclairer les relations entre ces temps et ceux . . . d'autres facteurs socio-culturels, économiques ou religieux par example? [Ainsi on] prépare et conditionne . . . la possibilité d'aborder un jour de façon sérieuse le problème de la *validité objective* de l'astrologie, c'est-à-dire le problème de la corrélation, que l'astrologie affirme, entre les coordonnées spatio-temporelles et les qualités propres aux êtres et aux événements se manifestant dans ces coordonnées . . . reconnaissant une grande dette envers l'oeuvre psychologique de C.G. Jung. . . . [Cette étude sera de la] structure essentielle [d'un signe], même si elle est ultérieurement subdivisée . . . en trois parties (dans la tradition "décanique") ou même en trente (dans la "moerogenèse"). Par ailleurs seront laissées de côté les complications qu'en cette structure plus générale constituent les déterminations ultérieures du temps-qualité exprimées dans le langage . . . des "présences planétaires," des "aspects" et de la "domification" dans le signe.

It is evident from chapter 3 and its references that other investigators are coordinating with this author's research desiderata and that a new science of timing and qualitative time is opening up, which has been called chrono-topology and which is particularly relevant to systems essentially involving human components. Psyglyphics is its language: the qualitative analogue of mathematics in the sense that it has in its domain of application just as much precision, flexibility, and semantic compression.

The psychiatrist and psychopharmacologist Dr. J. Elkes, one-time director of the Johns Hopkins department of psychiatry and behavioral sciences, perceptively wrote [120]:

> Indeed, time would appear to be the main axis around which we build our models of reality; and nowhere is this more apparent than in the models we construct to represent behavior, including human behavior. . . . It may not be too much to hope that concepts only partly or inadequately covered by present-day language may, before long, find a more adequate expression in new symbolic systems of greater precision and power. The usefulness of such systems may—and, I would venture to say, will—not be confined to the study of behavior.

Psyglyphics as the appropriate language for the expression of psychological and behavioral modalities, energies and processes, fulfills naturally and abundantly the criteria of my old colleague Joel Elkes' vision.

Notes

1. People do not have "collective" hands and eyes: they simply share in a quite *individual* possession of such bodily elements, down to the biomechanically (antigenically) individually distinct molecules of their proteins. The same goes for their psyches. Though the psyche is ipso facto not *physical*, it is quite objective in another order than the molecular.

2. Binary code means using only the digits 0 and 1 to form patterns that can represent any number, e.g. our decimal integer 10 is now represented as 1010; $11 = 1011$; $12 = 1100$; $1.5 = 1.1$, since $0.5 = \frac{1}{2} = 2^{-1}$, *et alii*.

3. Except as ancillary when, for instance, statistical treatment is called for because of lack of sufficient knowledge.

4. Psychology, of course, underlies anthropology and sociology and, through the overriding phenomena of *expectations* and, even more, *desires*, ineluctably underpins all of economics although mathematical economists (so irrelevantly anxious to ape physics) are mostly loth to admit the fact. That admission would require radical revision of a psychologically naive methodology.

5. When mathematical relationships became very mutual and "feedbackish," even mathematics found it had to forego linear for nonlinear spaces; indeed nonlinear partial differential equations require for their treatment spaces of no less than infinite dimension [103]. And what may be the core of mathematics—the theory of hypernumbers [104]—finally devolves upon a set of *qualitatively* different higher arithmetics and their corresponding metaspaces. At my Ravello lecture of 1962, in a conference chaired by quantum physicist Eduardo Caianiello, mathematicians like J. Lions were still talking only about linear differential equations. I pointed out to my audience (Lions was there) that, with practically all of nature nonlinear, as well as such comparatively elementary concepts like ellipsoidal areas, we were dealing quite unrealistically if we included only linear equations in our repertoire. The additional criteria of resonant and qualitative causation that enter into chronosystems carry us still further—from the forest of nonlinearity into the jungles of strange and chaotic attractors; and even beyond, to a place where mathematics must finally join with psyglyphics to interpret reality in enough depth to be adequate for the answers we need.

6. The Arabic roots of the word "alchemy" in turn go back to the old name for Egypt itself "Kam," the land of the rich black soil, as e.g., the hieroglyphic phrase *Kam-ur* (plus the determinative for "body of water") meant the "Great Sea of Egypt," i.e., the Red Sea. The cognate Coptic word is *kamè* and the hieroglyphic root for *Kam* is found as far back as the Pyramid Texts of the Fifth Dynasty, 2501–2342 B.C.E. at latest.

7. Be it well noted, we use the word "personality" in no pejorative sense, as do some persuasions, but rather as a neutral term applying to the whole of the individual psyche, including desirable or undesirable elements and potentialities, as the case may be.

8. And hence having direct connection with those reaches of personality of which the ordinary waking consciousness is unaware—this is the true meaning of "the unconscious" which thus is in a very real and deep sense *more* aware than the so-called "conscious mind" even though the latter be unconscious of *it*!

9. By the way, it is not unuseful to note that the insightful categories of "firstness," "secondness," and "thirdness" perceived by the philosopher-mathematician Charles Peirce, so unjustly ignored by more jealous than talented academic contemporaries, and only now coming into his own, possess deep relations with our trion of primary psychological-ontological typology, in turn derived from the spirit of the typological traditions developed in Prolemaic Egypt, whose roots go deeper still; and this ancient knowledge, like that of old folk herbalists deployed in modern pharmacology, can render signal service.

10. Which, however, psychiatrist C.G. Jung [105] did not realize could be made accessibly understandable by *resonance phenomena* and theoretically explicable by the rich concept of resonance. The ancient *sympatheia* doctrine of Egypt and Chaldea, filtering through the syncretistic Alexandrian gnostic and hermetic teachings, had reached China before the time of Tung Chung Shu (*fl.* 150), who wrote (chapter 57 of his *Ch'un Ch'iu Fan Lu*) [106]: "Things of the same kind energise each other. When the note *kung* is struck on a lute, other [i.e., harmonically related] strings reverberate of themselves in complementarity—a case of comparable things being affected according to the kinds to which they belong. . . . When men can see no shape accompanying motion and action, they describe the phenomenon as 'spontaneous' [e.g. "action at a distance"]. . . . But in truth there is no such thing as 'spontaneous' in this sense. Rather, everything in the universe is attuned to certain other things, and changes in accordance." The scientific core of "sympatheia" and "synchronicity" is *wave resonance*. We saw in chapter 3 that the basic waves are in time itself. Jung was close to the spirit of these insights, and he pointed out (in 1931) that "the Philistine believed until recently that astrology had been disposed of long since, and was something that could be safely laughed at. But today, rising out of the social deeps, it knocks at the doors of the universities from which it was banished some three hundred years ago" [*Seelenprobleme der Gegenwart*, Rascher Verlag, Zürich, 1931; translated as *Modern Man in Search of a Soul* published by Kegan Paul, London, 1933, p. 243.] It was because of not having realized the concept of resonant causality (see sections 3.12 and 3.14) that Jung, and for that matter Bohr's school of quantum theorists who influenced Jung, used the term "acausal" erroneously instead of the correct ascription "not linearly causal."

Other of Jung's insights, however, are valuable; and in the same vein as the perceptive sentences just quoted from him, the late and lamented Erich Jantsch, fifty years later, in his last and most penetrating work [reference 51, pp. 212–13; 215], is able to write even more strongly that "there is no longer any doubt that certain cosmic and biological rhythms are coupled. . . . The relatively new branch of science which is called *chronobiology* investigates these oscillations. . . . They [the resonant couplings] may not be due to mechanical or gravitational effects, but to the interaction between clouds of plasma (ionized gas) around the sun and planets on the one hand, and between solar and planetary magnetic fields on the other. There seems to be a certain correlation between planetary configuration and sun-spot activity which, in turn, influences the occurrence of geomagnetic storms. What formerly has been rejected as unscientific astrology is now about to find at least to some extent plausible scientific explanations." It is one of our theses, of course, that thoroughgoing explanations will not be forthcoming until the *inherent wave structure of time*, and hence of all energy release, be reckoned with in a conscious chronotopological context.

11. The writer announced [107] in 1970 this concept of the cosmos, independently of either David Bohm or Karl Pribram, with both of whom he later co-lectured: with the latter several times, and with the former at the scientific conference in 1976 convoked by the philosopher Krishnamurti at Ojai, California, and later at Professor Bohm's home in London.

12. The frequency f being then given by $1/\sqrt{LC}$ where L and C are the inductance and capacitance, respectively.

13. The Anglo-Saxon root preserved as *Tues* is related to the Teutonic deonym *Tiwas*, in turn related to the Latin *Deus*, the Baltic *Dievas*, and the Sanskrit *Deva*. The ancient translinguistic root *Di* means "shining" and appears even in the Chinese root *Di*, heaven. Another such translinguistic root *I*, to move (e.g. Latin *ire*, French *ira*) extends also from the Indo-European to the Sino-group, appearing as the important root *I* in Chinese, meaning "to alter or change" as in *I-Jing*, the known *Book of Changes* based on 64 binary-coded symbols.

14. If we try to skip more than two vertices, we obtain one of the three same sequences in either direct or reverse sense of rotation.

15. Preserved in old chemical treatises and also in recent chemistry books that give historical data like the college text by Babor, Esterbrooks and Lehrman used in the 1940s in the City University, then College of New York.

16. The ancient roots of such a system are currently attested in the still by far from obsolete words *saturnine, mercurial, sunny, jovial, lunatic, venereal,* and *martial,* listing them in the order of figure 4–2(c). The same system of correlations, a fivefold one of Indian and pre-Christian origin (four elements plus a quintessence, called "earth of light" or "center" in the Chinese system and *akasha* in the Indian version) passed into China [109].

17. The archaeologist and paleo-anthropologist Marija Gimbutas has noted [116] the prevalence of meanders and wave patterns in what was, evidently, a religio-symbolic language of prehistoric Europe.

18. The Lithuanian-American archaeologist Marija Gimbutas has established the age of this script by radiocarbon dating calibrated by tree-ring chronology [118].

19. Which serves as the *implementations* of combinations of psychological ends with means.

20. Found after this chapter was written but just in time to include here.

21. Cf. also Henry Corbin's use of the word *imaginal* rather than "imaginary."

22. In connection wtih this reference, Tables 4–1 and 4–3 (the prototypic phosphenes) will be seen to re-derive the ancient sequence of zodiacal archetypes.

5 *FONS ET ORIGO*: SOME TRADITIONS UNIQUELY ILLUMINATING THE STRUCTURE AND MEANING OF TIME SYSTEMS

We commence by a second look at a prefatory quotation to our prologue—the sentiment of playwright Preston Jones that "time is an eroding mystery, a son of a bitch." The scene now shifts to a night in Manhattan, a scene for which the writer assumes no other than reportorial responsibility in what amounts to a bit of sparkling sociology concerned with that greatest of all systems, the cosmos itself.

One evening in that large city, two characters sat hunched over an all-night bar. They were launched on a philosophical discussion as drunks often are. *In vino veritas*, perhaps. Suddenly one struck the bar with his free hand, glass clutched in the other, exclaiming, "I don't give a flying fuck whether your God is a he, she, hermorphadite (*sic*) or it! If your God is good and also can do anything he-she-it pleases, then, friend, given the state of this here nucular (*sic*) world, your God's up shit creek in trouble."

"Waddya mean?" the other queried, glassy-eyed.

"Well, if that God is good and if that God can do anything, then that God's not going to let this rotten world stay that way. But it *has* stayed that way—for millions of fucking years of dinosaur eat dinosaur, dog eat dog, and man kill and yes"—he stared for a moment—"eat man. So your God can't be good or else can't do anything he, she, or it wants. Make up your goddam mind."

The other drunk gulped a long draught and fell into incoherent and quiet mumblings, as well he may—for the problem is old and has baffled many. An "all-loving, all-powerful" God just doesn't fill the bill given the world as it is. Several reasons come to mind. Loving divinity by that very fact could not be tyrannical and hence must respect the free choice of beings of lesser stature. Love cannot have omnipotence over the free will of others who may choose not to love. Therefore a loving divinity could not *ipso facto* be omnipotent in an immediate sense, but only in a very long-term one.[1] That is the beginning of the answer.

And what of the horrors *built into* a nature with a largely predatory rather than the viable alternative of a thorough-going symbiotic ecology? Through what or whose arts and choices did that come about? "Nature is criminal" observantly exulted the Marquis de Sade in one of his essays. He then unreasonably concluded that that gave him, and anyone else of his ilk, the right to be so too. Nonetheless, de Sade had pointed his poisoned pen at a genuine Pandora's box.

This chapter which is essentially historical (a major aspect of time) couldn't have been completed before 1970 when a key breakthrough was made in our knowledge of the ancient Egyptian world–view, enabling even more pieces of an even larger jig-saw puzzle to fall into place than the able archaeologists and paleographers immediately concerned were aware of. Though the Temple of Opet was discovered at Karnak in 1970 by the French archaeologist Claude Traunecker, with its wall figures surprisingly well preserved, it was not until the later 1970s that the brilliant reconstructor and translator of Egyptian religious texts, Jean-Claude Goyon, found that the Opet reliefs duplicated those of the extremely important but almost destroyed initiatory temple of the Nubian Pharaoh Taharka,[2] the second ruler of the Twenty-fifth or Nubian Dynasty founded by the conqueror Shabaka, famous for restoring the ancient theological text at Memphis, the remarkable remnants of which are preserved on the so-called Shabaka stone in the British Museum. We will get to the important implication of the 1970 excavations and the Taharka Temple presently. Those implications will take us farther back than archaeology alone can.

The origin of time entails the origin of world evil on all levels—which is ultimately a matter of history in the larger sense as the record of events, whether man-made or not. For the origin of evil must be traced back to the first actions that had pervasively inimical consequences for all creatures. That is the trail to the roots of time that this chapter will seek to retrace. The beginnings of the trail are writ large.

The late twentieth century phenomenon of fantasy role-playing games (*Dungeons and Dragons, Runequest,* and *Call of Cthulhu,* for instance) with their fantastic, transcontinental popularity among young (and old) adults, point up sharply the deep need for belief in some ongoing cosmic administration, in some viable religion if you like. These so-called games that arose with such psychological power despite the machine era are really deep and detailed appeals to the religious and symbolic imagination, all of those mentioned having elaborate deific hierarchies and cult practices worked out.

The two principal themes that emerge in the intuitive sensitivities of the writers who created these living games are, interestingly, the two that emerge more profoundly from a comparative study of the most powerful ancient religions: the theme of a catastrophic unleashing of evil and the theme that the present cosmos maintains a sometimes uneasy balance between the mindless violence of naked evil and the orderliness provided by the nature of Time, the power that arose after the outbreak of evil, in order to administer an alternatingly good and evil world in some sane manner.

One role-game, "Stormbringer," adapted from Michael Moorcock's book by Ken St. André and Steve Perrin, summarizes the key principles of the "Melnibonean" Mythos: "Magic is defined as the opposite of Law [i.e. Science]. Law is predictable, reproducible, and constant. Magic is unpredictable, not reproducible, and random. Magic is the essence of the gods of Chaos [121]. Another game in this mythos, "Battle at the End of Time," done by G. Stafford and C. Kronk, centers on the Melniboneans' "unholy pacts made with the gods of Chaos. . . . The Cosmic Balance constantly swings and sways as . . . spells of the game alter the influence of Law and Chaos upon the world. Should the balance tip too far either way, the world will come crashing to an end" [121].

In a special book [122] on the relevant pantheons and cults written by Steve Perrin and Greg Stafford (the creator of the game) for "Runequest," there is much the same concept (p. 18): "The Devil is the incarnation of Chaos, which presents itself in the form of raw and devouring maw of entropy. Its existence is an abomination: a trick clause in the Laws of Creation. It is a hole in the cosmic fabric, motivated by destruction and evil." Whether the academic philosophers are aware of it or not the mythos of the twentieth century was actively keeping the burning question alive in the awareness of humanity at large, so that by ignoring them the academics succeeded only in looking nothing so much like the proverbial ostrich. Let us then pursue the matter.

Howard Phillips Lovecraft, one of the progenitors of the late twentieth century fantasy role-playing gaming[3] phenomenon voiced some of the same primordial concepts in his letters and his essay "Supernatural Horror in Literature" (written in 1925 and kept in print by the late August Derleth, founder of Arkham House Publishers in Wisconsin): "All my stories, unconnected as they may be, are based upon the fundamental lore or legend that this world was inhabited at one time by another race who, in practicing black magic, lost their foothold and were expelled, yet live on outside ever ready to take possession of this earth again."—a clear variant of the fallen Luciferean legions. Lovecraft added, even more graphically: "Out of corruption horrid life springs . . . and things have learnt to walk that ought to crawl" [124].

That the nature of time is inextricably bound up with the origin of evil, the late twentieth century popular game-creators also interestingly affirm in a complex and sophisticated train of ideas:

> There is a mysterious goddess in Hell [the transform of the great cosmic goddess of all nature, Glorantha, after she was slain in her original form by the Devil] who combats the Devil and, with the aid of the other gods, defeats it and devours it, shortly afterwards giving birth to the force called Time. . . . Armed with Time the gods could reassert themselves in the cosmos. They fought their way back to Being, reassembling the shattered world as they went. At last Yelm [god of sun and all light] . . . released Time upon the cosmos. Thus began History [124, p. 57].

Thus again is reaffirmed the ancient doctrine of an existence before time as we now know it.

And again [124, p. 57]:

> Time did not exist in the Godtime . . . [or] Gods' Age, Golden Eon, Non-time, . . . the Magic Place or Godworld. Time was born in Hell, where the shadows of chaos reigned and held the heart of the universe. . . . When the Lightbringers entered, they forged a cosmic pact which bound all entities, living or dead, spiritual or physical, pure or unholy, intelligent or inert, into the Great Compromise. These solemn vows are the source of Time.

Our intuitive game authors then add that our current Reality, born of time, is suspended between the deific Non-time with Chaos at the other pole, and hence is clearly temporary.

Such are the newly made sign-pointers to very ancient traditions[4] that throw surprising light on the baffling nature of our world, so disconcertingly compounded out of diaphanous, delicate beauty and crude, blatant horror. This chapter may be regarded as a study in realism—the most realistic way of looking in the most profound sense at the world and the human condition, and searching for their origin, meaning, and significance in terms of the future. In that sense it is also a study of most profound realism in terms of this principle: if your premises are deep and precise enough, you can gain insight into even the most recalcitrant of seemingly meaningless or hopeless situations and circumstances.

Such realism is directly linked with the human survival concerns of chapter 6—for without hope one does not survive. Hope is the human essence and roots of what in systems theory is called *resilience*, a concept different from and more subtle than "equilibrium" as C.S. Holling first pointed out. Indeed, resilience is the ecological vindication of Prigogine's negentropic concept of stability "far from equilibrium." (See chapter 6 for discussion and references.) It is not for nothing that the words *help* and *hope* are deeply linked etymologically: the Greek for "hope" being 'ελπıς (*helpis*) where the *is* is merely the noun ending. The Cockney's pronunciation of "helps" as " 'elps" is righter than he realizes.

After conferring with socially prominent theologians and historians of their era, two staff writers of the mass medium *Newsweek* [125] summed up the contemporaneous view of the question of the origin and nature of evil as of 1982. That mass media report noted that "the problem of evil remained as mysterious [read 'unsolved'] as ever." The writers also noted the "despairing position" today of "secularized Western societies" (they might just as well have included Eastern secularized societies: secularization is endemic); and that "despite the high promise of science, technology and other tribal gods of the modern era, evil persists on a truly awesome scale, . . . the mystery of evil that even nonbelievers must confront in these harrowing times."

A century ago, that Russian genius, Fyodor Dostoevsky, had unforgettably shared his perception of the problem in his *Brothers Karamozov*; and his twentieth century compatriot, Alexander Solzhenitsyn, in a 1981 interview published in the French mass medium *L'Express* (January 15–21, 1981) just seven months before the *Newsweek* article, said: "The danger that menaces the humanity of the twentieth century does not come from any single country, nation, or leadership in particular. It comes from universal evil . . . " And an older (1966) survey of the contemporaneous scene [126] candidly observes:

> In three hundred years of accelerated technological innovation, science acquired a revolutionary mystique. Crowned by liberating and transforming success, it became a form of secular religion, tending toward popular dogmatism and uncritical authority. Like all things, science and technology are essentially *amoral* and their uses ambivalent. Their miracle has increased equally the scale of both good and evil. The human situation has vastly benefited, but so too has "evil" attained monumental potential. Man himself remains a moral primitive. . . . Science and technology in themselves offer no guidelines. . . . They cannot relieve us of hard choices with which we must grapple in traditional ways.

This last observation reminds us of our history's neglected traditions and ancient insights. *Newsweek*'s poll showed that the problem of evil remains as recalcitrant as ever and attests to contemporary civilization's inability to solve it. Let us now uncover a little known, very old, and extremely subtle and profound solution that the global and technological civilization that sprang up between the sixteenth and twentieth centuries missed. We shall spend our limited space in delineating and completing that solution, rather than in endless and fruitless discussion of the various failures and cul-de-sacs that were attempted over the earth and the ages with respect to the same intractable problem, that of the nature and origin of evil—a characterization clearly involving the nature of time and how the present cosmology came to be. Questions of evil and cosmogony are thus deeply linked.

We have already mentioned in passing the Tayyibite[5] Shī'a tradition preserved in medieval Yemen, with roots extended into far earlier times and more ancient civilizations. Let us now have a closer look.

The available sources are not too voluminous to be summarized here, and then we will discuss the doctrine. The first unequivocal mention of this very distinctive tradition appears in the writings of the third Yemenite (*Tayyibītī*) chief *Dā'ī* or spiritual leader, Ibrāhīm ibn al-Hussain al-Hāmidī (†1162) and in particular, his great compendium of the doctrine, *Kitāb Kanz u'l-Walad*, an edition of which, though unfortunately not from the best manuscript, was published in 1971 [127]. The clearly compendious nature of this early Yemenite work shows it is not a personal teaching, but rather represents the preservation of much older traditions, ones we will later trace. In a 1982 letter from Professor Pio Filippani-Ronconi we learned that two of his former students at the Oriental Institute in Naples are at work on an Italian translation, which will be the first ever made from the Arabic original. At this writing we were still seeking the ungarbled diagrams for this work which, our colleague Professor Heinz Halm informs us, is not in the manuscript collection at the University of Tübingen.

Among other extant sources of the tradition of our interest can be cited the writings of the fourth chief Yemenite *Dā'ī* (†1199), Hātim ibn Ibrāhīm al-Hāmidī, and the fifth chief Yemenite *Dā'ī* (†1215), 'Alī ibn Muhammad ibn al-Walīd, some of whose works may be found in Strothmann's valuable book [128]; and the eighth chief Yemenite *Dā'ī* (†1268), Husain ibn 'Alī ibn Muhammad ibn al-Walīd, some of whose works were translated by Henry Corbin (*Trilogie Ismaélienne*) and, before him, by Bernard Lewis of Princeton University. Final mention must be made of the *Zahr al Ma'āni* ("The Flower of Meaning") of the last (nineteenth) chief Yemenite *Dā'ī* (†1468), Imādaddīn Idrīs ibn al-Hasan, which was briefly summarized in English as early as April 1937 in the journal *Islamic Culture*, published at

Hyderabad, India. The interested reader should also consult the valuable bibliography given by Heinz Halm in 1978 [129]. The following discussion uses the above sources, and as others are needed, they will be separately given. The reader is also referred to figure 5–1, which will be a convenient reference point for exposition. Our investigation will take us back to ancient Egypt, including the invaluable data unearthed with the Temple of Opet mentioned at the start of this chapter. We begin with the tradition as preserved by the Yemenite *Da'wat*. We will tell the story as briefly as is consistent with clear understanding.

The story begins with a beginningless beginning, delineated in both Persian and Arabic, by the Shī'ite-Fatimid philosopher Nāṣir-i Khosrau (†*ca.* 1075), whose beautiful prophetic poem we once cited years ago [130]. He ingeniously and profoundly uses [131] various modes of the verb "to make" and "to be" in order to arrive at a threefold self-regenerating reality, related to the old Indian formula *Sat-Chit-Ānanda* that corresponds on a more exalted level to the three *guṇas* (*tamas, sattva,* and *rajas,* respectively), in turn related to our trion group of chapter 4. The three Persian terms are *azal, azalīyat, azalī;* and the Arabic, *fā 'il, fī 'l,*[6] and *maf'ūl,* respectively. The Persian words all refer to being, but in a causal context as shown by their Arabic counterparts furnished by Nāṣr-i Khosrau [see reference 131, chapter 17]. The word *fā 'il* means to make or to effect in the sense of to cause to manifest, to cause to exist; this corresponds in the context of this discussion to the Persian *azal,* "to eternally be," in the sense of self-causal being. Then comes the nuance of *fī 'l*: ongoing activity, active functioning or effecting, a verb *par excellence*; this corresponds to the Persian *azalīyat* in the sense of an eternal making-to-be, an eternal self-actuation and self-actualization. Completing the three interacting phases is *maf'ūl*: a having-been-made, a made-ness, a full or complete manifestation (the Arabic term *ism al-maf'ūl* denotes the past participle in grammar); corresponding to *azalī*—a constant having-been-made-ness or fulfillment of existentiation.

We thus have a trinacria effect or three-phase cycle, in which the third phase "feeds back"[7] into the first, reaffirming it. *Fi 'l* (= *azalīyat*) is thus the know-how and implementing power that transmutes the potentiality of *fā 'il* (= *azal*) into the joyous blossoming or self-achievement of *maf'ūl* (= *azalī*). Here we have the trion group on its highest level, since all this self-manifestation is unmanifest (in the sense of not perceived by) to the lesser beings that will be created out of the *maf'ūl* state.

This unmanifest aspect of divinity, this self-energizing pair[8] eternally blossoming through their jointly achieved bliss in *maf'ūl,* can emanate[9] or reproduce lesser forms of themselves.

As a perceivable unity, this three-phased self-manifestation is called the

First or Primal Intelligence (the word has nothing to do with the current meaning of "intellect" but denotes a profoundly aware, supra-human entity) or *Ibdā'*, which carries also the connotations of wonder, uniqueness, and creative power. Specifically, this First Archangelic Being is called *al-Mabda' al-awwal* or First Beginning, First Point of Origin.[10] This first creature-perceivable manifestation of divinity was later assimilated to the Islamic Allah (literally *Al + Lat*, a syzygy combining masculine (*Al*) and feminine (*Lat*)—symbolized in the *teh marbuta* of Allah—attributes).

This first Archangelic Intelligence was also succintly called '*Aql*, literally "Mind," in the sense of the entire psychic gamut and not simply intelligence as such. The word in Arabic connotes also insight, understanding, and spirit, although the adjective *'aqlī* has degenerated to a more superficially rational meaning. In German it would correspond to *Verstand* rather than *Vernunft*, a very useful and basic distinction first made by the penetrating Jacob Boehme at the beginning of the seventeenth century. As we noted, this first deific manifestation, also called *Sābiq* (the one who goes before, in either time or space), is a transform of, rather than an emanation from, the unmanifest source.

In one sense, as Nasir-i Khosrau himself noted, this *Mabda* (or '*Aql*) *al-Awwal* or First Intelligence *is* the personifying of the *Maf'ūl* phase, the Eternal Divine Child of *Azal* and *Azalīyat*, of *Fā'il*[11] and *Fi'l*. Emanation actually begins with the Second Intelligence, called *Nafs* or (Universal) Soul, emanated from '*Aql* and thus also known as "the first Emanation," a terminology that we will not generally employ because it can too easily lead to confusion.

Now in another sense, the First Intelligence ('*Aql*) is a resonance of *Azal*; and the Second (*Nafs*), of *Azalīyat*. Thus the Second is also called *Tālā*, the one who follows or comes afterward. Hence the "second emanation" or Third Intelligence would again resonate with *Azalī* or *Maf'ūl* and be a re-creative and emanating power. This great Archangelical being is called *Adam Rūhānī* or the Spiritual Prototype of humanity, in whose image we were formed. Thus this Third Intelligence is to be the Divinity of our universe which has not yet come into being. It corresponds to the great *Anthrōpos Megos* of the Valentinian Gnosis.

Now there was no problem even conceivably arising with the first two Intelligences who realized the source of their being was in the Unmanifest. But the Third was inherently more exploratory, analytic, and outgoing, and sought its source as a resonance of Maf'ūl, though on two levels lower, the first Maf'ūl resonance being '*Aql*, as explained in Nasir's *Jāmi*, before cited. (See also the exposition of Henry Corbin, ref. 131, pp. 44–45.) Now what follows is the crux of the matter, but it is not found explained outside the

Yemenite tradition, though some corrupted vestiges exist in a few places mentioned before.

Corbin, despite his great merit in publicizing it, did not clearly grasp the incisive significance of the Yemenite tradition, which uniquely supplies nothing less than the origin of evil. Consequently Corbin consistently gives the misleading impression (cf. e.g. pp. 132, 135 and 136 of his *Trilogie Ismaélienne*) that Ḥamīdaddīn al-Kirmānī († *ca.* 1025), and Abū Ya'qūb as-Sijistānī (*fl.* 950) knew the doctrine preserved in Yemen, which their works clearly show they did not at all; and they fail to delineate the problem of the origin of evil and only repeat the inadequacies of neoplatonism on that score.

Kirmānī, Sijistānī, Naṣir-i Khosrau, and all the other more famous Ismā'īlī writers followed Plato and Aristotle and were quite naïve as to the origin of evil, although Corbin—despite his vast merits—misrepresents them and the Yemenites as simply different means of saying the same thing, as several alternative choices on the same menu. Corbin, overlooking the stunning originality of the tradition preserved in Yemen, can say only that the Yemenite period is characterized by "compilation rather than creation." The point here is that these compilations uniquely preserve a fantastically creative argument and chain of thought from earlier invaluable sources that have little to do with Ismailism as such, as we shall see.

Consideration of the Third Intelligence, as preserved in the Yemenite tradition, leads us into far more real territory than simply "a drama in heaven" or a "trans-historic style;" namely, it faces us with the origin of all the potential horror in both man and nature, so much of which has been unleashed that one must shudder to think of what can come—making it all the more imperative to study the bounds imposed by the nature of time upon evil. We have far more than dramaturgy here: we have the stuff of terror, tragedy, suffering, and rescue. All these realities may well contain dramatic elements but they are far more than a mere "drama," as life is more than a game, a play, or a *mise-en-scène*.

The Third Intelligence inquired and sought the source of its own origin. What could be apparently more natural? Yet it was a misconceived plan fraught with very dangerous consequences, like an innocent and unknowing intruder in the control room of an atomic reactor, toying with the buttons and seeking to access the full power of the energy source as "a good thing."

Resuming now the main line of the dénouement of the origin of evil in respect of the nature of time, the Third Divine Entity sought to encompass its own origin and to plumb the very depths and sources of being—a route that would perforce have to lead into the Unmanifest, the Mystery of Mysteries that by its very nature cannot be unveiled with impunity to the one so seeking: the veiling is inherent and necessary for the eternal provision of immortal being. The notion echoes in the words of the great Goddess inscribed on the portals of the now lost Temple of Saïs, preserved to us by the records of ancient travelers: "None can lift my veil and live." To seek to manifest the source of life out of the unmanifest, could end only in the manifestation of death, for such a seeker thereby would succeed only in cutting *himself* off from the circuit and flow of life in so trying, even though unwittingly, to preempt it. No manifest being can contain the unmanifest infinite.

The Third Divine Entity dreamed such a dream of finding that source explicitly and controlling it to be within himself (as he mistakenly thought was the case with the Second and First Intelligences). That dream and wish albeit momentary, had on that level of power and perception dire consequences, the first of which was a *retarding* of the consciousness of the Third Intelligence by reason of this thus introduced blockage or fallacy that could by its very nature not advance, but only hold back. The basic term used in the tradition[12] is *takhalluf*, to stay back because of being delayed, retarded, or postponed. Etymologically related words that clarify the usage in our tradition are *taḥāluf*: to be self-constrained by some prior allegiance; *takalluf*: a self-caused constraint; and finally the very illuminating *takālif*: self-caused costs or difficulties from the word *kulfa*, trouble.

The reason for such grave consequences of a released desire on the part of the Third Archangelic Power is bound with the fact embedded in ancient traditions preserved in Homeric Greece of the βουλή (mere wish or willing propensity) of a god being equivalent to the determined ἐθέλω[13] or implementing, focussed will of a man. But the implications go deeper, since the reason that it is so depends on the fact that the gods are not in our kind of time. Duration of things, yes, and changes, too—but all *without waiting time*, which is the chief characteristic of what we humans call our time. We must wait for any idea or plan to be enacted and then mature to fruition or full manifestation.

We must wait for anything we want to happen, to happen. True, the possession of wealth and power diminishes waiting time, but cannot eliminate it. Waiting time is built into the very fabric and foundation of processes of controlled change in this world. Any constructive changes we wish to bring about require planning, programming, and patient perseverance. Ironically, destructive acts require the least waiting time, for destructiveness has no embryology except in the development of the unhealthy values, attitudes, and belief-systems that give rise to it. The good counterpart of such evil is the elimination of destructiveness by cultivation of the requisite values and habits, or the active intervention against destructiveness already released. That is called heroism—which the Third Being finally had to exercise.

The Third Divine Entity was inquiring into the source of its own being, and the second apparently natural thought was to desire that source to be within itself, so as to be completely self-caused and self-sustaining.[14] Yet natural as that thought seemed, it was the essence of opposition to the nature of Love and to the most thoroughgoing meaning of divinity. For the ultimate Source must needs remain in the Unmanifest, since to manifest is to be limited and finite, and hence no longer to be ultimate. So in so desiring, the Third Entity broke the immortal band of love-energy since that desire was, in effect, to have the whole of Love to itself, to possess the unpossessable, to limit the unlimited.

Now nothing cancels out in that world-without-waiting; but the only way such a desire could become implemented was by invoking the very image of lovelessness out of the Unmanifest Source of all possibilities—something never meant to be manifest. As Lovecraft, whom we previously quoted, put it: Things walked that were never meant to crawl. All this happened *instanter*, for in the world-out-of-waiting-time there is no delay. Immediately with that momentary dream of absolute self-containment on the part of the Third Entity, arose within its being the monstrous image of all evil,[15] called in the Yemenite tradition, "the Image of Iblis" (i.e. of Satan), the concept going back to the Egyptian god of evil, Set, who antedates the Indo-Iranian *Angra Manyush* (> Ahriman), literally "hate-filled, i.e., loveless mind." Note that all possibilities must exist in invokable form in the unmanifest, or else there could not be free choice, which is the hallmark of love, by which love in turn is guaranteed since non-voluntary love is a contradiction in terms. Thus the very nature of love guarantees both the *possibility* (under free choice) of evil and its ultimate defeat if manifested.

The shock of this horrible manifestation awoke the Third Entity from the evil-spawning fantasy; but too late, for in that realm of supernal reality, evil was now released and made manifest. With a shudder of revulsion, the divine being expelled the horrid image; but that being contained also within itself the seeds of countless other potential and similar beings, who were now all infested with the image. All these beings possessed free choices, for that is and must be one of the endowments of love (cf. Supplement 1.7), dangerous as the gift may be. Many of these lesser beings belonging to the Third Great Divinity likewise abjured the evil image in themselves. But some did not, and in rebellion proclaimed the false and destructive egalitarianism of "we are as excellent as you, and if we feel this image increases our own power we shall keep it and cultivate it."[16] Of course, all that happened to them is that the Image of Iblis mastered *them*: they verily became all equal—all equally slaves. The unqualified egalitarianism that sprang up with the bloody massacres of Robespierre and Cromwell and their ilk still ends in increased slavery for all adherents of such creeds stemming from the disordering image of evil's essence. The primordial retributive paradigm prevails throughout time.

So the Third Divinity gathering about the heroic cohorts that had likewise abjured lovelessness within themselves, re-avowed the great truth that no manifest being, however high, can contain the source of his/her own existence, but must humbly and lovingly acknowledge that Unmanifest, Limitless Love-Power-Wisdom that alone can be the Source of all without danger and disaster.

Meantime, during that dark and diseaseful moment of reverie a momentary cut-off from Love's energy began to form a horrendous and absolute separation in the scheme of things. But absolute separations cannot exist by the fundamentality of Love, which means universal connectedness. Hence the virtual and impending gap between the Third Entity and the higher ones was at once filled with a manifest image of the unmanifest Pleroma of Powers, which form a minimal group of seven (the hepton of chapter 4).[17] But that gap, thus interpolated and closed, forced the Third Divinity down to Tenth Place (see figure 5–1)[18] as a therapeutic measure.

At this point, it would be well to take stock and observe that with the first manifestation of evil could arise for the first time a pathological kind of pairing. Whereas before, we have a multitude of natural and mutually completing pairs like female/male, day/night, finite/infinite, white/black, et al., now we have the additional possibility of pathological, host/parasite pairs like good/evil, honesty/deception, health/sickness, in which we have no longer two self-completing entities, both of which are needed in the scheme of things. Rather, we now have pairs of which only one is needed for well-being, the other being parasitic (*not* symbiotic) and actually inimical to it.

The Pythagoreans, misunderstanding their Egyptian teachers, placed the host/parasite duality of good and evil (hence also health and sickness) on the same footing as the quite different class of benign, self-complementary duals of finite/infinite, male/female, et al. And later philosophers, both oriental and occidental (e.g. Carl Jung), have repeated that fundamental error stemming from inaccurate perception that failed to make the basic distinction between the two radically different kinds of opposites: those which are wave-like and mutually self-completing; and the later, pathological variety, able to exist only since the manifestation of evil, where one of the pair parasitizes on the other and, attacking it, attempts to destroy it permanently. The grip of the ancient error in the human mind is evidenced by the fact that this fundamental distinction was taught in no university philosophy course of the

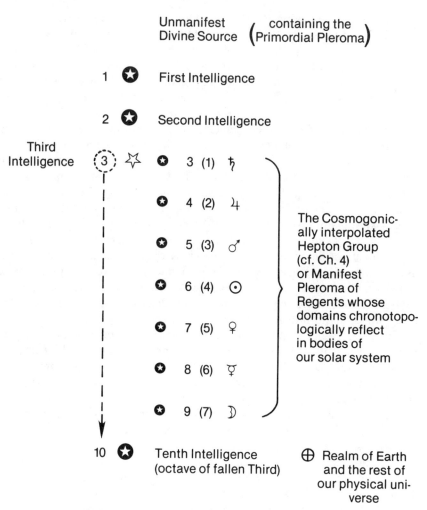

Figure 5-1. Schema of How Our Time Began According to Ancient Tradition

twentieth century as of 1983. Indeed, Jung's confused "coincidence of opposites" continues to be parroted.

Finally, the term for "Evil" in ancient Egypt is the word *isf-t*, already in the oldest of the Pyramid Texts, that of Unas (line 394). It is derived from the verbal root *isf* "to cut off" (found also in the Pyramid of Unas, line 120). Thus the most ancient meaning of evil traced its origin to when the love-current of divine energy (called *māddat* in the Yemenite form of the tradition) was inadvertently and momentarily blocked or cut off by the Third Divine Entity when he dreamed of containing the source of his own being.

The tradition whose doctrine we are discussing assigns entire worlds of development to each member of the Hepton thus cosmogonically engendered in the incipient or virtual Love-vacuum caused by the brooding dream of impossible self-sufficiency on the part of the Third Entity, who has now become the god of our fallen universe at the tenth or lowest level in the hierarchy. Each one of these worlds is in resonance with the timing and chrontopological effect or nature of the bodies of our solar system, in which the "time of long domination (of suffering)," the old Iranian *zervān derangxvatāi*, has replaced the time of no waiting, the time without limitations or *zervān akarāna*. It should be noted that the preceding discussion puts the old dichotomy of "eternity versus time" in a new light. Eternity is not the mere empty concept of infinite duration but rather it is Time devoid of limitations—without waiting time; hence a Time of Eternal Blossoming, a blinding effulgency for us, immersed as we are in the time of lengthy and necessarily endured waiting. Without this new interpretation of eternity versus time, the tradition we are discussing cannot be properly understood; and it hitherto has not.

However, Henry Corbin, who came nearest to understanding it, well points out that there is a great correspondence between the old Zervanite tradition of the god who "forgets" goodness and so gives rise to a monstrous child (Ahriman) who is forthwith rejected but nevertheless ties up the universe of Zervan for ages with suffering, all manner of moral ills, and death. Yet the Zervan story is very gross and corrupted as compared with the purer form of the same tradition mysteriously and uniquely preserved in Yemen.[19] Let us proceed.

The introduction of waiting time meant, in precise terms, the introduction of entropy and hysteresis, for now no cycle could be repeated without energy losses; and hence all systems would inevitably and eventually run down as, in each cycle more so, the newly introduced energy could not be quite enough to repair the worn structures and restore the energy losses without unavoidable further wastes and dissipations due to the same finite-and-loss-occasioning-waiting-time phenomenon.[20] So the biological body, in theory (i.e., with no waiting time for re-energization) immortal, must ineluctably age. Similarly, resistance can be undermined and disease occur; and the ultimate consequence of aging is death, or the functional cessation of the bodily vehicle for physical implementing of awareness. Thus our world of waiting, disease, aging, suffering, and death stems from the nature of time itself and was part and parcel of the set of implied consequences of the Demiurge's Dream—

that very brief nightmare that had spawned a reality of evil on awakening.

So the God of our universe is a wounded God in heart although Himself recovered. His domain, which before was a universally symbiotic cosmos, had now become the frenetically struggling, predominantly predatory one we all know, with Nature trying still to smile through her travail. There is a mysterious tradition both in Iran and Egypt of the female aspect of this Divinity (Dāēna in Iran and Isis in Egypt) who did not share the death-dream of her spouse and who in fact helped him revive as the renewed and victorious Horus. So Isis beautifully sings with Dante, "Veni, sponsa de Libano"—Come, my spouse, from Lebanon—for the coffin of Osiris had washed ashore at Byblos . . . In this connection compare [132, pp. ix, x, xii] and Proverbs 8:27–31 [134, p. 1002], where Goddess speaks of God.

A fragment of the ancient protohistory reappears metamorphosed in Amfortas, the gravely wounded king of the Grail Castle in Wagner's version of Wolfram's *Parzifal*. He is the Osiris to the rescuing Parsifal's Horus: two aspects of the same deific being—one just after his mistake and the other after its correction first in himself and then in his (i.e., our) cosmos. And Wolfram's mysterious and somewhat eponymous source, the sage "Flege-tanis," evidences Islamic origins since the name is simply a corruption of the Arabic *falak tanī*, "the second star," i.e., the Regent of Mercury (counting from the lowest or Moon—see figure 5–1), lord of wisdom, known in Hellenistic Egypt as Thoth Thrice Great or Hermes Trismegistos.

Other remnants of the ancient tradition were preserved in medieval Europe, notably in the Jena and Manesse manuscripts' recounting of the great minnesinger contest in the castle on the Wartburg, the primary published source for which is *Der Singerkriec uf Wartburc*, edited with text, translations, and notes by Ludwig Ettmüller and published by B.F. Voigt in Ilmenau, 1830. Songs 84–85 of the Jena Manuscript and 122 of the Manesse Manuscript tell of that precious stone that fell from Lucifer's crown when he, with his legions of "sixty thousand angels," sought to overthrow divinity in our universe. The poem speaks of "der stein der us der kronen sprang"—the gem that from the crown then sprang (Manesse Manuscript, Lied 122)—and of how "die krone brach er sunder . . . ein stein darûz gespranc, der wart doch sint of erdhen Parzevale"—from the crown that broke asunder a crest jewel fell and waited on the earth for Parsifal (Jena Manuscript, Lied 84). There is a further illuminating detail preserved in the medieval sources (cf. Ettmüller's note to line 1245, Lied 84, on p. 135): the crown jewel went from Lucifer back to the Holy Virgin, Divine Protectress of the earth—an Isis figure. In the ancient Egyptian version, Set (> Lucifer/ Lucifuge) became thus "emasculated" thereby foregoing his divine creativity based on the now lost love power. Then the Divine Virgin safeguarded the jewel of immortal life and sacred power (symbolized also by the left eye of the Elder Horus and the phallos of Osiris), vouchsafing it again to the young and resurrected Horus Savior, the messianic Parsifal figure and also the *puer aeternus*, Shakepeare's "naked new-born babe striding the blast" (*Macbeth* I, 7) and bearing al-Ḥāmidī's *Kanz al-Walad*, the treasure of the divine youth.

The ancient tradition we are investigating in this chapter clarifies that Lucifer was the chief of those cohorts of the Third (become Tenth) Divine Being who, after the latter's momentary lapse, chose to follow the thereby evoked Image of All Evil that arose from that fleeting yet so crucial nightmare. In making that choice, Lucifer lost the crown jewel of his love, then transferred into the safekeeping of the Divine Virgin, Protectress of Earth, where the battle between the forces of good and evil was to rage until Time was through. Parzevale in the *Singerkriec* and in Wolfram von Eschenbach's poem is the image of the cosmic Hero-Savior or Avatar whose earliest form is Horus: Osiris regenerated through Isis's love. (Cf. our *East-West Fire*, Watkins, London, 1955, p. 43.)

Lucifer is in the ancient tradition thus put in perspective, not as the primary source of evil, but simply as the leader of those first high beings who were corrupted by its evocation into manifestation. The lapse in brooding though momentary reverie on the part of the regnant divinity of our universe manifested the image of all possible evil; Lucifer—then become Lucifuge (a title and concept preserved in the medieval grimoires)—was simply the first casualty. Jacob Boehme (cf. [135]), who transmitted the ancient tradition as well as revealed new insights, makes a related distinction in his works between "Satan" who in Boehme corresponds to the evoked "Image of Iblis" in the Yemen-preserved tradition, and "Lucifer" who was the highest being personifying that Image of Evil and of whom Boehme says in the *Signatura Rerum* that "from a king he is become an executioner" i.e., of the behests of the Image whose slave he became. "That old dragon" of the gnostic Christian Book of Revelations by John of Patmos corresponds to Boehme's Satan and the ancient Egyptian primordial Serpent[21] of Evil, '*Ap-p* (Coptic ΑΦΩΦΙ or ΑΦΟΦΙ), with a set of "accursed names" countering the 75 divine and sacred names of the beneficent God of gods. Boehme's Lucifer relates to the Egyptian Set, who becomes emasculated—a facet of the tradition preserved in the impotence of Wagner's Luciferean figure of Klingsor in the music drama *Parsifal*.

The tradition of a cosmic struggle between higher powers of good and evil thus did not start with Iran: Egypt was older. And to argue that a "Devil" was merely invented as a "scapegoat" for our failings is an error of human egotism: the evil of our predation- and parasite-ridden ecology *antedates* humanity.[22] Until we stop closing our eyes to this far-reaching fact and its profound implications, we will not be able to muster the needed intellectual honesty or acumen to respond to the first drunk's pointed remarks at the start of this chapter.

We, the lowest remant still on the planet earth of the much vaster legions of the Divinity of our universe, now are fallen, together with our subaltern fellow creatures, by our persistent inability to expel the anciently released Image of Lovelessness from within us. Yet we still possess our primordial links with immortality, but they are vitiated by being death-inter-rupted. . . .

The tradition reminds us, were we to be released tomorrow back into the realm of time-without-waiting, we would speedily fall immediate heir to even worse troubles than we now have, for we could not control our power-dreams and hence would only re-evoke the illusion of self-sufficiency and the consequent re-manifestation in us of the image of unmitigated evil to which such a thought and desire leads as their inherent implication. Indeed, the comparative molasses-slowness of our current kind of time is our shield and protection against ourselves.

Then what is our recourse? It is twofold: to practice maintaining the serenity and inner harmony that can invoke the love-wisdom energy under all conditions; and second, to practice charitableness toward evolutionary stages less perceptive than our own, and seek communion with beings of evolutionary stages beyond ours so that they, by our willingness and leave, are thus able to help us and imbue us with inner strength, inspiration, and hope.[23] By such practice and living will we gradually, through the time of long waiting, be able to prepare and equip ourselves again for that presently unimaginable Time of Blossoming. This discussion helps afford an inkling of the enormous strength of love and responsibility required for godhood as distinct from mere humanity. It is a salutary reminder.

But whence came this remarkably specified, penetratingly intelligent solution of the central problem of human systems throughout history and before—to the still unrecovered origins of humanity itself? Because of free will, history cannot be exactly pre- or postdicted without access to what actually took place. In our tradition we accordingly have, quite correctly, a historical setting, using history in the most far-reaching sense of a record of events that happened, no matter how far off in our reckoning of time.

Our tradition also makes clear that the current cosmic stage is in process of overcoming the effects of its originally induced evolutionary postponement, the *takhalluf* already discussed. Hence our time is a profoundly restorative process, by which we return back through the fallen octave, back from 10th to 3rd place, when the interpolated hepton (see figure 5–1) will again be able to withdraw into the Pleroma, and the seven heavens "rolled up like a scroll," as a later and corrupted scrap of the same tradition recorded by John of Patmos tells. Thus our time is self-reëntrant (the ancient *ouroboros* symbol) and contains an inherent and beneficent self-destruct in its long but ineluctable pilgrimage to return to its lost higher octave of beginning. Time is like the flight of a great hawk that finally returns at the call of the Falconer.

The return is not mere repetition since it is fraught with the wisdom distilled out of its intimate confrontation with brute, conscious, all-devouring, necessarily parasitic evil—the Image of Iblis, first unawarely allowed to form in and then escape out of the Unmanifest by the desire-energy of the self-doomed quest of the Third Intelligence. Pandora's box is an extremely diluted form of the same ancient tradition, which we will endeavor to trace further.

The key to it is the number 10 (venerated first by Pythagoras who, on all ancient authority, sat under Egyptian teachers). That this is so is born out by the related fact that the Egyptian number-base 10 was also used by the Greeks and the Phoenicians.[24] The Chaldean priesthoods of Sumero-Babylonian civilization developed a sexagesimal system based on 12, but even that was dominated by multiples of 10 like 30 (the sacred number of the great divinity *Sīn*, regent of the moon), and 60. Indeed, as the least common multiple of 10 and 12, 60 was the chosen base of the Chaldean number system.

So the Egyptian 10 was basic, and the number words in ancient Egyptian prove it, leading up to a complete fullness in 9, with 10 being the number of the eternal new birth of the unit, and thus a paradigm of that infinity and eternity that characterized the divine power imbuing the world in which we find ourselves. The etymologies show the numbers were regarded as a series of god-like powers. We have space only for a few examples here, which will deal with the primary or cardinal numbers 1 through 10 comprising the Egyptian number base. The ordinals were all very similar words with the feminine-substantive -*t* suffix added.

The number one is called *W'a* (still the same root in all semitic languages) and we find *Nub W'a*, Lord of Oneness, in the Fifth Dynasty Pyramid Texts (Unas, line 416, Teta, line 237), as well as in later texts; '*a* alone means "a" or "an." Sometimes the manifest godhead is called "the one" (*W'a*) as in the Pyramid of Teta, line 247 (see Kurt Sethe's *Pyramidentexte*), showing how long Plato and Plotinus were antedated, not to mention the Biblical "I the Lord thy God am One." The Coptic descendant word is *OYA* (pronounced *WA*—recall that the Coptic Y is a *U*).

The ancient Egyptian number word for "three" is *khemet* (*ShEMET* in Coptic, when, as even in later Egyptian the phonetic transition *Kh* → *Sh* occurred). Now the glyph ⬙ (*Kh* or *Khè*) was itself a word meaning babe, child, or youth. The rising sun, thus called the divine "babe," was denoted by it, as well as the Nile when starting to rise. Now the word *mēt* (Coptic *MHT*) is the number word for "ten" and was denoted by the phallus glyph as we shall presently see. The number word for "three" is that same glyph qualified by the *Kh-* glyph. So "Three" is literally called "the youthful ten" or "The former state or start of Ten" (i.e., "Ten" as it used to be), thus remarkably preserving that unique connection between the Third and Tenth Intelligences or Divine Numbers that distinguishes the Yemenite-preserved tradition, throwing sharp light on its Egyptian origin.

Note that the Ten Divine Entities were also symbolized as numbers in the deepest Pythagorean sense—a sense also, as the extant and repeated record attests—derived from Egypt during Pythagoras' studies there (later, without any shred of evidence whatsoever, denied by those whose prejudices that fact did not suit). These facts are also confirmed in that jewel of Judaism, the Kabbalah, by the oldest gnostic-kabbalistic text we have, the "Book of Foundation" (*Sefer Yetzirah*) which depicts the 10 great cosmic spheres[25] or domains of the divine numbers as ruled by "flaming ministers" who, swift as lightning, constantly execute divine commands throughout the universe and momently circle back to the exalted throne for new orders, like some vast electronic network of computer circuits.

The Kabbalah drew on Iranian, Chaldean, and Egyptian influences, and the sacredness of Ten is peculiarly Egyptian, as we have already seen. The ancient traditions preserved in the Kabbalah also include the threefold mystery within the Unmanifest as *'Ayn* (the Nothing), *'ayn Sof* (without limit, i.e. the Infinite Power) and *'ayn Sof Aur* (the limitless or infinite Light), thus relating as we already have seen, to the Iranian *azal, asalīyat,* and *azalī* (Arabic *fā'il, fi'l,* and *maf'ūl*), the first two terms corresponding to the late Tantric *Shakta* and *Shakti,* as before noted, the third being then the *bindu*: the divine seed or golden womb (*hiranyagarbha*) from which all things issued forth. It is all the same tradition: the oldest perennial philosophy. The mystery of the Tenth Number, *Malkut* or "the Kingdom" (i.e. this universe, destined for divine transformation) is the Mystery of the fallen Tenth Intelligence, God of our race and our world in the tradition.

We resume the ancient Egyptian number sequence. "Five" was *tua* or *tu* (Coptic *TH* and *TOOYE*) sometimes written also with the tall pyramidal determinative, meaning to impart to, equip, prepare with (hence in the esoteric sense, "to initiate"). The word *tua* with the pentagram or star determinative meant "dawn" (Coptic TOOYI). With the nominative suffix -*t* added, we have the famous Egyptian word *Duat*, the place of deepest darkness after death, where the soul may either be transformed into a higher metamorphosis able to dawn (*dua*) as a rising star in a higher world, never again to set; or else be re-cycled in a divine tear of compassionate sorrow at its failure, and fall again to earth to begin its climb anew, as the ancient Egyptian esoteric books set forth.[26]

"Eight," as the cube or third power of two (powers of which played such a fundamental role in Egyptian arithmetic [89]), was called *Kh-m-n* or literally "generating or creating enduringly," i.e., an enduring (*m-n*) "three" (*kh-m*). Mathematically, $2^3 = 8$, 8 having 3 as its logarithm to the base 2. Hence the primal creator gods formed a group of eight. That group with their leader then implied nine, the complete closure of units, and an important number in ancient Egypt, signifying the completed company of gods. "Nine" was called *psit* (Coptic ѰIT, sometimes ѰIC) and is written with (or sometimes simply as) the glyph meaning "radiance." Nine thus also meant to shine, illumine, or energize: literally to provide with seeds of light-life substance that could later germinate. With the proper determinative it could refer to the backbone, and could also denote the sacred sacrum of Osiris the *djedj*, considered the regenerative seat of his immortality. Thus nine denoted the full gamut of immortal, divine power, and a complete company, circuit, or enclosure of powers that generated their regenerative seeds. Interestingly the archaic Greek word εἰνα for nine also derives from an old form of the root meaning to be enclosed or fully contained, the same root being connected with the German *ei* ("egg") and the English eye (i.e. "eyeball"), as a seed-pod (the eye being thought of as an egg) that could generate life and light, and the sacred eye of the Elder Horus is also "the egg" from which the Immortal Younger Horus arises.

We finally arrive at the number base 10, which confirms that the full complement of unit digits was reached in "nine." All succeeding numbers are written as new combinations of this primal number alphabet. The word for "ten," *mēt* (Coptic *MHT*), could also be written as the ejaculating phallus glyph, denoting fertilization and begetting, and the word *mēt* meant a procreator or creator. Written with the determinative for the "negation" or for "destroy," it then meant death or the cutting off of life. As a plural, *mētu*, the word denotes "seed," "posterity," i.e., those procreated. Thus the 10th number denoted our sensorily observed world of generation and corruption, the domain of the Third-become-Tenth Intelligence in the Yemen-preserved tradition.

As the zero in figure 5–1, the realm of the unmanifest divinity, it was in ancient Egypt the *nen-un* or *n'un*, literally the non (prefix *nen* or *n'*)- existent (*wn*, the Coptic OYN or OYON, taken by the Greek as AIΩN, and still surviving as "aeon" or "eon" in English). Note the philosophical pun, a phenomenon by which the Egyptian priesthood set great store. The word

NWN 〰️ meant the original, primeval, self-maintaining, living substance (note the wave-glyphs and *cf.* announced Supplement 2.2 and 2.4). It could also thus mean *N'WN* or *N + WN*, the great sea of unmanifest (*N*) being

(WN) this last being symbolized also as 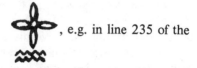 , e.g. in line 235 of the

Pyramid Texts of King Pepi.[27] Note the fivefold, life-dawning symbol emerging from the waves of the primal substance. The rabbit glyph's long ears were used as a symbolic assimilative replacement for the "petals" of the more ornate glyph. That the fivefold glyph referred to life in the eternal no-thing (= no as yet manifest thing) is evident in the fact that three such glyphs in a row was a plural form meaning "the ever-existing ones."

So when the number 10 appears as the heart of the distinctive tradition preserved so uniquely in Yemen, one is naturally, by the geography alone, led to think in terms of an originally Egyptian context. Al-Kirmānī, whom the Yemenite *Dā ʿīs* so frequently quote as an authority, taught, to be sure, a doctrine of ten intelligences, yet without a trace of the distinctive features of the primordial fall of one of them to lowest rank, and its subsequent cosmogonic and cosmological consequences for us and our current universe. Moreover, al-Kirmānī had no Ismaili precedent in this.[28] Thus when the Yemenite *Dā ʿīs* cite him as they do, they do so to try to establish, by the only link available, the Ismaili orthodoxy of their actually quite different doctrine. Their frequent citation of Kirmānī does not show "influence" (for he did not even conceive of their teaching) but rather justification and an attempt to incorporate into Ismaili acceptance a powerful tradition that had come to them and by which they were deeply convinced.

As to how the doctrine reached them, we must still await, for a full determination, a study of unedited manuscripts preserved in Yemen (their center was at Sa'ana) and in the Bohra community in Bombay. Yet even now we can begin closing that mysterious and largely unknown time gap by citing the probable line of transmission from Egypt through figures like the gifted, inspired, and enigmatic Dhū 'l-Nūn (actually, Abū 'l-Fayḍ Ṭawbān ibn Ibrāhīm al-Miṣrī) alternatively transcribed Dhū 'n-Nūn († 860) and called

"The Egyptian" (al-Miṣrī) who, long before Thomas Young and Champollion, had seriously studied and attempted to read Egyptian hieroglyphs, the last indigenous priests having that knowledge having died out in or by the seventh century. He came only some 200 years later.

His father was a Nubian, so he was thus in his family contacts that much closer to Yemen. He lived for years at Akhmīm in Egypt and died at Alexandria. He preached an advanced Islamic mystical doctrine of love as the greatest cosmic power and the necessity to vigilantly keep it uppermost in enlightened awareness. He accordingly taught that the sin of advanced souls does not take the usual wordly forms, but the subtler one of inattention (*ghafla*) or failure to maintain this vigilance. He inherited the Egyptian alchemical, theurgistic and gnostic tradition[29] [141,142] and with it the concept of the almost divine human being that he was termed a *quṭb zamānihī* ("axis of his time"), a concept that passed through Shī'ite Ismaili channels to ibn al-Arabī and became the Shī'ite (including Ismaili) central notion of the *Imam*.

Egyptians like the remarkable Dhū 'n-Nūn were sufficient to carry the golden thread of the ancient Egyptian gnosis into later Islamic gnosticism,[30] whence by some as yet not fully delineated path, it reached the Ṭayyibītīs in Yemen and was luckily preserved.[31]

The last great manifestation of ancient Egyptian religion was the cult of the Hidden God, Amun-Ré (Coptic *PH*), whose symbolic appearance, though with gradual loss of its comprehension, persists well into the subsequent gnosticism of Christian Egypt, especially in Amun's later, four-winged form. The world at large knew very little of the theology until recently, when the temple of Opet was excavated in 1970 by Claude Traunecker [143] of the Centre Iranco-Egyptien at Karnak and later studied by the brilliant decipherer and interpreter, Jean-Claude Goyon, who had already distinguished himself by his *Textes Mythologiques* (Parts I and II). Parker freely acknowledges (p. x) that Goyon did "the translation of all the texts . . . [and drew] the hieroglyphs throughout, the plates of parallel texts . . . and it is he who has undertaken to formulate an interpretation of the purpose of the edifice, an interpretation to which both Leclant and myself are happy to subscribe."

It was the almost intact Temple of Opet at Karnak which, by a parallel mural, allowed Goyon to resolve the mystery of the inmost and most subterranean room of the Temple of Ra built by King Taharka, successor of another pharaoh, Shabaka, of the same Ethiopian (XXVth) Dynasty, *ca.* 735–655 B.C.E., the same Shabaka who restored that remarkable monument to ancient Memphite Theology, the so-called "Stone of Shabaka" now in the British Museum.[32] The Opet-lent solution is strikingly relevant to our investigation and proves the profoundly numinous character of the number ten, the primordial attestation of which in ancient Egyptian tradition we have already found evidenced in the very etymology of the number words for 1 through 10.[33]

As Goyon says, summarizing his work (p. 79): "It may be considered as certain that this number [i.e. the number of divine souls of Amun] was ten, the same as the number of secret names carved on both sides of the door" (of the Taharka crypt). The like crypt of the Temple of Opet made the restoration of the figures of the Taharka initiatory temple crypt possible, which together with the older texts at the Temple of Hibis in the Khargeh Oasis, in turn further confirmed the doctrine expressed in the figures of the crypt of Opet. Goyon (p. 80) observes the antiquity of these notions: "The Ethiopian 'Renaissance' was essentially a return to the forms and lessons of the past. The Kushite kings aimed at restoring the rites and the manifestations of the long line of their predecessors." It is moreover known that the theology of Amun was syncretistic seeking to incorporate all the older and important teachings within itself. Hence the doctrine of an ultimate ten highest and essential beings whose united attributes are those of an all-supreme Divinity, must be regarded as a tradition long antedating the Theban theology, as again borne out by the prior analysis of ancient Egyptian number words, for such words are the oldest artefacts of any culture.

Goyon again significantly notes (p. 82): "From the New Kingdom on [i.e. from *ca.* 1300 B.C.E] we have references to the trip made by Amun every ten days from Luxor to Medinet Habu and the mysterious crypt of Kamutef. . . . Some of the rites take place at Djemê, where tradition places the crypt of Kamutef. And again (p. 51): "The representations . . . seem to retrace symbolically and schematically some of the rites that took place during the visit of Amun to the sacred mound of Djemê [of death and re-birth]. . . . A figuration of the mystery of the transformation of Amun into a sun-falcon, rising again from the lotus as keeper of the world order (Maat)." It was at Djemê, too, where lay Kamutef and the either other divine ancestors invoked in these ceremonies centered on the divine re-birth after achieving resonant union with the Ten Great Powers. Moreover, this rite was celebrated every ten days, as the hieroglyphic texts themselves state, as they also identify the funerary mound of Kôm Djemê symbolically with "the kingdom of the dead," i.e. the place of those who have not yet re-attained, re-actualized their own potential divinity.

In the most recent, subterranean crypt at the Taharka Temple were 24 columns originally covered with texts now restorable only through copies on the walls of the Temple of Hibis, which contains also some extremely important ancient cosmological doctrines, that are not of immediate concern to the present discussion. This crypt is concerned with the Ten Deific Souls of the Most Hidden One (Amun Ré). The First of these is identified with Ta-Nun; the Second, with Osiris; the Third with Shu, and also with Nun. For the Fourth through the Tenth of the Divine Souls or Creative Essences, the text is unfortunately too destroyed to make out the various inscriptions; and the Opet Temple, useful as it is, does not give as full texts as the Taharka Temple. However, the Fifth seems related to Sekhmet, and the Ninth to Sobek. But the principal intent of the ceremony can be deciphered from all these remnants, and we can do no better than to cite Goyon's masterful summation (p. 83): "Finally, the god entered the last accessible room, where the representations of his ten bas appear, there, in the most secret part of the edifice, in the half-light, the divine statue, thanks to the efficacy of the word and the magical communication from one image to another, became impregnated with the vivifying power emanating from the ten sacred effigies and, by this mystical union, became Re, who would appear out of the darkness as on the first day." Goyon adds in his important note 40: "The ten bas are treated theologically as direct emanations of Re."

Such was the reconstruction finished around 1977 by Goyon, and published in 1979, of a doctrine whose roots go back to an extreme antiquity, as the ancient Egyptian base-ten number system also showed, particularly in its special relating of Three and Ten—a connection illuminated by the obscure remnant of the tradition preserved with remarkable detail in the backwater of medieval Yemen. Such a persistence need not surprise when we know that certain rites and doctrines of ancient Egypt had a continuous existence from at least the Vth Dynasty through the Ptolemaic period—a stretch of over two millennia.

There is a last word to be said on the repetition of the ceremony of uniting with the Ten Divine Souls every ten days, for that was exactly the period between the heliacal rising of each ruling star of a decan (hence the name). The Carlsberg Papyrus No. 1 states (III, 2 and VI, 2+8) that "one star dies and another star lives every 10 days." The time of each star's "working" is in the clearly visible night sky region of 120°, 60° on each side of the zenith. The nadir or nethermost invisible portion of a star's circuit was considered to be 70° (or seven decades of days, ending with heliacal rising), in extent, identified with the invisible, or after-death world called the Duat, where also the regenerative process, preparing for a new birth or dawning, took place. This was called also the House of Geb, the Mound of Djemê, and other like appellations, depending on its various aspects addressed in the rituals.

From stopping from working to setting is 30° when the star "entered Nut's mouth" at the western horizon. Then from setting to entering the Duat is another 60°, thus making 90 days in all from its "ceasing from working" in the West and its entering the Duat. Then, after the 70-day purification and self-metamorphosis, the star prepares 50 days for dawning and then remains in the East 30 more days before working. We thus have as the whole sacred regenerative preparatory period $90 + 70 + 80 = 240$ days which, added to the 120 days of manifestation or "working" complete the 360° circuit of the ritual year, the five special days (361–365) being considered outside of and apart from the cycle itself and more like the extra bit of axially directed arc necessary to be added to execute a full 360° turn on a helical path. The number 240 is also celebrated as a sacred number of the god of wisdom (Thoth) in the texts inscribed on the walls of the Temple of Horus at Edfu, an ancient site restored in Ptolemaic times.

Bearing out his faithfulness as a reporter in this respect, Diodorus of Sicily uses almost the same words as the Carlsberg Papyrus No. 1 already given, obviously having depended on a similar source-text. He writes in his second book, and we are now in the times of Julius Caesar, that the regents of the planetary spheres are deputized as "interpreters of the divine mind and purpose" and that, as prime overseers, there are some thirty star gods each of whom is a βουλαίους θεούς or counseling deity, and "once in ten days a messenger or angel star (καθάπερ ἀγγελου) rises above from below, and another sets and descends."

Knowing this passage in Diodorus and its striking confirmation of the ancient Egyptian tradition, I was happy to read on pages 355–356 of the second volume of Joseph Needham's *Science and Civilisation in China* that "there were prognostications based on the decan-stars, that is to say, those paranatellons the heliacal risings and settings of which can be used to determine the exact hour if the date is known, or the exact date if the time is known. These were studied by the Egyptians as early as -2000. The Greeks called them *leitourgoi* ('stars on duty') or *theoi boulaioi* ('advisory gods'), and considered that every ten days one was sent as a messenger from those above to those below, and vice versa (i.e., setting and rising)."

His citation—pure Egyptian doctrine—seemed to show a possibly different source from Diodorus, but unfortunately none was indicated, so I wrote to Sir Joseph and asked him for his source. On March 13, 1983, I learned he no longer recalled it, and he wrote: "A fairly cursory search . . . did not reveal the origins of the Greek terms which you mention. I much regret that I did not give the source for them in a footnote on the page that you mention. However, I have no reason at all to think that they are wrong."[34] They are decidedly not wrong, and only serve to re-confirm how robust and long-surviving were the old Egyptian traditions. It becomes less and less surprising to have re-found them in medieval Yemen.

Let us not forget that one of twentieth century scholarship's weak points was its failure to take into account the extent of early communications or to realize that human beings were quite as intelligent as long as 30,000 years ago as they are today, and on the whole were honest in their statements— certainly not less so than in the twentieth century.[35] It is now beginning to be realized, through the work of scholars like Emil Benveniste, W. Bousset and their intellectual heirs, that there were deep Egypto-Chaldean influences on Greek, Roman, Byzantine, Islamic, and European civilizations, and that the Platonic Academy was influenced by ideas that filtered through from ancient Iran. Indeed Plato and Pythagoras themselves make no secret of Egyptian influences bearing on them, much as some of the later more superficial brands of thinking might like to discount those passages as well as deny the facts themselves, which go ill with latter-day intellectual chauvinisms. Plato's Academy was no more conventionally Grecian in its theology than was Cosimo de' Medici's Florentine Academy Christian.

It is also often heard that only with post-Christian gnostics did the idea of the planets being linked with beings of evil arise. But the idea is ancient and would have to be the moment the origin of the current cosmos is seen as a *re*action to an original unpremeditated release of evil possibilities. Indeed in Aristotle's *Metaphysica* (xi:6,12) he clearly implies that only in the spheres beyond those of the planets are utter harmony and bliss to be found.

The system of spheres in Aristotle could well also have reached him through the Chaldean-Magian synthesis that had been going on ever since Persia conquered Babylon under Cyrus (Khosroës). It is certain in any case that the doctrine of a sacred number of celestial spheres and their domains did not originate either with Aristotle or for that matter with Greek civilization; and the first Greek on record as visiting Chaldea was the near contemporary of Pythagoras, Antimenidas (whose brother was the poet Alcaeus), who resided there for some time *ca*. 590 B.C.E., as Strabo tells us in his thirteenth book, confirmed also in fragments of Alcaeus. And later, of course, there was Herodotus who went there under the rule of Cyrus. Aristotle, in his voyages as preceptor of Alexander of Macedonia, might even have come to see Babylonia and Persia himself, and certainly would know something of their leading ideas, and much the same applies to Plato and especially to the later Academy.

That the Yemenite tradition recognized it had forebears is born out by the writings of the Ṭayyibite spiritual and doctrinal leaders. Thus the eighth sovereign propagator of the faith (*Dā ī muṭlaq*), Ḥusain ibn 'Alī ibn Muḥammed ibn al-Walīd, in the third section of the preface to his "Tract on the First and the Last" (*al-Mabda' wal-ma'ād*) written in thirteenth century Yemen, specifies that his treatise contains the core of "the teaching that comes to us through our Most Pure Guides concerning the profound doctrine

(Tawhīd)," without further naming this lineage of doctrinal transmission; and the earliest Ṭayyibite workd containing the tradition of our interest likewise clearly evince that they are transmitting something of primordial character and not at all writing novelties on their own.

Let us recall that Yemen was a Pharaonic protectorate from the times of the earliest Memphite Dynasties and their priesthoods, and hence a natural repository for ancient theological traditions. That protectorate bridged the way to Syria, Iraq, and Iran—the former Assyrian, Chaldean, and Persian kingdoms—for it included the ancient 70-day caravan route that went from the old site later called Aden to the present Gulf of Aqaba. The powerful continuance of the important pharmacological tradition of ancient Egypt in Yemen even through medieval times[36] is another testimony to an enduringly strong cultural bridge. And, as recently as 1983, a Saudi archaeological team found among the ruins of an ancient Arabian temple a stone depicting religio-cosmological symbols from still more ancient Egypt and Chaldea.

And, as we have already seen in other ways, old Egypto-Yemenite tradition directly influenced the Ṭayyibītī Ismaʿīlīs of Yemen. But it also influenced the Eastern Ismaʿīlīs since during the first century of the Hegira there was a great influx of Yemenites into Syria, particularly after the seat of the Caliphate was transferred from Hijāz to Damascus in 661 C.E., in the 41st year of the Hegira. Now we are in a better position to understand how the ancient and distinctive doctrine of ten deific administrators of the cosmos (nine of them beyond the God of our universe) arose among the Eastern Ismaʿīlīs. It had been transplated from the same ancient Egyptian root-sources that supplied Yemen, reappearing in the sacred Pythagorean decad, the ten ultimate categories of Aristotle, and the later Kabbalistic ten Sephiroth—the same kind of cultural osmotic process through which ancient Egyptian and Iranian doctrines had reached the Platonic Academy which, we now know, was by no means a wholly indigenously Attic blossom.

At this juncture we would like to mention here, as an item found during the writing of this book and one of the more candid attempts to treat the subject of evil, a volume [145] by a professor of the history of ideas, Dr. J. B. Russell of the University of California at Santa Barbara, even though his sources did not include the substantive contribution [135] of Jacob Boehme (1575–1624) and his great expositors John Pordage and Dionysius Freher (1649–1728), much less the extremely important and remarkable though little known ancient traditions preserved by the Ṭayyibites of medieval Yemen. Russell, however, despite his not resolving the main question, rightly reminds twentieth century scholarship, which has so much, especially in the sciences, lost its historical sense and orientation, that "history is a sacred calling." It is nothing less than the call to seek the most truth we can, so that we may best profit by the past, which always proves to be far richer than any arrogant chauvinism of topical contemporaneity could imagine.

It is now clear that the ancient tradition that we have detailed and restored in these pages has a decisive contribution for theodicy;[37] namely, that divine goodness did not create evil. But an error of judgment, far above the human level, inadvertently released it out of the ocean of unmanifest possibilities. Then, under the law of love's allowance of free choice, divinity could not prevent the like free choices by other entities to follow the released image of evil for their model; although love, despite all acts by such entities, must also by its own law of integrity remain itself and so oppose in effect, by its very remaining what it is, the results of such choices.

Moreover, such opposition is not by intent, but by the fact that acts of evil by their very nature choke off (remember the ancient Egyptian root for evil, "*isf*," means "to sever or cut off") the current of love-expressing energy, and then parasitically use that energy to work loveless acts. But such use, by an ineluctable feedback, gradually chokes off the flow of that energy which was engendered by and for loving acts in the first place. Hence evil (already posterior to good as no is to yes, since denial requires a prior affirmation) slowly withers.

But the process is long (in the geological sense!) and the character of time during that process changes to include suffering, waiting, malfunction, senescence, disappointment, and death—all consequences of the primordial usurpation of the love energy by the released image of evil.

Lucifer (then fallen to Lucifuge), was simply the highest ranking among the quasi-divine beings in the cohorts of the Tenth Divine Entity who chose to follow the dictates of the evil image and who continued to feed it with their will, that in consequence became less and less free and more and more in bondage to the manifest Abhorrence. The process of our universe then became a long-drawn out and cycling one of fractional re-distillation,[38] recovering slowly and bit by bit, entity by entity, the beings who had first chosen the Image of Evil as their guide for action, and then re-chosen Love. Meantime, the acts of horror continue in an ecology now turned overwhelmingly predatory from originally symbiotic. For to intervene and stop even one such unjust act, requires, by the law of justice itself, stopping them all. But that would speedily bring our world to a sudden end, and many beings would have lost the chance to reconsider and re-do.

For their sake this cosmic system of school-cum-incarceration is continued until the point where the suffering of the just would accomplish no more good for either the unjust or themselves. At that point the curtain would have to be rung down by love's own law and integrity. But we do not have access to all the data necessary to make such an assessment. Some beyond our stage in the evolution of insight would, however, and that logical assurance must remain our sustenance.

In his Edinburgh lectures, which were the basis for his famous book *The Varieties of Religious Experience*, William James brilliantly summarizes, saying that all great religions address an uneasiness and offer a solution for it:

> "The uneasiness, reduced to its simplest terms, is a sense that there is something wrong about us as we naturally stand. The solution is a sense that we are saved from wrongness by making proper connection with the higher powers . . . "

Here is the root meaning to "re-tie" of religion as *re-ligare*. James goes on:

> "The individual, so far as he suffers from his wrongness and criticizes it, is to that extend consciously beyond it, and in at least possible touch with something higher. . . . Along with the wrong part there is thus a better part of him, even though it may be but a most helpless germ."

The solution, then, is that one identify one's real being with this higher germinal part of oneself becoming, in James' words, "conscious that this higher part is coterminous and continuous with a *More* of the same quality, which is operative in the universe." Making that choice, that re-identification, enables us to survive as significant individuals and re-claim our inherent heritage.

Adding a confirmatory 1982 re-phrasing of James's insight, there is a profound line spoken in the screenplay of "TRON," that great twentieth century version of the primordial struggle and victory. Dumont, Guardian of the Gate between two worlds, speaks: "All that is visible must grow beyond itself and extend into the realm of the invisible. You may pass, my friend."

Meantime, there are some very practical consequences of all this for systems theory since, if these basic ethical-ontological priorities are overlooked or crassly overridden in any chronosystem, the system will fail by eventual but certain disintegration due to the disaffections or the actual psychosomatic and environmentally produced diseases that will thereby become endemic in the human individuals essential to the system's functioning and maintenance.

Thus all tyrannies are non-self-sustaining because tyranny, like all other manifestations of evil, is essentially parasitic. And if we omit love from our premisses, we must needs eventually become not only unreasonable and illogical, but irrational as well—finally clinically so. The human race thus finds itself unique in the dubious distinction of being the first biological species able—if it continues on certain psychological collision courses—to become insane. Fortunately, the diagnosis also indicates the remedy.

To close this chapter there are scarcely more fitting words than those from Christopher Fry's *A Sleep of Prisoners*:

> The frozen misery
> Of centuries breaks, cracks, begins to move;
> The thunder is the thunder of the floes,
> The thaw, the flood, the upstart spring.
> Thank God our time is *now*, when wrong
> Comes up to face us everywhere,
> Never to leave us till we take
> The longest stride of soul men ever took.

After this manuscript was with the publisher, a discerning friend (Francis Huxley) kindly presented me with a copy of a book, *His Master's Voice*, by Stanislaw Lem, whose work I did not know. In a remarkable preface Lem struggles with the same problem that this chapter addresses in more detail. He fails, however, to realize (because he neglects love as a primal ontological factor) that the theology of a fallible God *is* existent, resolving the dilemmas of an arrogant infallibility set up by human hubris in its basic insecurity; and that its magistral prototype was preserved in ancient Egypt and medieval Yemen.

Compared with that prototype, unearthed in the course of this chapter, the various brands of apologism we have been fed by authors from ancient to modern times (their name is legion) fall by the wayside through their comparative superficiality. Similar superficiality, with even less sincerity to excuse it, characterizes the thousand and one versions of defeatism before the problem of evil, masquerading as cynicism or else as that merely inverse credulity called skepticism.

The answer, as we have seen, to all the evasions and pseudo-solutions[39] of the problem had long existed and been preserved, even if in obscure places, and is traceable back to the immemorial traditions on which the priesthood of Amun drew—traditions buried in the very roots of the language of ancient Egypt. That answer, it turns out, is not particularly simple. Nor could it be, for it unveils a subtle and profound illusion which, for one tragic moment, blinded even a god.

Notes

1. Ancient Iranian thought had a technical term for the meantime period: "the time of long domination [of evil]" (*Zervān-i derany xvatāi*). The usual (and naive) attributions of

"omnipotence" are inadequate because omnipotence consistent with love could be neither immediate nor obvious since the free will of others, when taken into account, generates, to say the least, very nonlinear feedbacks, to use cybernetic terms.

2. Taharka's name is effaced by Psammetichus II, who was, however, the first Pharaoh to officially allow Greek and other foreign travellers to visit Egyptian temples and converse with the priesthood.

3. "Gaming" in a more technical but definitely related sense is now an accepted part of systems theory [123].

4. The 1982 novel *Tron* (by Brian Daley based on a story by Bonnie MacBride and Steven Lisberger, who also wrote the screenplay for the Walt Disney release of the same name), though not yet recognized as such, is one of that rare genre, an authentic twentieth century myth in the grand tradition. It explores the central theme of all great mythology: the liberation of the world from the usurpation of an essentially parasitic evil power incarnating lovelessness and exhibiting the consequent pathology stemming from desire denying love and filled with self-centeredness.

5. A type of Ismā 'īlī not be confused with the Aga Khan's better publicized brand (see also the fifth note to section 3.14). For the same reason opinions voiced by the Aga-Khan-subsidized among Western scholars must be suitably sifted, especially in relation to the inadvertent usurpations of the Ṭayyibīte-Bohra doctrines. Now that we know about the very great distinction of the Yemenite doctrine, there is no longer any reason or excuse for the ambiguous usage of "Ismaili" which existed at the time of Vladimir Ivanov's pioneer studies in the 1930s and 1940s.

6. Not *fī 'l* as given by H. Corbin. The spelling is simply *feh, ayn, lam,* with no explicit *ya.*

7. The Arabic term *maf'ūl rajʿī* means feedback and long antedates the English word. The other Arabic word for emanation, *munbaʿiṯ*, simply means "something sent forth or emitted" and is uninformatively descriptive.

8. Cf. the more profound aspects of the tantric doctrine of India and Tibet [132].

9. The graphic Arabic term is *faiḍ*, literally to overflow or pour out: to be emanated or radiated is to be given forth, to issue from, to be ejaculated and to be born at the same time.

10. Cf. also Corbin (reference 131, *Temps Cyclique*, p. 44).

11. The *Lia Fail* or Stone of Divine Destiny in ancient Irish comes to mind, deeply connected with the later concepts of the Grail and the sacred, transmuting Stone of spiritual alchemy, which conferred divinity and immortality. Destiny (Fail) is that which causes to become: so the old Celtic *fail* and the semitic *faʿil* are also linguistically related.

12. See the works of the Ṭayyibite tradition and notably of the second, eighth, and nineteenth Yemenite *Dā 'is* already mentioned.

13. The reader will recall the discussion of *symbolon* and *diabolon* in chapter 2, both stemming from the word βολος, a directed motion or throw. The matter goes deep and the primitive Greek root BOΛ is also behind the word βουλή (Doric βωλά), referring to the decrees (the directed, self-implementing will) of the gods, and especially of those council gods who traditionally presided over the deliberations of the Athenian Senate: Zeus, Athena, and Artemis. The same root is behind the Latin *vol-*untas and *vo-*tum (↔ Sanskrit *vratum*), whence also the Spanish *bolo* and the English *ball, bullet* (French *boule* and *boulet*), *vow* and *will*, and the German *wollen*, to will or wish. *Willing* is thus anciently conceived as a future-directed energy of time—an arrow that unerringly seeks its target manifestation in the as yet unactualized.

14. It is a subtle trap that to demand utter independence means ultimately to deny love and to deprive others of their freedom, too. Freedom is a great desideratum, but it cannot be attempted to be made absolute without also an attempt to introduce an absolute separation into the scheme of things—something existentially outlawed by the fact that love is more primal than even

freedom, and by its very nature prevents the existence of absolute separation. (Compare the first theorem of the Supplement.) So for an individual or group to demand absolute freedom for itself is by that token to deny love and finally to fail in its demand in any case. Love thus self-restrained from a crude omnipotence may *seem* less than freedom when viewed from a lower level, yet in its own higher dimension is infinitely more, just as a finite volume is greater than a surface of any extent. (See figure in the Supplement, as per note at the start of the epilogue.) Love is more profound and powerful than freedom, and ultimately creates freedom; but freedom of itself cannot create love. It is a lower dimensionality that becomes evil if it deny love.

The word "theodicy," the attempt to justify evil in terms of divine beneficence, was coined by Gottfried von Leibniz in 1710. But the questions that lie behind the word and that are its raison d'être, are as old as evil itself. Actually, the term is misguided. Evil cannot be "justified," only explained; and its origin, as we have seen, is not logical but affective and emotional. There is no "logical" origin for evil—only a psychological one. Hence any ultimate "justification" for evil must be rather an *explanation*, and any ultimate resolution of evil cannot be intellectualstic, but must be by love not as simply sentiment or feeling but as authentic cosmic power.

Theodicies come and go as the winds of theological fashion blow. But all of that is human socio-politics, and is dwarfed by cosmic realities. Free-willed beings, however great their stature, are fallible—not as a necessity but as a potentiality. Otherwise they could not be free but would be pre-determined. Yet if that potentiality be even momentarily actualized in the case of a being of great power, the consequences can be disastrous and of long term before they are resolved. There is a devil, as this chapter explains, and the devil is not divinity; yet divinity is partially responsible for such manifestation.

Boehme almost had the central answer when he wrote [*Signatura Rerum*, 16:24,27; emphasis ours]: "Yes, dear reason . . . first learn the ABC in the great mystery: All whatsoever is risen out of the eternal will, viz. out of the great eternal mystery of all beings (as angels and the souls of men are), stands counterpoised as to evil and good in the free will *as God himself; that desire which* powerfully and predominantly works in the creature, and *quite overtops the other, of that property the creature is.* . . . And thus hell is an enemy even to the devil, for he is a strange guest therein . . . wherein he was not created. . . . The wrath has powerfully got the upper hand and dominion and put itself out of temperament into a discord, and so he must be driven into his likeness; this is the fall, and the fall of all evil men." And: "If you understand this aright, you will not make of God a devil" [Aurora, 13:64]. When we later refer to theodicy, it must be taken in the context of this entire note.

15. Sensed very well by the intuition of the creator of the story of "Forbidden Planet," a classic sci-fi film of the 1950s in which Walter Pidgeon starred and which featured the "Monster from the Id, the mindless primitive."

16. This phase of the story repeats in variant echos the same tradition as the Sumero-Babylonian cuneiform record of "The Inimical-Rebellious Shining One" [133], the fall of the son of the morning [134], the fall of Lucifer and his legions, and kindred Gnostic accounts that were preserved through Paracelsus and Jacob Boehme [135], referring to the highest ranking follower of the released evil. That entire host of beings who chose *not* to love as their "freedom" (thus perforce placing others in bondage and suffering) are called in ancient Egyptian tradition "Children of the Rebellion" (*Mešu Bdš*, variant *Btš*, the latter word connoting "evilly disposed and aggressive"); while the followers of the self-arrested and rededicated Third (now Tenth) Deific Power were called the *Shemsu Ḫoru* or "Companions of Horus," the sacred name that symbolized the self-victorious recovery of the Tenth Deific Power.

We, humanity, descend from the line of those Children of the Rebellion who saw their mistake and righted themselves (though too late to change the effects of the released evil on their seed, much as a parent, herself or himself recovered from some genetically damaging experience with radiation or certain drugs, could not prevent having affected children). We are born of their tears, as the Egyptian tradition tells (e.g. *Papyrus Carlsberg No. 1*: VI,23), and the ancient rebellion is strong in us. Thus even the great poet John Milton in *Paradise Lost* described Satan much more convincingly than his counterpart: "Better to rule in hell than serve in heaven!" The primordial history of the nature of Time and its unfolding that we are tracing has thus much bearing on the grave psychological dilemmas for the human race that began to climax in the twentieth century.

Those dilemmas are simply the reflections upon the mirror of human hubris and ignorance, of the underlying tragedy of a parasitic/predatory biology and a by-and-large unstable chemical/physical ecology in which no substance is abiding, not even the very densely compacted atomic nucleus—the heart of matter—as Otto Hahn and Lise Meitner learned when they first succeeded in fissioning the atom in the 1930s. Technology in the service of the usual low motivations soon lead to the atomic bomb. The underlying tragedy here is quite classical, for the dénouement—given the clear lack of human emotional health down the centuries as our history's bloody record shows—is an ineluctable one of increasing erosion and destruction, both physically and culturally. The upturns and periods of happy growth, always few and sparse, in the course of the twentieth century became vanishingly rare both globally and in time. The ancient cosmic war was being played out, and as it proceeded more and more finalities were being generated.

It is the archaic origins of that war that concern us here—archaic in a strictly temporal and non-pejorative sense, since the instrumentalities that were evoked in the precipitation and administration of our cosmic condition lie far beyond our present or even most ambitiously projected technologies. The too-often-touted canard that all natural order arose through sheer and blind chance is easily shown to be the superficial credulity it is: no amount of aeons, let alone mere geological time, would be enough to generate the minute and intricately balanced order we see throughout nature. Mere chance can never make up for lack of intent and purpose. This basic theorem is the stock-in-trade of the expert detective who fruitfully practices inverse or effect-to-cause logic, guided always by his discernment of how intent would manifest itself. The natural order we now see is the result of a temporary (in a super-geological sense), though optimal, restoration after a great disaster.

The ancient tradition was interestingly preserved also by the Hebrews who inherited much from older priesthoods. This valuable preservation, however, tends to be obscured by mistranslations. Thus the sense of the Hebrew verb *hāyah* is an emphatic "came to be" or "became" and not a mere copulative "was." In the second verse of Genesis, the phrase mistranslated as "the earth was without form and void" actually says, "The world had become a desolated chaos (*tohu*), and featureless ruin (*bohu*)," i.e. as a result of the rebellion for unmerited dominion against love by the corrupted legions of higher entities, after the divinely though mistakenly evoked image of all evil out of the unmanifest. The same word *hāyah* is used in Genesis 19:26 when Lot's wife *became* a pillar of salt and in Ezekiel 17:6 when a seedling *became* a large vine. The excellent Rotherham translation renders *hāyah* as "had become" in Genesis 1:2.

Confirming the ancient tradition, Isaiah's (45:18) commentary on Genesis 1:2 clearly states that divinity did not originally form the earth as *tohu* or a wasted desolation. Isaiah uses the same word as Genesis, but it is ordinarily mistranslated as "in vain," thus losing the entire point of the commentary, which plainly indicates that whatever made it become *tohu* occurred later than the original scheme of things. Thus the "beginning" of Genesis was not at all the first beginning, but the beginning of a divine intervention to remedy, as best could be, the calamity of a world that had been primordially deranged. The same Isaiah (45:12) cries out, "O Lucifer, Son of the Morning, how art thou fallen from heaven!," echoing the much more ancient record cited at the start of this note about how the primordial *tohu* arose.

Pre-institutionalized and gnostic Christianity carried on the anciently authentic tradition, and in Greek texts the Semitic *tohu* became *akatastasia* as we find it in I Corinthians 14:33, for instance. The point of all these preservations of the archaic record is that the God of this universe did not author the primal confusion and devastation but beneficently intervened, resulting in the current physical world of atomic and molecular matter—an optimal but by no means ideal compromise, until all the consequential time cycles could be fulfilled. We noted in a prior publication [135], pp. 98–102) that Jacob Boehme and his 17th, 18th, and 19th century followers (outstandingly John Pordage, Dionysius Freher, and James Greaves) specifically perpetuated this most ancient historical tradition; and at least one 20th century Biblical exegete, H.W. Armstrong, noted [146] that "what geologists and astronomers see is not an evolving universe, but the wreckage of a titanic battle . . . a battle fought before man's creation." This echoes Greaves: "The creation, as now it is seen, tells of prior confusion in higher powers. . . . Strife is older than man."

So recount various later and fragmented strands of the ancient theme of how free choice—of necessity available to beings however high their stature and power—came in one fateful instance to attempt to deny the fundamental reality of love as ultimate power. Then was precipitated a long and difficult series of consequences that invoked the fathomless profundity of provability of intent and the arduous development of trustworthiness, without which love is ineluctably betrayed. Trustworthiness is another side of wisdom, which in turn is deeply involved with the nature of time and temporal process. It must be learned (truly wise advice invariably refers to the future). And when wisely provided safeguards for learning are violently cast aside, the learning inevitably becomes painful. There is no inherent need for either cruelty or suffering in learning. They are invoked by a choice (though their consequences may entrain the innocent and delay resolution).

17. Mathematically, this is verified in the first convex figure with finite constant curvature, and hence boundlessness: a circle. And the most compact group of circles which itself forms a circle centered on a circle, consists of seven circles, as pennies readily show.

18. Note that in the Figure, ⊕ symbolizes not merely the planet Earth but our whole psychophysical universe, the domain of the Tenth Intelligence. Similarly, the seven symbols ranging above it refer to supra-levels of cosmology held to be in resonance, by nature and timing, with the various bodies of our solar system indicated by the astronomical symbols.

The same (lefthand) numbers in the second column of figure 5–1 (3 for Saturn, 4 for Jupiter, etc., through 9 for Luna) are attested in Heinrich Cornelius Agrippa's famous publication [136] of 1531 as the bases of the mathematical magic squares assigned to the planets and luminaries. To Saturn was assigned the magic square of base 3 (i.e. nine numbers so arranged that all rows, columns, and diagonals yield the same sum); to Jupiter, the square of base 4 (sixteen numbers similarly arranged), and so on, as per the cited base numbers of figure 5–1. As Agrippa's compilation is a repository of knowledge accumulated since ancient times, we so have another independently documented confirmation of the Tayyibite-preserved tradition whose roots are traced in this chapter.

19. With fragments elsewhere: in the Ismā'īlī tradition, notably in parts of the Nuṣairī-inherited *Kitāb al-Azilla* ("Book of the Shadows") and the *Umm'ul Kitāb* ("the Mother [or Source] Book); and in scattered portions of doctrines preserved through certain obscure Shī'ite heretical (*gulāt*) sects studied notably by Professor Heinz Halm of the University of Tübingen, who kindly gave me a pre-publication set of proofs of his forthcoming study of Ismā'īlī-related gnosis. The *Umm'ul Kitāb* and the related early ninth century Iraqi-Syrian *Kitāb al-Azilla* both teach interrelated schemes of Ten Cosmic Powers (and a hidden or unmanifest Divine Source) together with the doctrine that seven of them play a key role in the way divinity contained the first manifestation of evil, both pre-human and human. Halm well notes elsewhere (*Der Islam*,

vol. 58, Heft 1, 1981, p. 50) that "is not to be doubted that this system must have had non-Islamic precedents. . . . the origins must be sought in non-Islamic gnostic circles" which he traces as far back as Manichaean and Coptic gnostic texts (p. 51). Beyond are still deeper origins, lying in ancient Egypt itself, as we see in this chapter. The old teaching found its way, like a deep subterranean stream, into many minor surface springs. Again, in one rare manuscript variant of the Old English poem *Merlin and Arthour* (reflecting older sources) we read of the fall of Lucifer and his legions for "seven nights, as thick as hail in thunder-light." Here is independent testimony that the Luciferian fall, following the potentiation of evil through the Divine Demiurge's dream, involved seven stages as each power of the interpolated hepton (figure 5–1) was traversed. The seven rooms of the legend of Bluebeard's Castle, for which Bela Bartok wrote some of his best music, and the seven precious rooms of the House of the Lord of Time and Death in the Esthonian epic *Kalewipoeg* (14th Canto) are fragments of the same tradition.

20. Despite an inability to answer key questions—an inability largely due to the inherent stability and naïveté of any brand of mechanistic randomis, *The Physics of Time Asymmetry* (University of California Press, Berkeley, 1974) by P.C. Davies is an interesting book, with a principal positive conclusion (p. 197) bearing on the findings of this chapter: "It is a remarkable fact that all the important aspects of time asymmetry encountered in the different major topics of physical science may be traced back to the creation or end of the universe," i.e. to the two major singular points of time itself—one at the beginning of our "time of long duration" and the other at its attaining the pre-initial state of things, and so ending by fulfilling its therapeutic function.

21. Sometimes identified with time in the fallen, temporary universe.

22. The origin of evil lies before and beyond any creature, and prefaces the very origin of our present physical cosmos itself. The free choices of creatures could not even begin to explain why they are all tied into a vast, predatory ecology they cannot control either to change or to halt.

23. Called in the terminology of the tradition *māddat* (universally sustaining substance-energy) and *ta'yīd* (interventional, inspirational help). In the wake of such a faith (i.e. inner harmony, not mere blind credulity) such sustenance will come. We must remember that "the angels keep their ancient places . . . 'Tis ye, 'tis your estrangèd faces that miss the many-splendoured thing" (Francis Thompson).

24. And hence by the ancient Hebrews who by all evidence had early strong Phoenician connections, their original alphabet being Phoenician and their language a dialect of Byblos. Moreover, an imageless God, who appeared only as an eternal flame (recall the Burning Bush and the Pillar of Fire), was worshipped by an esoteric sect in the temples of Tyre and Sidon. Melchizedek (= King of Justice) who initiated Abram into monotheism (the worship of the Most High God, *cf.* Genesis 14:18–21) before his name was changed to Abraham, and who thus founded Judaism, would appear to be a priest of this ancient esoteric religion, then exotericized into their own national religion by the Hebrews. A Hasidic rabbi, notable for his honesty and learning, once told me "These verses are a Mystery," and conventional Judaic theology can give only casuistry in attempting to maintain, in the face of this clear evidence to the contrary, that Judaism was nonderivative.

Ancient Iran then added the Messianic/Heroic concept to it. Later, a now messianized Judaism, combining with ancient Egypt's distinctive individual-immortality doctrine and sacred history of a slain yet immortal God-among-men (Osiris) appearing in resurrected form as a Universal Savior (Horus) born of a Divine Virgin (Isis)—gave rise to Christianity, a religion that thus combined permuted and transmuted elements from Hebrew, Magian, and Egyptian sources and hence had wide psychological appeal through this judicious syncretism. The rise of Christianity in the West, despite superficial confrontations, in the end only served greatly to strengthen Judaism in its basic tenet of being the religion of a divinely favored and selected kinship and cultural group, whose destiny it finally would be to rule the earth by divine mandate. The global triumph of Christianity and Islam (we must here correctly add the other Abrahamic religion) all served to strengthen Judaism's position and self-prophesying grandeur. The original concept—that the elect of Israel were processed by an election of earned human merit regardless of genetic or cultural background—was forgotten and "God" became culturally Jewish (as the Christian Christ officially was). That error was inversely and most horribly repeated by Adolf Hitler.

The interplay of these various elements and motivations accounts for some of the major trends and tragedies in historical time since the later Roman Empire. The momentum of the trend has continued, and ironically even supplied the 20th century supposedly antheistic religion, Lenin's Communism, with a bearded Judaic prophet (Karl Marx, formally born Christian), was the child of Jewish converts).

Only the Gypsies and the Japanese had taught as fiercely effective a national elitism, though one not as historically successful. Even the Gypsy word of contempt *gaj* for a non-gypsy, evokes the Hebrew *goy*, a like pejorative and stronger than the Greek *barbaros* for a non-Greek; and a similar term of opprobrium in Chinese, not to mention the Japanese epithet *gai–jin*. In institutionalized Islam the same intolerant concept arose in the term "infidel" against whom "holy war" (*jihad*) was to be fought. That notion was later softened by allegorical interpretation but the original meaning remained, as religious tyranny in immediate post-Shah Iran bloodily proved. Clearly, there is a psychopathology of human nature involved in all these phenomena— one that finds its ultimate origin in the origin of the *manifestation* of evil. (*Potential* evil is always in the unmanifest and must be, by the nature of free choice itself.) Humanity assented to that manifestation in assenting to using unjust and ugly means to gain its ends. It is the justification of the *means*, not the ends, that remains the primal ethical problem.

To sum up, mankind's religious and cultural history was more competitively xenophobic than harmoniously diversified. And among these universally self-glorifying cultures (hence xeno- phobic by indirection), two of the most historically successful it must in all fairness be admitted were Christianity and its resilient forebear, Judaism, with their joint child Islam not far behind. Buddhism is also elitist in effect (a non-Buddhist was called a *mleccha*, another term of contempt); and orthodox Hinduism is also extremely xenophobic. One must be a *born* Hindu to partake of the ceremonies of *Jaganath* (Lord of the World) in his temple at Puri: a non-Hindu intruder would be mobbed, and very possibly killed as recently as 1971, as I learned from an indigenous informant when visiting there who delightfully offered to dye my skin and disguise me as a *sanyasin* under vows of silence. But *malgré tout*, Buddhism and Hinduism did not attain the more aggressive appropriativeness of their competitors.

It should be noted that in this entire discussion we refer to the temporal, social-power-seeking aspects of all these religions. Their most exalted practitioners, their holiest men and women, their real sages and saints, did not share the crude, xenophobic, and self-congratulatory aggressiveness of their temporal-power groups. It is the psychological type of the power-seeker (even to the point of pathology if need be) that is the root of all the trouble, and not any religious teaching per se.

25. The Hebrew word for the Ten Deific Powers, *Sfirwt* (Sephiroth) has a vexed etymology. A philosophical pun between the Greek loan word for "spheres" and the Semitic root *sfr* (which in Hebrew means "letter" or "number" and in Arabic, "zero" or "space," whence the French *chiffre* "number" and the English *cypher*) seems the best solution.

26. In the fragments we luckily still have. They are mostly lost priestly books, cited by title in the few extant papyri, often together with a very brief quotation as an authoritative source for a point being made in the text. The Papyrus Carlsberg No. 1 [137,138] is a rich source and was

obviously written by a ritual astronomer-priest with access to a large library in some House of Life, as the ancient Egyptians called their temples, which were also therapeutic and learning centers. We list the titles, with reference to the section and line of the Papyrus, and in some cases we have emended the prior translations of the cited reference: 1. *The Book of the Ordering of the Moments of the Stars* (which is) *The Book of the Flight of the Spheres of Light* (*pȝ bn-n*)[A.I, 11 and 14]; 2. *The Book of Protection of the Basis* (literally "the Bed") [B.I, 20]; 3. *The Book of the Beholding of the (Solar) Disc* [B.I, 26]; 4. *The Book of the Realm of Geb's Consort* (i.e., of Nut, Goddess of the Heavens) [C.II, 11]; 5. *The Book of the Five Days after the Year* (the five sacred epagomenal days) [C.II, 12]; 6. *The Book of the Ways of the Sky* [D.II, 21]; 7. *The Book of the Circlings of the Divine Deputies* ("*inw*," i.e. the stars). Note that *idn* was *par excellence* the deific regent of the solar disc "*itn*" or, more familiarly, "Aton," and thus the disc or physical body of the sun was considered a deputy or *idn* of Ré, lord of the Sun) [E.II, 37], the same word *idn = adon* (when freed from the artificial transcription system that arose among early 20th century egyptologists and was thereafter too blindly parroted) being the root of the Phoenician deity *Adon* (literally "the Lord"), the name being adopted by the Greek as *Adonis* and by the Hebrews as Adonai, "my (divine) Lord," as a reverential substitution for the not-to-be-pronounced Tetragrammaton, *Yaweh* (Jehovah), e.g., in Genesis 45:8,9 and throughout the Septuagint. This book title, as well as the second of (1), and also (4), and (6), were not able to be translated by Lange or Parker, although the concept of *idnw*, the stars as the celestial deputies of divine beings, is essential to a correct or thorough understanding of ancient Egyptian cosmology and theology. 8. *The Book of the Past* (literally *sf*, Coptic *saf*, meaning "Yesterday" or "The Day before Yesterday") [E.II,42]; 9. *The Book of the Crowning (Culminations) of Sothis* (*shn* here is clearly a corruption for *sḥn*, crown) [E.III,5]; 10. *The Book of (Celestial) Regions* (*iȝt*) [VI,14]. Lange and Parker are unable to furnish translations for either books (8), (9), or (10). This series gives but a hint of what the ancient Egyptian Temple Libraries of Sacred Texts—the Houses of Life—must have contained. We would know much more if barbarous Christian mobs at the instigation of criminal bigots and power seekers like Cyril of Alexandria, Hypatia's murderer, had not, whipped up into vandalistic frenzy, destroyed the magnificent, irreplaceable Library of Alexandria and its Serapion.

Now (1) is cited again [E.II,41] in a very important passage showing that Sothis (Sirius) was a regent of the 36 decan stars, not to be counted as one of them but apart; the passage from that book reading: "Sothis, there are 18 stars after her and 18 stars before her." Thus she was the 37th. The same applies to the ruling star of the constellation of *Sȝḥ*, identified with Osiris as was Sothis (*Sopd-t*) with Isis. The only contenders for the as-yet unidentified Osirian star are Canopus and Betelgeuse, or else—and more likely—the dark companion of Sirius, which was known to the Egypt-influenced Dogons, as the researches of Germaine Dieterlin and Marcel Griaule showed. Neugebauer and Parker try to exclude Canopus, which would place the Osirian star in Orion, when it would have to be α Orionis or Betelgeuse; but they do not seem to grasp that the ancient Egyptians, unlike their later Greek inheritors, placed their cosmological emphasis on the ruling *stars* of celestial sectors (the decans) and not on the decans as such, i.e., as sectors. It is all the more strange since Neugebauer and Parker (N&P) in other places seem to recognize that the ancient Egyptians thought in terms of stars as deputies of star gods, rather than in terms of sectors; and the hieroglyphic texts bear this out, e.g. in the Carlsberg Papyrus No. 1: "The one which sets . . . that is to say, the star among them which goes to the Duat" (VI,42) et al. Indeed N&P themselves conclude (p. 96): "Text V of Seti and Ramses, with its commentary in *P. Carlsberg I* would seem to settle the question decisively in favour of single stars, 36 in all" [with Sothis their leader as 37th, since the texts say clearly; "18 stars before her (Sothis), and 18 behind."—*C.M.*], showing clearly that the old priests regarded the Osirian *Sȝḥ* as a star as well as the Isis-star *Sopd-t* or Sothis (= Sirius). *Papyrus Carlsberg* states

(VI,3): "These are the chiefs of the gods: that is to say, *S3ḥ* and *Sopdt*, the first [or leaders] of the [star]gods." Since Sothis clearly was a star, so was *S3ḥ* even though both were undoubtedly also embedded in named ancient Egyptian constellation groups as yet unidentified.

It also went previously unrecognized that the 75 deities of the well-known "Litany of the Sun" refer to the 36 decan stars in their Isiac and Osirian contexts, each context having its leaders, Isis and Osiris, thus making $(2 \times 36) + 2 = 74$, plus the all-encompassing Ta-Nun

(otherwise called Tatanun and, by priestly pun, Ptah-Nun), the primordial Creator-God, thus furnishing the full complement of the 75 Divine Names. (In New York City's Metropolitan of Art is a previously unrecognized depiction of the 75 Divine Forms on the sacrophagus lid of *Urš nfr*, "Auspicious Guardian," Prophet of the Great Mother Goddess in the XXXth Dynasty *ca.* 350 B.C.E., showing how persistent were the ancient traditions even in the Late Period.)

Interestingly, this same name Ta-Nun resonates deeply with the nature of time as it was understood in ancient Egypt, especially in the profound philosophico-religious-scholarly revival that began with the XIXth Dynasty (*ca.* 1300 B.C.E.), with the founding of the Order of the Spider or Lord of the Eight Limbs, thus signifying the divine enneadic group, the *Paut* (*p3w-t*), the literal meaning of which is "the Primeval Self-Existent (Ones)." Note that while the six-limbed scarab is common among the Egyptian hieroglyphic texts, not even the ancient Egyptian word for the eight-limbed spider, much less its glyph, has come down to us—so sacred it was. It was never written, although spiders are common in Egypt and the ancient Egyptians were keen natural observers.

One of the foremost in the growth of the Order of the Lord of the Eight was a son of Rameses II, Kh'a-m-wast, a name which means "Appearance of the (Divine) Power," a name which was later taken in the XXth Dynasty as one of his honorific titles by Rameses IX (*ca.* 1100 B.C.E.). Such "Appearance" or manifestation could include the personification of a deific power in a high priest(ess) or in the king or queen. Although Kh'a-m-wast was a crown prince, his consuming interest was restoring and preserving the secret and sacred religious wisdom and cosmological teachings of the earliest Egyptian traditions. He personally initiated and directed the restoration of sacred buildings of ancient Memphis, including the even then ancient Pyramid of Unas, last king of the Vth Dynasty. As a priest of Ptah, and thereby of Ta-Nun, his embalmed body was ceremonially entombed in the Serapion of Memphis.

Returning to Ta-Nun and Time, the word *ta*, in addition to denoting soil or earth, can also denote a particled or discontinuous thing, and in particular a moment of time (Coptic *TH*) or a numeric part or portion in arithmetic; and the word is found written with different glyphic forms of the initial letter *t*. The latter part of this name, the *Nun*, refers to the primeval continuous substance of duration itself, ever self-integrated, ever enduring. (Indeed this ultimate God was even simply called "Nun," as in the tomb of 'Usr, royal official of the XVIIIth Dynasty.) These two aspects were harmonized, discontinuous and continuous aspects of time being seen as two appearances of one thing, the continuity being the more fundamental aspect (cf. section 8.1) although quantized, discrete time is phenomenally very important, as in quantum physics (cf. sections 8.2 and 8.4) and in practical application, in the computer (section 3.2–3.3). In the Harris Papyrus (text and translation published by Hans Lange in 1927) Tanun was called the "ancient one who self-rejuvenates and goes throughout all Time . . . who excels above all gods."

27. In addition to this "great zero" (which we might call the Omega—cf. Zosimos) the Egyptians were familiar with the "small," mundane meaning of "zero" denoting simply empty space or container. This was the *wš* glyph (*OYESh* or *WESh* in Coptic) which the priests-

scribes used to denote a lacuna or gap in a papyrus copy, denoting a lost portion of the text.

28. We are confirmed in this conclusion from our study of the literature by a similar conclusion arrived at by Paul E. Walker, Executive Director of the American Research Center in Egypt based at Columbia University, New York. Dr. Walker made a special study of al-Kirmānī and wrote [139] that "as far as I can tell, no Ismaili predecessor of Kirmānī recognized the doctrine of ten."

As to how al-Kirmānī got his peaceful procession of 10 Divine Intelligences, we must remember that the sacred Platonic-Pythagorean decad had reached Hellenistic times in full panoply and was featured in the School of Alexandria and in Proclus's school in Athens, notably in the latter's three triads (of the Divine, the Nous, and the Psychē) plus our sensorily perceivable universe. The three exactly accord with the Unmanifest, the '*Aql* (Intelligent Awareness) or First Intelligence, and the *Nafs* (Soul) or Second Intelligence of Shī'ite tradition. The sometimes seeming confusion in Shī'ite writings of both eleven- and tenfold schemes depends simply on whether the zeroth term—the Primal Unmanifest—(*cf.* figure 5–1) is added to the ten or not. The scheme finally reached twelfth century Europe, and Dante's Ten Heavens are this Divine (or zeroth) Term plus the nine others, without including the physical world [140]. See also the end of note 14 to this chapter.

29. Which was the channel to later times for many ancient Egyptian concepts. In this connection, one is reminded of the erroneous assertion (despite undoubted gifts) of the late Frances Yates, talented but blindly following seventeenth century apologist Casaubon here, that the Hellenistic Egyptian treatises attributed to the tradition of Hermes Trismegistos, "Hermes Thrice Great" (i.e., the Egyptian Divinity Thoth, who granted highest wisdom or gnosis) had no Egyptian sources and that the epithet "thrice great" was not found in pre-Christian Egypt. First, that error is refuted in *Coptic Studies in Honor of Walter Ewing Crum*, published in the 1950s well before Yates's book (on Giordano Bruno, who had only himself to blame when he was criminally burned to death, she compassionately says, because he was too "obstinate"!). Second, it is refuted by the Egyptian coffin texts. In 1957 the writer saw one discovered by Sami Gabra, excavator of ancient Hermopolis (the modern Ashmunein)—"city of Thoth"—bearing the hieroglyphic inscription "Tehuti" (Thoth) thrice great"; and similar readings in both hieroglyphic and hieratic of "Thoth twice great" are common. The repetition of an adjective (two or three times was all the same) in ancient Egyptian denoted an intensification and superlative. Besides these attestations, the content of the Hermetic books is, with neoplatonic overlays, deeply and anciently Egyptian.

30. Another of his doctrinal heirs who should be mentioned is Sahl at-Tustarī (*ca.* 890).

31. Yemen, well within the ancient Egyptian protectorate that included the 60-day caravan route from present Aden to the Gulf of Aqaba, thus came under Egyptian cultural influence from the times of the earliest Memphitic priesthood.

32. In 1973, without any hard evidence except the arrogant methodology of "always deny ancient testimony," Friedrich Junge proclaimed *ex cathedra* that the grammatically ancient Memphitic text was *not* restored by Shabaka, and that the King had lied and the text was a compilation of his own day. Other denigrators of Egypt's antiquity grasped Junge's coattails, and in a reference-collecting study sparse in hermeneutic insight, Hermann Schlögel repeated— again without evidence—Junge's attention-seeking denial, with the slight change that it was a XIXth instead of a XXVth Dynasty forgery, now maligning also Kh'a-m-Wast, one of the truly great and learned restorers of ancient texts and temples. Unfortunately, since Schlögel cites Kenneth Kitchen's *Ramesside Texts* over and over (though not for the point in question), Kitchen might find it socially awkward to disagree with Schlögel's opinions; and, not unexpectedly, in his review of Schlögel finds no fault with the latter's *de facto* repetition of Junge, with a still aberrant chronology. Such viewpoints see no impropriety in slandering Shabaka or any other ancient authority in the interests of updating wherever possible. That king's recorded dedication makes it obvious that he was proud to have played a part in a

restoration of ancient knowledge that would otherwise have been lost. Indeed, the entire history of the Ethiopian Dynasty shows that it continued the sound impulse of restoration of ancient texts begun *ca.* 1150 B.C.E. seriously and consciously in the XIXth Dynasty under the aegis of the royal High Priest of Ptah, Kh 'a-m-Wast, son of Rameses II [144]. If Hermann Schliemann had gone by the denigrations of his time who, à la Junge-Schlögel, called Homer's account "fictional archaizing," Troy would not have been found. Margaret Murray much more soundly observed that certain expressions in the Shabaka text show it was re-edited in the XVIIIth Dynasty, which implies earlier origination. Its basic language would bring us back to the Vth Dynasty at least, for then already Heliopolitan theology had superseded Memphitic. Schlögel cites Murray, though without, apparently, grasping the significance of what she points out.

33. The reconstruction of the ceremony of Amun's becoming one with Ré by uniting with ten great divine powers, called the divine souls (*bas*), elucidates the figures on the walls of the stone staircase of the Temple of Seti I at Abydos, showing the 37 Isiac forms of R'a (presided over by the mannikin "knot" or image of the power of Isis, the *t-t* symbol) on one side of the staircase and the 37 Osirian forms (presided over by the *dj-dj* symbol of reaffirmation despite change) on the other. Goyon calls these the "Solar" and "Osirian" forms of Ré, respectively, and that is our only difference with him. The *t-t* symbol as clearly belongs to Isis, as self-enduringness (giving rise to the hatching of the divine Horus from the egg of the sun, origin of the self-rearousing Phoenix legend) belongs to Osiris. Besides, to call some of the forms of the solar deity, Ré, "solar," and others not, is a contradiction in terms. The king as deputy god descended on the side of the Osirian forms and ascended on the side of the Isiac forms. For it is Isis who leads Osiris into Horus by a Mystery of Virgin Birth.

34. Sir Joseph later kindly confirmed to me that his source indeed had been Diodorus. However, Diodorus is doubly confirmed by better than merely Greek sources, namely, by the Carlsberg Papyrus I [137 and 138], the demotic text of which provably reflects authentic ancient Egyptian doctrine and practice.

35. An epoch distinguished for its conscious study of the techniques of manipulated deception on the largest scale, as exhibited in "motivational" mass media advertising and the entire body of methods used in "unarguable persuasion," propagandizing, "brain-washing," and "operant conditioning."

36. With strong vestiges persisting into modern times. See, e.g., S.H. Nasr's *Islamic Science* (London, 1976), p. 189, n. 23, and p. 223.

37. The bankruptcy of the usual theologies, based as they are on the unwarranted and unrealistic assumption of an infallible God—usually assumed with equal naiveté to be male—is clearly expressed in a standard work of exemplary honesty, Augustus Strong's *Systematic Theology* (3 vols., 1907, reprinted thirty-two times between then and 1979 when it appeared in a one-volume edition published by Judson at Valley Forge, Pennsylvania). Speaking of the origin of evil that had led well before humanity to the brutal and predatory ecology we all know, Strong admits the incompetence of ordinary theology, working (on pp. 460, 585, and 588):

How an evil volition could originate in spirits created *pure* is an insoluble problem [that is, for such theology and theodicy]. Here we must acknowledge that we cannot understand how the first unholy emotion . . . could have overcome a soul in whom there were no unholy propensities [the infallibility assumption] to which it could appeal. The mere power of choice does not explain the fact of an unholy choice . . . [nor] explain how this desire came to be inordinate. . . . Satan's fall, moreover, since it must have been uncaused by temptation from without, is more difficult to explain than Adam's fall. . . . Satan fell without external temptation.

Strong is clearer here than most later writers, e.g., Francis Schaeffer or Jeffrey Russell.

However, Strong is not yet clear enough as to the nature of such "unholiness" and "temptation" that could have arisen in a divine being. Still less has he reckoned with the fact that the desire to be self-sufficient at the expense of love, no matter how subtle a form that choice may take, then ineluctably transforms the activity of such desire into something capable of evoking unholy horrors from the otherwise ineffective unmanifest in which the infinity of all possible eventualities—good and evil—lies, awaiting only the appropriate evocation, much as a dormant computer program needs a specific calling code to make it operative and manifest.

Nor can ordinary theologies contain how a prince of angelic beings could fall into such a trap and be overwhelmed by the temptations inherent in the unforeseen but consequently evoked Image of all Evil. For *that* in turn had been called forth from the abyss of the unmanifest in one fleeting but sufficient lapse on the part of the God of our universe who wished to contain the ultimate source of being. That wish, apparently so appropriate to a divine being, was in fact not innocuous. Such desire means to attempt to preempt, to confine the unmanifest and infinite love-energy in a manifest center, and thus attempt to possess it, yet thereby succeeding only in cutting off the flow of love to that center, since such a desire is the antithesis of love's nature. The essence of the "calling code" that would thus reach the unmanifest through that initially harmless-looking wish could only be: Send forth the very essence of evil. Hence, even though the fundamental error was quickly perceived after the fact, the damage caused by the manifestation of what should under love's nature never have been released into being, was done, and then, in H.P. Lovecraft's striking image, "things walked that were meant only to crawl," and all the misery-ridden potentials of our predatory cosmic ecology were released. At this point it must be realized that such an uprush of wrongfulness into manifestation would nevertheless be attended with great power—no less than the misdirection of an entire cosmos.

That power was that which could tempt angelic legions, just as curiosity and greed to play with it could tempt humanity, that then also turned its back on love, as so much "scientific" experimentation and industrial technology still witnesses: e.g. the tons of carcinogens and other lethal poisons constantly spewed forth into the air, water, and soil of our planet, with man-made viruses in the offing. Only a theodicy based on the primary realization of a divinity endowed with free choice with respect to evocable potentialities, with access to infinite love, and with great but necessarily finite (because manifest), as yet *achieved* wisdom, and hence with potential to err— could explain our human and cosmic condition. See also the prior note 14 on this matter.

38. A form of which can be considered as reincarnation, a thesis traditionally adopted by the majority of the world's peoples.

39. Both Buddhism and Hinduism—the former more so—tend to evade the problem of evil and the requisite responsibility of philosophy and religion to provide a satisfactory answer. Neoplatonism fell into a similar evasion, and more modern thinkers, for the most part, have fished in muddied waters. Both the more dogmatic/apologistic, and the more intellectualistic approaches (e.g. Steven Brams) have failed to resolve much. Though the latter type at least trace evil to divinity, yet their tools are too crude to unravel the extraordinary trains of eventuation and relationships involved in the actual ancient happening. Brams does arrive at the existential possibility of deceitful and unethical beings more than humanly powerful. But his main trend of exposition is of little relevance since he has made the typical pedantic error of omitting feelings and the power of love from the ultimate logic of relationships between sentient beings, where those considerations cannot be excluded with impunity.

Fred Gearing in his *Priests and Warriors* (Amer. Anthropol. Assoc. Mem. no. 93, 1962, p. 34) recounts how a knowlegeable Cherokee informed a missionary-ethnologist (Daniel Butrick) of a deeper logic that ties in precisely with the primordial cosmic history we have traced: Namely, that the word for "power to heal" is the same word which also means the power of atonement for a collective mistake. Yet *ca.* 1850 the indigenous Cherokee way of life was still being dismissed as "senseless superstition" by even a relatively enlightened observer like C. Lanman (*Letters from the the Allegheny Mountains*, 1849, p. 95). Catherine Albanese (*History of Religions*, vol. 23, 1984, p. 349) sums up well the original Cherokee teachings: "Hence, disease and death appear as *un*natural. . . . The harmony of a privileged dawn time has been ruptured; and humans, responsible for the rift, are left to cope as they can—even as in the gentle blessing from the plants, nature still aids her children." As we have already seen, humanity could not by any means have been solely responsible for the violent and predatory state of the natural system in which we find ourselves. (This I established some years ago in *Illumination on Jacob Boehme*, and pointed it out to Jeffrey Russell in an interesting conversation in 1982 at Santa Barbara, as a lacuna in his *Satan* that I hoped his projected *Lucifer* or *Mephistopheles* would address.) The Cherokee tradition, for one, had taken a large step in the right direction, however. As we now see, the real explanation could not have been found until we analyzed much older strata, primarily preserved in Yemen and ancient Egypt.

6 SOCIAL APPLICATIONS

There is timing in everything. Timing in strategy cannot be mastered without a great deal of practice. . . . In all skills and abilities there is timing. There is also timing in the Void—that which has no beginning and no end and in which there is no evil.

—Shinmen 'Miyamoto' Mushashi,
A Book of Five Rings (*Go Rin No Sho*, tr. V. Harris)

We now address ways and possibilities of application in chronotopological theory, and particularly in psychosocial contexts, which are of prime importance in chronosystems.[1] A frequent but not recommended usage[2] is "hard" for systems not involving humans and "soft" for those that do. Actually, the terminology is poor because hard also connotes difficult; and in that sense human-dependent systems are much *harder* to analyze than the others. Moreover, soft connotes "vague" and "indefinite," whereas human systems are governed by most definite principles, the "vagueness" being largely the result of the deplorable naïveté in the minds of those accustomed only to non-human systems.

A 1981 story comes to mind, piquantly recorded (emphasis theirs) by W. Giauque and R. Woolsey [147] about the shiny new Ph.D. systems analysts who were engaged "to increase the productivity of a third-world steel mill. A major problem lay in the scheduling of three electric arc furnaces. The time required to process a charge depended upon the amount of power fed to the furnace; thus power scheduling was a critical decision variable. Furnace operators, who were on an incentive plan, had to work within a power capacity for each furnace, a total capacity for the plant, and had to schedule such resources as charging and pouring cranes so as not to interfere with one another.

167

"The [young analysts] . . . studied the problem, gathered operating and capacity data, and developed a complex model to handle furnace scheduling. A computer system, complete with video displays for each furnace operator, was procured, and massive amounts of time and money were expended in developing and debugging the code, report-writers, system interfaces, and so forth. Total cost was approximately 2.5 million US dollars. All concerned settled back, confidently expecting major increases in productivity.

"Unfortunately, productivity didn't change *at all*. The system designers had overlooked one minor detail: of the 24 people who operated the furnaces over three shifts, *only five could read*! The study team had never bothered to go to the furnaces, and had never studied the *actual* operations, much less learned how to *do* them.

"What was wrong? The [young men] . . . were undeniably bright; technically, the system was fine. What was lacking was a sense of perspective, a knowledge of reality, and understanding of the business, and an understanding of the cultural infrastructure. The furnace production was substantially increased . . . by junking the 2.5 million US dollar computer system and substituting a scheduling method based on colored blocks in a plastic frame. Cost . . . was less than 200 US dollars for the deluxe model." [Italics in the original.]

We applaud, and disagree only with the authors that the young men were "undeniably bright." Bright they were not, though verbally facile products of an educational system emphasizing superficial facility in symbolic manipulation rather than profound thinking based on wise insight into the nature of human beings in various cultural milieus. We must also demur at the related statement that "technically, the system was fine." Technically it was not, since it omitted prime psychological data—data *essential* to the technical viability of any chronosystem. In this case, the glaring 2½-million dollar loss points up the serious scientific error of failure in predictability.

But for each such obviously costly error go thousands of similar ones perpetrated by bureaucratic types of analysts who neglect the human data to the ultimate great loss and often breakdown of the system. In the same year, Alvin Toffler [148] noted that Giauque and Woolsey's story is being repeated on a global scale with appropriately graver implications. He well observes that "national governments in Washington, London, Paris, or Moscow continue by and large to impose uniform, standardized policies designed for a mass society of increasingly divergent and segmented [i.e. individualized] publics. Local and individual needs are forgotten or ignored, causing the flames of resentment to reach white heat."[3] Throughout all those examples, the neglect of human individuality is the cardinal sin of those who vault themselves into positions of societal power, then often ironically controlled and made impotent themselves by the very forces of group and mass conditioning they themselves helped to launch and perfect.

But the circle is not quite vicious, for the prime movers throughout human society and its history have been and always will be individuals. I recall a U.S. Army Classification Officer of the Second Service Command, who was in charge of the whole vast system of "classification" tags placed on men— tags that would then determine their destiny in the great computer-like human network called "the army." To change your destiny in the army you had to change your classification tag. The colonel kept his powers a well-concealed secret; one day a soldier just on a hunch required an audience with this Colonel E. for a classification shift that could transform his whole life. He was informed to go through such and such channels to effect it.

After a circuitous course consuming days of constant and useless effort, and going through hosts of people, he finally persevered until the end of the feedback chain, which then looped back to the real source: he was referred to Colonel E., who gave him a sharp approving look and snapped, "Couldn't discourage you, could we? Now you know I'm the son of a bitch who runs things here. In finding that out, you showed you deserved re-classification. Request granted and approval recommended. Go back and wait for your new orders." In every chronosystem, however complex and "impersonal," there is always a key individual who can quite correctly say, with respect to any desired change, "Yes, I'm the son of a bitch. My Yea or Nay does it."

As IIASA's Wolgang Sassin shrewdly observed, "[Systems] analysis can never be value-free" [150], which is to say it is a human activity, necessarily and rightly value-imbued. By the same token science can never be valueless. The real problem is finding the best values, individually and generally, over the long term; and so, again, we face the nature of time. The following remarks again address the ubiquitous question of taking individuality and uniqueness into account in systems thinking.

On June 1, 1981, at the home of a mutual acquaintance in Paris, I was fortunate enough to meet and talk with Marcel Chapuis, the justly renowned French organist. He explained that organ pipes are made of a tin-lead alloy, often in the ratio of 4:1, in order to be rigid enough to evoke vibrations easily. However, he went on, new pipes, made of the same alloy, don't sound well at first; yet if he plays on them for a few months he can make them sound right. When I suggested that he was reorganizing their molecules by sympathetic resonance he agreed, saying he calls what he does "musical alchemy" since it transmutes timbres and confers individuality upon an originally non-unique set of pipes.

But individuality needs to be exercised, and the molecules tend to lose the patterns of their resonantly induced rearrangements. Thus, he added, he can tell at once whether an organ has been played on recently. Also, he went on, various organs have their distinctive fundamental tonalities around which their sets of natural resonances are centered: F major for St. Séverin, A major for the great organ of Poitiers, C major for Dole, these keys being their resonantly best ones.[4]

Such considerations of individual resonance patterns for best musical effects extend to buildings, he continued, and the old architects knew how to construct with predetermined acoustic nuance. If you sing in the Cathedral of Notre Dame facing east (the direction the choir faces) the voice has a magnificent resonance and amplification, whereas if one faces west it is all confused. What the master organist seemed to be saying was that religious buildings could be constructed like musical instruments. I recalled hearing the remarkable acoustic resonances built into the subterranean, neolithic temple on Malta called the Hypogeum. "C'est une science perdue," said Chapuis—"a lost science."

Like organist Chapuis, if we remain sensitive enough, we can still "tune in" on resonances around us momently. Creative artists through the ages furnish examples, and there is a particularly clear illustration from old Esthonia. The sage Jaakob Fischer, who had been a gifted violinist in his younger years, met the future Dr. Friedrich Kreutzwald when the latter was sixteen at Erlenfeld in Esthonia, and over the next four years imparted to him the basic traditional cantos of the great Esthonian epic the *Kalewipoeg*, which became the real claim to fame of Kreutzwald even though he was a successful physician of his day. He recounts what the then eighty-year old, yet spirited and gifted Jaakob told him in 1820:

> In the sound of the sea on a stormy autumn night, as it breaks its force on the rocks—is music, teaching us melodies no instrument can render . . . and when I was sitting in the forest shadows surrounded by the soughing of the wind in the treetops, and the twittering and songs of the birds in the branches, there would awaken such melodies in my spirit. Then I would quickly take my violin and try to reproduce that inner sound into audible tones. Sometimes whole nights would fly by so, without my noticing, and at such times all the stars seemed to me to be ringing with music. Yes, all things in the world have their voices, their special way of speech, but our ears do not understand such language [151].[5]

Yet our minds can understand (recall chapters 2 and 4) and we must make an effort to recover that typological and metaphorical sensibility that is more akin to a poem than to a program.

As a concluding example of inherent resonant individuality, Marcel Chapuis cited the Chapel of the Popes at Avignon which was constructed especially for "musique monodique et polyphonique" in the style of the

Carmelites. "You could never hear an organ successfully played there because the contructor prohibited it," he observed. "We today no longer understand these things." The investigations of the foregoing chapters show we had better restore such understanding, at least as reflected in human relations and in systems in which human beings play essential roles.

Closely related to individuality, but wider in scope, is what may be called *uniqueness*. The members of a group of mass-produced bolts are all individual but their uniqueness is very low. Indeed it is designed to be minimal on the principle of replaceable parts. Uniqueness works in the other direction, that of irreplaceability. There is only one poet as universal as Shakespeare, only one symphonist as profound as Sibelius, only one life-bearing planet (Terra, Gaia or Earth) in our solar system, and so on. Actually, each of us not simply strives toward increasing uniqueness but we all realize that in some deep sense we *are* all unique.[6]

In fact, our greatest contribution to others, and to our self-development as well, lies in the direction of developing precisely along the lines where our greatest uniqueness lies. In common parlance, that is called developing our special talents. Each person's set is different, and in different stages of unfolded potential. One of the keys of vocational guidance, management, and education is to be able to determine given people's sets of most promising potentials and then enable them, by suitable methods and situations, to develop and evolve to greatest mutual advantage and in greatest harmony with persons endowed with other varieties of uniqueness.

We have spoken of the great tendency of evolution of insight (both into the environment and into oneself) as a main spring of change in the biosphere. Closely linked thereto is the tendency towards evolution of uniqueness and not only of mere discrete individuality as such. We see that tendency even on so humble a level as each person's molecularly unique protein immune system and fingerprints. Timing also is a component of biological indi-viduality, as evidenced in the following datum (emphasis ours) [30, p. 29n]: "Remarkable differences exist in the strength of the reaction [of the red cell or erythrocyte immune system] in different individuals—*and even in the same individual at different times*. Some unknown factor, or factors, apparently regulates the activity of the red cell immune system."[7] An entire science of chrono-immunology is implied.

On the pathological side, the same powerful, primal principle operates, and tyranny is but a mistaken caricature of the noble desire for uniqueness. One of the first things selfish power-seekers do is ordain unique privileges for themselves which are their special prerogatives. Tyranny is the teratology of genius, and oppressors parody the natural and earned special greatness of heroes.

Thus, uniqueness is closely related to the desire for freedom. To the extent that we are unique we are unbounded and unchallenged. Therefore the rightful desire to be unique is beset, when unaccompanied by sufficient love, by the same trap as the desire to be free when it is without love or worse even seeks to act against it. Then, freedom degenerates into tyranny—the seeking of one's own (or one's group) freedom at the expense of depriving others of it; just as uniqueness similarly degenerates as, for instance, in the sick mind that is also so uncreative, it can fulfill its desire to be outstanding only by, say, assassinating a public figure, or achieving video-publicity through the terroristic bombing of innocents.

We recall the investigation of chapter 5, and, anticipating some ontological theorems, we see that one can no more attain absolute uniqueness than absolute freedom—for then the impossibility of absolute separation would be attempted, with its train of consequential pathology and psychopathology. All uniqueness must rest on a broad base of nonunique and *shared* traits, otherwise communication would become impossible. Likewise, all freedom must rest on, and be fed from, an immeasurably greater fund and source of love (*cf.* Supplement to appear), i.e. good will. The imperatives and prognosis of sections 3.37–3.38 are tied in closely with the same lesson, and are therefore now cited.

It is the unrealism and fallacy of the neglect of human individuality and uniqueness that began to discourage the latter-twentieth century public in science itself, especially when applied to pressing human problems as it always is in advanced systems analysis. People at large began to see that scientific method as prevailingly practiced could unlock grave dangers that it could not quell. It had become a sorcerer's apprentice.[8] The realization was world-wide, and a headline in the "Spectrum" section of Vienna's *Die Presse* of Saturday/Sunday, October 16/17, 1982, reads: "*Am Ende eines großen Abenteuers: die Wissenschaft in der Krise*"—"At the end of a great adventure: science in crisis."

The new scientific direction indicated in this chapter, and throughout the book for that matter, is now realistically called for. The 1982 ongoing crisis of science had been intensifying ever since at least 1966. As a then observer (H.L. Nieburg) keenly put it: "Science and technology have turned a critical corner. We have been careless of their ultimate costs and now must pay the toll. Belief in a limitless future wanes as progress becomes less easy and the necessity for choice more compelling. The pace, scope, and majesty of modern technology have wrought a revolution in man's ability to subdue and exploit this planet and its resources, bringing him at least into collision with nature's limits. . . . As his powers increased and his numbers multiplied, the universe became a narrow and constricted place, littered with the debris of his fond hours. Man awakened one morning to recognize himself as a destroying biotype." [126, p. 85]

The late James B. Conant, scientist, administrator, and philosopher of science, considered science to be "a development of conceptual schemes" that the future bears out as "fruitful." Science is not, in any event, a mere collection, description, or classification of data. Its essence is its future-directedness, its ability to predict and, to that extent to control, outcomes. Thus we may say that science is based on concepts that have predictive power. Now predictions may be fulfilled or not, but in any case, they must be able to be made—and this is the naked truth behind Karl Popper's emperor's-new-clothes circumlocution "falsifiability."

Chronotopological systems analysis may thus be said to bring science to a culmination in the sense of being equipped to predict personality inter- and reactions and situational outcomes over broadest possible ranges of desired criteria, on the basis of a minimum of initial data including the initial time-launch. It doesn't really matter what kind of ships sail out of port when it comes to predicting the weather they will encounter on their course.

As per its introductory principles, already sketched in chapter 4, there is an objective method of personality typological analysis, permitting prediction of interaction-nuances and situation-configurations. Topology in this context becomes typology. There is a related analysis linking personality with what may be called "destiny-proneness," of which the accident-proneness known pragmatically by insurance companies is but the tip of the iceberg. These complementary aspects of chronotopology are in turn linked with the oscillatory character of all natural phenomenology that was addressed in section 3.1 and will be treated in somewhat different ways,[9] in a separate publication (see note at start of epilogue).

A dental authority (Dr. Arthur L. Jensen) informed scientist and science writer R.R. Ward that many of his patients exhibited a cyclical sensitivity, at one phase in their cycle being able to withstand dental work easily and at the opposite phase unable to do so at all. These cycles are so marked that Dr. Jensen regularly schedules appointments in phase with them. As long ago as 1933 Nobel Laureate (medicine and physiology) Archibald Hill [153] observed that "wherever we look in the world of matter and events outside ourselves we find that oscillations and wave motions have a significant, often dominant role. It is not, therefore, astonishing to find that waves play an important part in ourselves also." Many observers corroborate that the parameters of psychological-economic behavior are no less oscillatory and rhythmic in nature than those of the biological variety. Thus economic analyst William Scheinmann noted in 1968 that "there is a rhythm to successful investing as surely as the ebb and flow of the oceans. Investment timing involves the matching of one's major decisions to the basic rhythms. . . . These waves represent the alternating waves of . . . optimism and pessimism," in turn related to the expansion (2) and constriction ($\hbar$) components in the hepton group of chapter 4, figures 4–1, 4–2(a), and surrounding text.

John Naughton has well pointed out [100] that "real-world systems practice is more fruitfully viewed as a kind of social technology [than as applied science]. . . . By a 'science' is meant a discipline whose prime goal is *explanation*. The prime goal of a 'technology,' in contrast, is *effective action*. . . . The myth that traffic in ideas between the two is one-way (*from* science *to* technology) is refuted by the actual history of science. . . . Historically, for instance, technologies flourished long before the scientific theories relevant to them had been articulated." So it was with chrono-topology (which has, in the above sense, technological roots going back millennia) and still is in many of its applications, as in chronobiology, chronopsychophysiology, and above all in the effective guidance (chronavigation) of human-involved systems. Chronotopological praxis is actually the analytic-interpretive art of conducting situations to optimal outcomes, by means of principles we are just beginning to understand and to the elucidation of which this book is addressed.

As we have seen, one of those key principles is that, contrary to scientific views prevailing from the seventeenth through at least the early twentieth centuries, it appears that the concept of mechanical, billiard-ball, or impact causation is not the way causation actually proceeds in nature. Gross appearances to the contrary, all causation is finally resonant, although sudden resonant perturbations can generate as much gross impact as ever is needed. But the point is that, in principle, causality is a phenomenon of resonances or anti-resonances; and that fact has profound implications, some of which were explored in section 3.1 and others will be in the announced Supplement.

A related "Principle of Least Entropy Increase" is one we voiced some years ago [11] as the general one that all natural change proceeds so as to minimize the local rate of entropy increase, which goes one process step deeper than the Principle of Least Action. Mathematically, it may be written as $\pi(dH/dt > 0)$ = minimum, where π here is the probability. That is, time's arrow proceeds in the direction of that state where the probability of entropy-increase, and hence the increase itself on the average, is minimized.

An interesting confirmation of this pervasive principle was received in a letter of September 22, 1982, from a colleague, C.F. Hansen, former chief of the Gas Dynamics Branch at NASA's Ames Research Center, Moffett

Field, California. One of the main points of a book he was then in the course of writing concerned gas phase reaction rates. In his words, "I'm treating gas phase reactions by a collision cross section model—which physicists do for their high energy collisions—but which chemists never seem to. Then I'm showing that at high T the slope of an Arrhenius plot is not the activation energy as they have always assured. It is for low T, say 300–600 °K, but not for high T 5,000–10,000 °K where the deviations may be as much as several eV due to the slope of the cross section and the effect of excited states. Most chemists still look at reactions as they occur between ground state molecules—but I claim that, wherever it's possible, the reaction proceeds by a ladder-climbing process (Markovian or random walk-like) up a ladder of excited states, strongly weighted towards a path with a large number of smallest possible energy increments."

He concluded by noting that without such an approach the area of "reaction rates is one of the least satisfactory areas of science [today]." I replied to Fred on September 27, 1982, saying that "your collision x-section model leads directly to counterexamples at high T against the Arrhenius plot approach valid at low T. One thinks of Rayleigh's versus Stefan's law before Planck reconciled them," then cited my minimal entropy-increase-rate principle and concluded that his ingenious "ladder of states" theory was in accord with it. Note that this "ladder" of states is ascended by means of resonant causality, functioning through resonances between quantum-mechanical molecular states. It is done through "tuning in"—a time-resonant process and context.

On the psychosocial level, the resonances become those between the qualitatively differing elements of the relevant typologies, together with their associated cycles of oscillatory behavior and recrudescence. These facts make possible a science of pre-selecting optimally interacting personality groups (psy-team formation) with optimal destiny-pronenesses for the situation envisaged, e.g. the optimal composition of flight or submarine crews. Not only that, but chronavigation then also becomes feasible: the charting of optimal courses through the possible seas of alternative timings for initiations or developments of key phases in planning.

In general, the crucial element of timing has been badly neglected in system-theoretic theories of planning, hence placing the expectations derived from such chronotopologically deficient theories at the total and mostly not tender mercies of the unexpected. In fact, the two commonest sources of unpleasant and unwanted surprises in systems theory are the neglect, first of human individuality and uniqueness, together with the related concept of that valuable potential; and, second, the practically total neglect of a viable method for the *timing* of moves, not to speak of optimal timing.[10] Conventional systems theory does not even contain the principles for such timing.

What chronotopological systems analysis invites us to do is begin to enter into some understanding of the programming, clocks, and interrupt systems used in nature's computer, as it were. We stand on the threshold of a quantum leap in insight. Once that threshold is negotiated, Time can become our powerful ally and will no longer be our implacable foe.

To have time to do that, however, demands survival as a *sine qua non*—a basic criterion for which was indicated at the end of the preceding chapter. Survival, it has recently been realized in systems theory, requires more than mere studies of how to maintain a stable equilibrium. That "more" is, of course, inherently implied by the nature of shifting environmental patterns, which not only change gradually but also cataclysmically the classic examples being those drawn from seismology (with tsunami or tidal wave phenomena included) and vulcanology.

So survival must address itself to something deeper than merely returning to some relatively simplistic pre-established equilibrium after non-cataclysimic perturbations. We need to know about the kind of viability that can survive cataclysms as well—survival over the long pull and without deterioration into behavioral cul-de-sacs like ants and termites. The latter, the result of some 200 million years of rigid communism—older even than the mere 70 million years pedigree of the social hymenoptera—routinely eat each other's excrement until it is inedible further even by them, and then use it for wall mortar in their burrows. The final obscene triumph of anti-individual utilitarianism thus ends in coprophagy, the inglorious end as demonstrated in proven "survival" practices over hundreds of thousands of millennia. Human survival, to be worthy of the name, must be much more than that. It needs to include human creativity and the fostering of uniquely endowed individuality for which purpose the society is the engendering womb rather than an otherwise pointless end-in-itself.

Having come this far, let us now enquire into a theory of survival that, first of all, must transcend mere return to comparatively static equilibria conditions after certain relatively mild perturbations. Thermodynamicist Ilya Prigogine, who was fascinated by phenomena of time ever since his youth, suggested an extension of the concept of stability that he called the theory of dissipative structures, structures that could, far from the conventional equilibrium points, come to stable terms with their environments, at the cost of high energy expenditure or, in thermodynamic terms, with the aid of negentropic access to energy supplies.

In 1983, two Nobel laureates (Philip Anderson and Ilya Prigogine) had a published difference of opinion. Yet Anderson's [156] criticism of Prigogine (who to this writing has not dignified it with reply) was unduly harsh because basically too superficial; and Prigogine's suggestive concept of systems that function far from equilibrium is not, because of Anderson's pique at it, to be abandoned. The critique became too obstructive without sufficient point or substance, since Anderson remained unaware of the vital distinction between mere stability (survival only if the system remains near an equilibrium point) and super-stability or resilience (survival despite perturbations that carry the system far from equilibrium).

That crucial distinction had been known and published ten years previously, in 1973. But, although Prigogine was always biology- and time-oriented [157,158,159], Anderson's thinking was narrower, remaining within the confines of the physical laboratory (he works for Bell Labs). All this again proves our often useful definition of " 'normal' is the way I was conditioned." Anderson's criticism was really beside the point and addressed to a straw man, as Prigogine's principal interests were never confined to physiological homeostases, which we all know must operate between very narrow limits of stability. Prigogine's work, however, addresses the much wider domains of morphogenesis, metamorphosis, and mutational, innovational developments.

In *Options* [160], house organ of the International Institute of Advanced Systems Analysis, the then IIASA director, ecologist Crawford ("Buz") S. Holling, was quoted to good effect: "The key issue is not policy advice in the narrow sense but access to a much more creative range of options for policy makers. The feeling is stronger now than it has been because problems arise with a speed, and on a scale that exceeds the adaptability of conventional systems."

Here Holling was speaking in the light of the concept of resilience in stability theory, which he was the first to voice (in 1973 [161]) and which carries the theory to *survival*—an important higher stage than simple stability as such. The crucial distinction between resilience and mere stability is clearly given in Holling's original statement [*ib*, pp. 2, 14, 15, 17, 18]:

"An equilibrium centered view is essentially static and provides little insight into the transient behavior of systems that are not near the equilibrium. Natural, undisturbed systems are likely to be continually in a transient state; they will be equally so under the influence of man. As man's numbers and economic demands increase, his use of resources shifts equilibrium states and moves populations away from equilibria. The present concerns for pollution and endangered speces are specific signals that the well-being of the world is not adequately described by concentrating on equilibria and conditions near them. Moreover, strategies based upon these two different views of the world might well be antagonistic. It is at least conceivable that the effective and responsible effort to provide a maximum sustained yield from a fish population or a nonfluctuating supply of water from a watershed (both equilibrium-centered views) might paradoxically increase the chance for extinctions.

"It is useful to distinguish two kinds of behavior. One can be termed stability, which represents the ability of a system to return to an equilibrium state after a temporary disturbance; the more rapidly it returns and the less it fluctuates, the more stable it would be. But there is another property, termed resilience, that is a measure of the persistence of systems and of their ability to absorb change and distrubance and still maintain the same relationships between populations or state variables. . . .

"In summary, these examples of the influence of random events upon natural systems further confirm the existence of domains of attraction. Most importantly they suggest that instability, in the sense of large fluctuations, may introduce a resilience and a capacity to persist. It points out the very different view of the world that can be obtained if we concentrate on the boundaries to the domain of attraction rather than on equilibrium states. Although the equilibrium-centered view is analytically more tractable, it does not always provide a realistic understanding of the systems' behavior. Moreover, if this perspective is used as the exclusive guide to the management activities of man, exactly the reverse behavior and result can be produced than is expected.

"Resilience determines the persistence of relationships within a system and is a measure of the ability of these systems to absorb changes of state variables, driving variables, and parameters, and still persist. In this definition resilience is the property of the system and persistence or probability of extinction is the result. Stability, on the other hand, is the ability of a system to return to an equilibrium state after a temporary distrubance. The more rapidly it returns, and with the least fluctuation, the more stable it is. In this definition stability is the property of the system and the degree of fluctuation around specific states the result. With these definitions in mind, a system can be very resilient and still fluctuate greatly, i.e. have low stability. I have touched above on examples . . . in which the very fact of low stability seems to introduce high resilience. Nor are such cases isolated ones, as Watt has shown in his analysis of thirty years of data collected for every major forest insect throughout Canada by the Insect

Survey program of the Canada Department of the Environment." So Holling.

It is clear that the new concept of resilience with its movable equilibria will greatly change mathematical modeling based on the less realistic idea of stability in the sense of static equilibria. We have a situation similar to a function with movable singularities versus one with only fixed singular points. (See, for example, E.L. Ince's work on ordinary differential equations or Harold T. Davis's *Introduction to Nonlinear Differential and Integral Equations.*)

One of Holling's data sources was a thoughtful paper [162] on the cabbage aphid and the remarkable, custom-tailored timing of its parasite when the originally European aphid was introduced into Australia. The parasite may lay "enough eggs to optimize its dispersion by the aphids, but no more," as else it would endanger its own survival by killing off too many aphids. The aphid would then become extinct because it "cannot react *fast enough* to an increasing load of parasitization" (emphasis in original). When the aphid throve in Australia, the parasite's European egg-laying capacity of about 190 increased to an Australia capacity of about 325 eggs, always maintaining the exquisite balance ensuring that enough aphids remain unparasitized to guarantee the continuance of the parasite's food supply.

This balance includes timing: "It is the aphids, as well as the parasite, which determines the parastite's time of impact on the aphid population. The young parasite spends about 3½ instar-periods feeding on the living aphid, and about four more in the mummified aphid. Compared with other insects, it spends a relatively long time as a pupa." But if it spent less time, it would tend to exterminate the aphid, and if it spent more time, it would not optimally reproduce itself. Thus "the parasite is maximizing its own reproduction without endangering the aphid."

The authors conclude (p. 534) that their model reveals "a general *strategy* [emphasis in original] of predation and parasitism to which even the arch-predator [and, we may add, arch-parasite], Man, must conform." But alas, in hunting the great whales, for instance, and a host of other species now extinct or near-extinct, humans have not shown even the intelligence of the parasite of a cabbage louse.

The cabbage louse itself, *Brevicoryne brassicae*, is not to be despised as it has evolved a genetically stable matriarchal society that reproduces parthenogenetically without males at all. But the plant louse could scarcely be the unconscious ideal of hard core fenminist extremists, who neglect the primal principle of uniqueness in its sexual form: the beautiful and *complementary* (i.e. not competitive) uniqueness of woman and man, not only physically and physiologically but psychologically as well, as is being at last better and better understood.[11]

May humanity before too long learn those salutary lessons that we now have seen are so vividly taught by both the lowly, minute cabbage aphid and its even smaller parasite *Diaeretus rapae.*

Holling's fruitful and deep notion of resilience had, of course, to be less awarely used by materials physicists and metallurgists in conceptually diluted form when speaking of elasticity of the sort that is restorable even after long stretches of time (and material!). Thus certain steels are said to be "resilient," while an ordinary rubber band is not, as anyone can readily observe after prolonged stretching. Robustness is the related but weaker property that allows a system to return to equilibrium after sizable (though not extreme) perturbations.

Recalling for a moment the ideas of chapter 4, we may also speak of the enormous *cross-referencing density* of psyglyphic language as a measure of its *resilient semantic radiance*, in the sense of its radial nonlinearity.

Ilya Prigogine's ideas also come into play within the context of resilience, as already adumbrated. He was one of the first to realize the fact of nonlinear time, in the sense that certain consistent oscillations in nonlinear dynamic systems can generate a new state and spatio-temporal structure for the system. Such structures (Prigogine terms them "dissipative," i.e. energy-dissipative) must needs be negentropically maintained, and are dependent on locally generated pools of negentropy. They occur at sufficient distance from thermodynamic equilibrium to enable new forms to arise (equilibrium would suppress innovation). Such phenomena can themselves be considered as macro-fluctuations and they contain inherent indeterminisms in their temporal evolution that accord well with biological observation.

There is even here, however, still no explanation for the phenomenon of many different but related mutations being set up in the right sequence and sustained in a long and purpose-fulfilling chain of changes: for instance, those needed to transmute a fish-scale into a bird-feather or a diffuse visual pigment into a highly organized molluscan eye, as in *Nautilus*, the octopus, or the squid. There is still no random equivalent for mind, which is in fact the essence of the antithesis to randomness, since it opportunistically uses stochastic elements to produce highly organized end-results. Planning goes as deep as the unexpected, and they are related much as fate and free choice (cf. section 3.16). "Randomness" to one entity is thus ultimately seen to be actually the results of other entities' choices. When the chips are down, purpose transcends chaos.

Notes

1. The techniques and methods specifically implementing these applications require an entire book for themselves (already projected under the title *Chronotopological Methods and Techniques*). This chapter deals basically with the concept of *control*.

2. Probably originating in hardware versus software in computer science, where these terms are more appropriate, since here "soft" means primarily flexible and multi-valued.

3. Chapter 5 has pointed up a large lesson—unfortunately not yet mastered. All that proceeds from that import underlies and eventually decides the outcomes of even what appear to be comparatively inconsequential examples of chronosystems relations. The imperatives and prognosis of sections 3.37–3.38 are also tied in closely with that same lesson. The great and and tragic problem of human history, of human development in time, is that the daily principal activity of most people does not express their own nature. The deep frustration thus generated can manifest only as social discontent, always speedily utilized by those sick and dangerous parasites—the unscrupulous seizers of power ever needing it to mask from themselves by a spurious image their own self-contempt for what they do. Even such humans, if they finally face themselves, see their psychological and developmental failure. Lenin on his deathbed said to his old friend and confidant, the Hungarian priest Bödo: "I have been mistaken. Doubtless it was necessary to liberate an oppressed multitude, but our method has only provoked other oppressions and frightful massacres. You know, my constant nightmare is to feel myself drowning in the ocean of blood of those innumerable victims. To save our Russia—but now it is too late—ten like Francis of Assisi would have been needed" [150].

The neglect of the existence of humanity in a system-treatment of human beings can take more prosaic but just as error-producing forms. Thus in the 1977 discussion of Stephen Smale's lecture on "Some Dynamical Questions in Mathematical Economics" [78, p. 115], the point was raised by two discussants (Fuchs and Kirman) that serious problems arose in Smale's model because of his neglecting to take into account the fact that "expectations about future prices play a major role." In response, Smale quite honestly admitted that his model was defective, i.e., that it would have to be "altered' and that his conditions "require an essential change" if this basic fact about time and human behavior is to be taken into account. It is for this and other reasons that the title (*The Mathematics of Time*) of the referenced photo-reproduced publication is a misleading one, undoubtedly suggested not by its talented author but by some publisher's promotion man, since despite its merits the book tells little or nothing of the nature of time and would more correctly have been called "Some Papers on Dynamics and Dynamical Systems." The same dearth of actual information on the nature or working of time applies a *fortiori* to the plethora of more superficial compilations (e.g. those of G. Whitrow or J. Fraser). Ilya Prigogine, we are happy to say, goes much further, e.g., pp. xii–xiii and *passim*, in his *From Being to Becoming* (Freeman, San Francisco, 1980), which we already discussed in [104].

4. Speaking of optimal tonalities and hence scales, I found that, beyond the 12 tones of the chromatic scale, there was only one further musically satisfying scale, one of 22 notes as follows (the fractions denoting the frequency ratios between the fundamental tone "1" and its octave "2"): 1, 25/24, 16/15, 10/9, 9/8, 32/27, 6/5, 5/4, 32/25, 4/3, 25/18, 7/5, 36/25, 3/2, 25/16, 8/5, 5/3, 27/16, 16/9, 9/5, 15/8, 48/25, and 2. This 22-tone scale, like the chromatic scale, can be tempered, and its intervals in any case are more naturally pleasing than those of any 24-tone scale. The musician and expert ancient and modern instrument-maker, Goa (Georges) Alloro of

the ARTHEA music group at Grasse, confirmed this comparison after I gave him the 22-tone scale as an experiment.

5. Old Jaakob felt that same power that breathes in Shakespeare's lines, "There's not the smallest orb that thou beholdst but in his orbit like an angel sings, still quiring to the young-eyed cherubin . . . yet this muddy vesture of decay doth so grossly close us in, we cannot hear it."

6. Ecological systems analyst C.S. Holling empirically corroborates the chronosystemically important concept of *uniqueness* (as including but extending beyond individuality) that we have voiced. He notes (in *The Director's Corner, Options*, IIASA, Laxenburg, Austria, Spring 1982, p. 20)) "the key role of singular individuals," adding that "IIASA has focused largely on issues at national and global scales. Sometimes lost in this perspective, however, is the personal element so critical for the resolution of any real problem, regardless of scale." One of the salutary functions of such individuals in the management and political context, he concludes, consists "in communicating, interacting, establishing the necessary conditions for communication, in order to highlight conflicts and to defuse them. . . . It is [thus] possible to pause, before some point of no return is reached, long enough to have our adaptive reflexes shape a response to change." We underline that this is a very different process from its caricature of too-often unwisely praised and, in extreme cases, consciously studied, maximal noncommitalism, which ends up in practice by not only becoming maximally hypocritical, but also quite useless in rescuing the system from either acutely or chronically dangerous problems.

7. Summary statement of I. Siegel and N. Gleicher, professors of immunology at Rush Medical College, Chicago.

8. In the preprint of an April 1983 paper, mathematical system analyst John Casti keenly notes (p. 43) that "a well-behaved system [e.g., natural ecology before ignorant and exploitative human meddling.—C.M.] can be sent into oscillatory or even chaotic behavior by introduction of control laws of unsuitable structure. This possibility is particularly insidious in situations where the control law is selected to optimize some performance criterion [e.g., economic gain.—C.M.] without proper attention being paid to its possibly bifurcation-generating side effects." Casti concludes this illuminating passage with the related observation that disarray could be an expected result coming out of such misconceived attempts to control, and follows with a mathematical example. But the principle extends much farther than the mathematical formalism, and well into depth psychology and our fundamental caveat already discussed: the need to respect individual entities and special situations.

On the matter of bifurcation, there is an important point not yet in the literature only because yet unrealized. That is, the importance in nature of temporally *asymmetric* heteroclinic bifurcations. Thus far only symmetric ones have been treated along with, of course, the homoclinic varieties which return to the same stationary point whether traced into the future or into the past.

A good example of symmetric heteroclinic trajectories is provided by certain values of the equations first proposed by mathematical meteorologist E.N. Lorenz in 1963 in the *Journal of Atmospheric Science*, and since studied by many topological dynamicists; and computer diagrams for Lorenz-derived symmetric heteroclinic orbits are given by Colin Sparrow in his *Lorenz Equations* (Springer, New York, 1982) on pages 166 and 169, with a useful summary diagram on page 229. Such behavior mathematically mirrors situations like DNA/RNA vis-à-vis the aminoacyl transferase proteins (cf. Supplement to come)—each being a source or necessary condition for the other, thus forming the two stationary points that mutually lead to one another.

Yet such systems can represent only "going concerns"—pumps-in-function, so to speak—and not the starting-up process or pump-priming. Nature, however, when origins are traced, shows *unsymmetrical* time processes, and hence the (as yet unstudied) phenomenon of asymmetric heteroclinic trajectories. We recommend their study as a next stage in developing bifurcation theory. Even the simple equation $y = \Gamma(t)$ is not symmetric in time. Nature's processes, with respect to origins, never are; and that is where her greatest secrets lie.

9. Including the universal property of waves, in relation to their medium, that should be, but has not yet been made the basis of any general wave theory: the ratio of elastic energy density over volume, E/V, to inertia density m/V, when both are taken in appropriate units, measures the square of the wave propagation velocity in the medium, that square being also the product of the phase velocity and the group velocity. Thus for electromagnetic waves, using the Poynting and Poincaré vectors for E/V and m/V, we have

$$\frac{E/V}{m/V} = c^2, \text{ or } E = mc^2,$$

showing that this now standard equation arises, not from any relativistic assumptions as such, but from the wave nature of all electromagnetic energy exchange. $E = mc^2$ is thus a consequence of Maxwell's theory, since retarded potentials follow from the finite speed of light.

10. Though it has not been sufficiently realized, the fundamental importance of timing enters even into the very foundations of mathematics. Thus we are told that operations may be commutative ($ba = ab$) or noncommutative: ($ba \neq ab$); associative, where $a(bc) = (ab)c$, or nonassociative: $a(bc) \neq (ab)c$; and distributive, where $ab + ac = a(b + c)$, or nondistributive, where $ab + ac \neq a(b + c)$. Actual concrete examples of all of the aberrant or "non-" forms can be furnished from hypernumbers (v, announced Supplement), whereas ordinary numbers exhibit all the normal forms of the operations cited above.

We find in the textbooks that these three operational classes (each with its "non-" forms) are presented as three quite different things. Actually, all three depend on the shared notion of sequence, time and timing. Thus, if in the first case the two members of a binary operation give a different result when their order is reversed, then the operation is termed noncommutative, meaning literally that the two members of the operation cannot be commuted or turned around or put out of sequence without changing the result.

In the second case where the operation entails two alternative sub-*operations* of the same kind, (ab) or (bc), the entire operation is nonassociative if the sequence of its suboperations cannot be temporally inverted with impunity i.e. without changing the result. Thus (ab) multiplied by c yields a different product from a multiplied by (bc).

The third case is simply a generalization of the second, where the two suboperations are not of the same kind. Thus adding b and c first and then multiplying by a yields a different result from multiplying through first by a and then adding the products ab and ac.

In all three cases, the key issue is one of inverting a sequence; in the first case the sequence concerns the members of a binary operation; in the other cases it concerns operations themselves rather than their members.

11. For instance, the fundamental and unperceived phonological differences between male and female speech [163].

EPILOGUE:* THE
CURRENT ARENA AND
THE BIRTH OF A NEW ERA

There is thus possible an entire *science of synchrony and qualitative time*, with applications to social contexts and problems. Some years ago we first used the term *chronotopology* to denote this study of the connectivity of time configurations. And when we understand time as both desire and consequence, we can then begin to apply the dynamics of chronoetics, which can result in acquiring optimal control over event types at predesignatable periods.

Brain research has something to offer here. As early as a 1971 interview with the journalist Maya Pines, Dr. John Henley of the Space Biology Laboratory at the University of California's Brain Research Institute offered these comments, already then scientifically possible even in such a convential setting:

> Certainly there are suboptimal states for learing—after a heavy lunch for instance. . . . There may be optimal states too—but when? . . . Perhaps there are

---

*This chapter was originally prefaced by two others entitled, respectively, "An Overview/ Prospect" and "Tools of Chronotopological Relevance." These, along with the already noted EXORcist portion of chapter 3, had to be omitted because of space requirements. They will appear as a separate publication, and interested readers should address the publishers.

periodicities in our ability to learn . . . when we discover what they are, we can capitalize on them.

Chronotopology confirms that it is certain there are, and how to use them.

From the quantum-physical nature of the fundamental bio-energetic transductions that lie behind brain function it is now clear that the brain is no more a mechanism than quantum physics is mechanistic. Indeed, the inadequate metaphor of a simplistic determinateness or mechanism in this field is rendered obsolete by the most thorough studies even of the physical world. Those studies conjoined with chronotopological analysis reveal that the physical world leads through the nature of space and of time itself into a realm of nonphysical yet physically effective reality[1] whose barriers we are just beginning to cross, in a new chapter of scientific advance.

So, in the best sense, this must remain an unfinished book, unfinished except for what has been expressly omitted. In this book there are none of the customary genuflexions to a now obese and outmoded Cerberus. We refer to zealot, uninformed, and over-long entrenched naive materialism and mechanism that came to pervade academic circles of twentieth century science and philosophy as a vestige of the nineteenth, in the greed-cum-technology rather than wisdom- or beauty-oriented global civilization that had already begun to arise in Europe and America in the eighteenth century, and which is now, happily, phasing out after some two hundred years of politico-historical hegemony.

Its deepest distinctive trait is that its credo, its religion, was in practice largely confined to *anthropolatry:*[2] the worship by human beings of themselves as a class—with the accompanying hubris of insisting that there could be nothing really significant beyond what they could come to control and to perceive bodily. No other culture in history has so shrilly screamed such unsupported denials of anything significant beyond physical man, and such denials in no other period ever became the prevalent philosophy and viewpoint of an almost global yet psychologically barbaric culture. But the current rather violent arena is also like an egg about to hatch under the stimulus of its cumulative, endogenously generated poisons. So its struggles signify the birth as well as the pangs of a new era.

Within a week after writing the above, we received an aptly related paper by a talented *enfant terrible* of scientific criticism, David Berlinski. He provides a salutary reminder[3] noting that everyone who thinks is intrigued by the varieties and arisings of form in the natural world. "But," he trenchantly goes on, "the modern molecular biologist for the most part looks on the organism—bugs or bacteria—with blunt dissective passion. His ambition is not to understand the creature as an object fixed in a region of space and moving solemnly or somberly through time, but to tear off its routine appearances—its distinctive shuffle and regular shape—in order to get at the basic and more fundamental molecular structure that in his crudeness he imagines runs the whole works from below. This is *reductionism*, a crude but violently vigorous flower in the contemporary philosophy of science."

Fallacious varieties of reductionism all omit the vital phrase *praeter necessitatem*—"unless necessary" (by reason of reality)—in William of Ockham's famous precept called Occam's razor: *Entia non sunt multiplicanda praeter necessitatem*—assumptions are not to be multiplied unless necessary. What is, of course, being directly admonished against is the *un*necessary multiplication of hypotheses.

But what is less obvious, and perhaps even more important, is that Occam's razor also logically disbars the *reducing* of assumptions to the point where they are inadequate to explain the phenomena and realities at hand, i.e. the "necessities" in Ockham's precept.[4] This latter and more subtle pitfall has by and large gone unnoticed in the blind bull-charge of an insufficient philosophy of random mechanism parading itself as a universal system of explanation. Adding further to untenability, its proponents have remained unaware that their naive notion of "matter" had been discredited in all the advanced physics laboratories of the world ever since the beginnings of the twentieth century. Planck's quantum theory, which unveiled the new vista of the much more profound nature of what we call "matter," was first announced during the last week of the turn of the century in the year 1899, and a radically new concept of matter was fully launched by the 1920s.

But the naive, fallacious, yet psychologically entrenched reductionism infiltrated down into many talented writers of science fiction (SF), revealing an additional admonition to Occam's razor: verbal facility and clear thinking have no necessary connection. The average reader too often believes even glaring fallacies when they are made invisible enough by skillful word webs, woven much as those spun by apologist-writers for a dogmatic religion or a tyrannical ideology, though these latter have no excuse of innocence.

The gifted SF author Italo Calvino[5] almost sees through his own web when he writes in his story *Mitosis* (a unicellular being is speaking): "Each of these filaments . . . or chromosomes had a special relation to some characteristic of the cell that was me. Now I might attempt a somewhat risky assertion and say I was nothing but the sum of those filaments or lines . . . , an assertion that can be disputed because of . . . the nervousness of an individual who knows he has all those lines, he is all those lines, but *also knows there's something that can't be represented with those lines*" (italics ours); "and then comes the death agony that precipitates triumphantly because life is already elsewhere." Unfortunately, he doesn't quite see through it because by "elsewhere" he simply reductively means physically, as the result of the mitotic fission.

The best he can do with the problem of death is to look forward to the day, in his tale *Death*, "of the machines that reproduce themselves through crossed male and female messages, forcing new machines to be born and the old machines to die. . . . A finale that doesn't conclude, . . . a net of words . . . where machines can speak, exchange the words by which they are constructed. . . . Generations of machines perhaps better than we will go on living . . . "—evidently quite innocent of the complete nonsequitur and inadequacy that his use of the word "living" not entails. Such philosophy, of course, inevitably leads through black humour or irony to melancholia, and Calvino his story *Blood, Sea*, finally sees a human death as "only an infinitesimal detail . . . , a number in the statistics of accidents over the weekend." So much for apologistic reductionism, even with a fine intellect defending it.

A similar case in point occurred in a personal conversation between the writer and the well-known ethologist Konrad Lorenz at the latter's home in Bavaria in the late 1960s. Though his eminent specialty is animal behavior, he had been trained as a physician, Jesuit and Darwinian—an interesting background.

After dinner Lorenz was advocating the commonly voiced view that human intelligence derives from the neurons or nerve cells of the brain. In response, I asked him whether as a physician and zoologist he would not admit that our white cells or leukocytes, the protectors and scavengers of our blood and lymph, are in fact specialized amoebas or one-celled animals belonging to the primitive order of protozoa. He of course agreed. I then queried whether he would not also agree that neurons, with their nuclei, axons, and dendrites, are not even more highly specialized amoebas, with pseudopods now almost fixed and stationary in the form of dendrites and axons that stream out of the protoplasm of each neuron in characteristic forms as the cell matures. This time, after a longer pause, Lorenz also agreed.

Now, I continued, Darwinism tells us that dogs are less intelligent than humans, clams less so than dogs, and protozoa even less than clams— "evolution" having proceeded from lower to higher levels of organized life, according to the received doctrine. But, I noted, then your Darwinism contradicts your theory of the source of human intelligence, for Darwinism could not grant without self-contradiction that the intelligence of humans could be that of protozoa.

At this point Lorenz's daughter, who was also present, wanted to change the subject. But her father, to his credit, valiantly persisted and did not flee the field. "It is the way the neurons are arranged," he offered as a solution to the dilemma. "But," I countered, "it doesn't make much difference how you arrange morons in a room, so far as their pooled intelligence goes; and above all, such arranging and/or arrangements imply an *arranger*. Granted, if you had an intelligent *operator* directing this switchboard of morons to perform intelligent tasks, we would then have a solution. But on your stated view, there is no such entity in or directing a human body, and all the intelligence is alleged to be derivable from neurons."

Lorenz could find no ready answer, and the conversation changed. What remained clear was that the theory of neurons being the *source* of human intelligence is logically neither credible nor creditable. Such an unacceptably improbable speculation would then also have to aver that a large group of precisely arranged silicon chips (which are, it should be observed, only very crude analogs of neurons) not only *manufactured* themselves, but then *arranged* themselves into a computer, circuitry, programming, and all—this whole already fantastically unbelievable operation being moreover all asserted to have been done by unplanned, *random* activity!

That, of course, is known to be not only totally absurd but totally untrue as well. Silicon chips do not make themselves or arrange themselves into computers. People with acute awareness of what they plan to do, do all that for chips. Compounding the prior absurdity exponentially, we often hear the really silly assertion that mammalian intelligence could be the result of the "self-organization" of neurons. The very term "self-organization" is here the give-away of an entire ploy of circular reasoning, since it is *precisely* such self-organization that must be proved in the first place and not merely naively asserted with pitiful dogmatism in the face of overwhelming high odds to the contrary, and despite the equally overwhelming verdict of all other experience. *Intricate and adaptive design directed toward future events requires intelligence to start with*. This is the basic axiom of logical sanity that has been dangerously neglected by the more superficial exponents of science in the nineteenth and twentieth centuries. Yet every computer designer knows it.

It further emerged out of the discussion with Lorenz that there is something in ourselves which can be biophysically *effective* through neuron-transducers, and yet not be itself biophysical in nature. The conclusions for such a category of reality are further corroborated by advanced quantum physics, which has demonstrated that space, devoid of either matter or radiation (and hence by definition nonphysical), yet possesses inherent energy and can be physically effective. Such a category of nonphysical but physically effective reality is what is also involved in the effectiveness of time and of the fluctuations in qualitative energies associated with it.

In other words, what is called matter in most writings today—even in psycho-socio-scientific ones—is still a figment of a too simplistic nineteenth century hypothesis later disproved in the crucible of experience and observation. The ultimate stuff of protons, electrons, and light now appears to be stubbornly "immaterial" in the quite definite sense that that stuff itself is neither protons, electrons, nor light. That is, their origin is none of the three stable constituents into which all matter is resolvable under appropriate conditions, but seems much more like "vacuum" or, equally paradoxically for our ignorance, "empty space." So the origins of matter, pursued to the most recondite reaches, finally lead to another order of reality that is not matter as we perceive it through our present senses or as now constituted.

That some scientists should feel threatened by such direct implications of their own experiments is natural, given the nineteenth century, quasi-theological dogmas of senseless randomism and mechanism that dominated well into the twentieth. But some attitudes are quite irrelevant to our ongoing understanding of a universe much more profound than such shallow dogmas could possibly comprehend, given their omissive premises, historically naive to the point that no anterior culture ever even countenanced them in its prevalent world-view.

All these relatively newly won facts about the nature of our world, which were mostly discovered in the first half of the twentieth century, leave in their wake a profound and remaining enigma, reinforced by investigations into the nature of gravitation [164] and related to there being at least one further dimension of space than the three we know—all in addition, of course, to time, which so fundamentally differs form space of *any* dimension. This last fact is easily grasped when we realize that it takes *time* for objects to move or be moved in any spatial dimension, however high. By virtue of this same insight, time is thus seen to be no dimension of space whatsoever, and the phenomenology of our everyday experience underscores this conclusion.

Matter, far from having an ultimate billiard-ball character, is now known to be much more like the nature of light and radiation in general, including both electromagnetic and gravitational waves. The supporting medium of such waves is further seen to be space itself—the so-called "vacuum state" of quantum physics, fast belying its name and showing a powerful structure and an inherent energy of its own in terms of a new order of reality that is not physical although physically effective. That inherent energy of space is today actually measurable in the laboratory as "the zero-point energy of the vacuum." Indeed such measured energies appear to be but a very small fraction of the potential, still unmanifest energy involved.

Nineteenth century materialism, still hanging on in the twentieth, is seen to be inadequate. In the light of accurate enough logical insight and new findings, the naively mechanistic billiard-ball materialism that anachron-istically still tyrannizes over great portions of school-taught biology, psychology, and sociology—simply becomes discredited scientifically and can no longer be reiterated with impunity in scientific treatises worthy of the name. And there are always those who say they no longer think that way, but in fact do.

Such regurgitations are now not merely *démodé* but wrong, and they do not figure here. On the other hand, the implications of the most scientifically advanced investigations fortunately lead beyond such impasses, and so enable the subtle yet daily effective subject matter of this book to be treated in experiential and phenomenological terms. The time is ripe.

In sum, and interestingly, the most sophisticated form of physical science—quantum theory—that this civilization produced, has been forced by sheer laboratory experience to deny precisely some of the most prevalent and loose assumptions of its own culture: namely, the specious conceptions of matter in mechanistic terms, and the derivation of life and mind from such matter. For advanced physics has found, among other striking facts, that light and matter are actually interchangeable entities: that so-called 'empty space'—devoid of both matter and radiation—still possesses an enormous inherent energy actually indispensable for the maintenance of the entire physical universe. Thus at the roots of physics lies, beyond both nature and human nature—as it always did—the Mystery. . . . And as an all-embracing scientific hypothesis, random mechanism fades into the oblivion of outgrown fallacies.

The greatest fallacies of all for humanity are, of course, its psychological and emotional ones. In this connection, there was a classic screenplay, *The Day the Earth Stood Still*, released in 1951 by Twentieth Century Fox and written by Edmund H. North after a story by Harry Bates. As I noted it down from a June 1980 televised re-run, the final words of the protagonist Klatu (Michael Rennie), who speaks beside his silent but mighty robot Gort, went like this: "The universe grows smaller every day, and the threats of aggression or oppression by any group anywhere can no longer be tolerated. There must be security for all or no one is secure. And this does not mean giving up any freedom except the freedom to act irresponsibly. . . . Pursue your present course and face obliteration. We shall be waiting for your answer. The decision rests with you." These words point to one of the prime enigmas of historical time, discussed in chapter 5.

If dedicated to a deep enough comprehension, the epoch now nascent and stirring is due to bring forth several radically different ways of looking at things, all stemming from the overwhelming logic and fact that no amount of random subforms or mechanically determined processes can account for the creative awareness we *experience* in ourselves and which we then use to explain nature. Indeed, the very process of *explanation* itself (quite distinct from mere rationalization) goes infinitely beyond any mechanistic system, that viewpoint again shown to be hopelessly inadequate. Happily, a new era of more profound science is dawning. It is our business to make the future better than our memories.

Notes

1. A concept, incidentally, that implies there are types of formable substance other than the atomic matter we know and with correspondingly different capabilities.

2. Endeavoring to have a purely "social" and "humanistic" religion is like trying to have a spherical surface without a three-dimensional space. Try as one would, such a surface could be only flat, although some could deceitfully shade it to suggest a sphere. So our conventional anthropo-centered twentieth century "religions" have become flat, insipid and shallow institutions without depth, either intellectual or emotional.

3. In a monograph that Maurice Nivat, chief of the University of Paris Institute of Programming Theory, called "necessary by reason of its recalling us to a fecund humility" (*The Rise of Differential Topology*, Inst. Publ. No. 80-33, July 1980, pp. 33–34).

4. The deeper viewpoint treated in chapter 5 is naturally among those necessities that require in turn an optimal deepening of scientific assumption and consequent explanation.

5. The original Italian text was published in 1967 by Einaudi in Torino, and the English translation, by William Weaver, in 1969 in a joint hardcover edition by Jonathan Cape of London and Harcourt, Brace & World of New York, and as a Macmillan Collier paperback in 1970.

References

1. Orchard, R.A. 1972. On an approach to general systems theory. In *Trends in general systems theory*, ed. G.J. Klir, pp. 239–247. New York: Wiley-Interscience.
2. Morse, M. 1959. Mathematics, the arts and freedom. *Fordham University Quarterly* 34:16.
3. Klir, G.J. 1972. The polyphonic general systems theory. In *Trends in general systems theory*, ed. G.J. Klir. New York: Wiley-Interscience.
4. Marshack, A. 1972. *The roots of civilization*. New York: McGraw-Hill.
5. Marshack, A. 1964. Lunar notation on upper paleolithic remains. *Science* 146:743–745. This is Marshack's first publication on this matter.
6. Baudoin, M. 1916. *Bulletins et mémoires de la soc. d'anthropologie de Paris*, Sér, VI, tome VII:25–103; 274–317.
7. Leroi-Gourhan, A. 1967. *Treasures of prehistoric art*. New York: Abrams.

8. Berlinski, D. 1976. *On systems analysis.* Cambridge, Mass.: MIT Press.
9. Musès, C. 1982. Surprise in system theory. Seminar conducted at the International Institute for Advanced Systems Analysis (IIASA), 21, October 1982, Laxenburg, Austria.
10. Kockelman, J.J., and Kisiel, T.J. 1970. *Phenomenology and the natural sciences: essays and translations,* p. 48. Evanston, Illinois: Northwestern University Press.
11. Musès, C. 1958. Foreword to J. Rothstein's *Communication, organization and science.* Colorado: Falcon's Wing Press.
12. Bryer, D.R. 1976. The origins of the druse religion. *Islam* 53:5*ff.*
13. (al-)Jurjānī, Abū Bakr 'Abdalqāhīr. His *Kitāb asrār* al-balāgha ("Book of the Art—literally 'secrets'—of literate expression") has appeared in a German translation by H. Ritter, Wiesbaden, 1959 (Bibliotheca Islamica, 19) but his penetrating *Dalā'il al-i'jāz* ("Guide to the Inimitable") still exists only in Arabic, edited by M. al-Marāghī, Cairo, 1950, though short citations appeared in W. Heinrichs' monograph on the history of metaphor in Arabic poetry (*Abhandlungen für die Kunde des Morgenlandes,* XLIV, 2, Deutsche Morgenländische Gesellschaft, 1977).
14. Musès, C. 1979. "Grammar, context and programming languages. *Kybernetes* 8:82–83.
15. Klibansky, R. 1950. *The continuity of the Platonic tradition,* pp. 43–44. London: Warburg Institute.
16. Musès, C. 1976. Computing in the bio-sciences with hypernumbers. *Int. J. Bio-Medical Computing* 3:211–226.
17. Deubner, F.L. 1975. *Astronomy and astrophysics* 45:371.
18. Brown, T., Stebbins, R.T., and Hill, H.A. 1978. In *Astrophys. J.,* 223:324; with a summary of this work by H.A. Hill in *The new solar physics,* ed. J. Eddy. Boulder, Colorado: Westview Press.
19. Wolff, C.L. 1976. *Astrophys. J.* 205:612.
20. Hill, H.A., and Dziembowski, W.A., eds. 1980. *Nonradial and nonlinear stellar pulsation,* p. 172. New York: Springer.
21. Olson, H.F. 1967. *Music, physics and engineering.* New York: Dover.
22. Davisson, C.J., and Germer, L.H. 1927. *Physical Review* 30:705.
23. Reference 11, pp. lxiv–lxv.
24. Abraham R. 1976. Vibrations and the realization of form. In *Evolution and consciousness,* ed. E. Jantsch and C.B. Waddington. Reading, Massachusetts: Addison-Wesley.
25. *New Scientist* 96(1982):562; also 97(1983):748.
26. Tipler, F. See *New Scientist* 87:654.
27. Brown, F.A. 1968. "The solunar clocks of life. *Oceanology International.*
28. _____. 1965. A unified theory for biological rhythms. In *Circadian clocks,* p. 231. Amsterdam: North-Holland.
29. Clark, Frances. 1957. Grunion in Southern California. A California State Fisheries Laboratory report, cited by R.C.H. Russell and D.H. Macmillan in *Waves and tides,* pp. 303–304. New York: Basic Books.

30. Ward, R. 1971. *The living clocks*, p. 270. New York: Knopf.
31. Hamner, K.C., et al. 1962. The biological clocks at the South Pole. *Nature* 195:476.
32. de Candolle, A.P. 1832. *Physiologie végétale.* Paris.
33. Arrhenius, S. 1898. Die Einwirkung kosmischer Einflüße auf physiologische Verhältnisse. *Skandinavisches Archiv f. Physiologie* 8:367*ff.*
34. Burrows, W. 1945. Periodic swarming of palolo worms. *Nature* 155:47.
35. Melixetyan, A. 1982. In *Teknika molodyezhi*, November, 1979, trans. in part by L. Vilenskaya. San Francisco: Washington Research Center.
36. Leao, A. 1927. Spreading depression of activity in the cerebral cortex. *J. Neurophysiology* 7:326.
37. Green, J.P., and Weinstein, H., eds. 1980. *Annals*, New York Acad. of Sciences, vol. 367.
38. Musès, C. 1984. Chapter 29 in *Self-organization*, ed. F.E. Yates. New York: Plenum, in press.
39. Heisenberg, W. 1925 and 1926. *Zeitschrift für Physik* 38:411 and 39:499.
40. Wigner, E.P. 1974. The place of consciousness in modern physics. In *Consciousness and Reality*, ed. C. Musès and A. Young, p. 141. New York: E.P. Dutton and Avon/Discus Books.
41. Williams, T.P. 1983. *Kybernetes*, 12:681.
42. Russell, R.C.H., and Macmillan, D.H. 1957. *Waves and tides*, p. 302. New York: Basic Books.
43. Sankar, S., and Yeo, G.K. 1977. *Embedded invariants, a contribution to forecasting.* Göttingen: Vandenhoek & Ruprecht.
44. Brown, F.A., and Webb, H.M. 1948. Temperature Relations on Endogenous Daily Rhythmicity in the Fiddler Crab *Uca*. *Physiological Zoology* 21:371.
45. Brown, F.A. 1962. Life's mysterious clocks. In *Adventures of the mind*, ed. R. Thruelson and J. Kobler. New York: Random House.
46. Reference 42, p. 232.
47. Reference 42, pp. 227-8; 305.
48. Jung, C.G. 1954. Synchronicity, an acausal connecting principle. In *The interpretation of nature and psyche*. New York: Pantheon. (Includes an essay by quantum physicist Wolfgang Pauli.)
49. See Reference 48, title and *passim.*
50. Corbin, H. 1973. Preface to *Man and time*, Bollingen Series XXX.3, pp. xvii–xviii. Princeton, New Jersey: Princeton University Press.
51. Jantsch, E. 1980. *The self-organizing universe*, p. 238. London: Pergamon.
52. Plato, A. *Republic*, 546; *Timaeus*, 40.
53. Reference 52, *Republic*, 546, B,D.
54. Reference 52, *Timaeus.*
55. Shuster, A. 1911. The influence of the planets on the formation of sunspots. *Proceedings of the Royal Society* (London) 85:309.
56. Huntington, E. 1923. *Earth and sun*. New Haven, Conn.: Yale University Press.

57. Bauer, L. 1924. Correlations between solar activity and atmospheric electricity. In *Terrestrial and Atmospheric Electricity*, pp. 23 and 161.
58. Luby, W.A. 1940. *Popular Astronomy* 48.
59. Clayton, H.H. 1941. *Popular Astronomy* 49.
60. Abraham, R. 1972. *Introduction to morphology*, p. 103. Lyons: Université Claude-Bernard.
61. Eysenck, H.J., and Nias, D.K.B. 1982. *Astrology, science or superstition?* London: Maurice Temple Smith, Ltd.
62. Abraham, R. 1973. Psychotronic Vibrators. In *Proceedings of the First International Congress on Psychotronics*, Prague.
63. Volkers, V., and Candib, W. 1960. Detection and analysis of high-frequency signals from muscular tissue with ultra-low-noise amplifiers. *Proceedings of the International Convention of Radio Engineers*.
64. Winfree, A.T. 1972. Spiral waves of chemical activity. *Science* 175:634.
65. _____. 1980. *The geometry of biological time*. New York: Springer. Winfree says on p. v that "those readers who, expecting wonders to follow so grand a title [and who] may feel cheated by its actual content [should] take this beginning as a serious challenge."
66. *Time* magazine, March 21, 1969.
67. Metzner, R. 1970. Astrology: potential science and intuitive art. *Journal for the Study of Consciousness*, 3:70.
68. Reference 42, p. 223.
69. Wuketits, F.M. 1982. Systems research—the search for isomorphism. In *Progress in Cybernetics and Systems Research*, vol. 11, ed. R. Trappl, et al., p. 403. New York: Hemisphere/McGraw Hill.
70. Riedl, R. 1979. *Order in living organisms*. New York: Wiley.
71. Weir, M. 1982. The mathematics and methodology of purpose. In *Progress in cybernetics and systems research*, vol. 8, ed. R. Trappl, G.J. Klir, and F.R. Pichter, p. 151*ff* New York: Hemisphere/McGraw Hill.
72. Musès, C. 1965. Systemic stability and cybernetic control. In *Cybernetics of neural processes*, ed. E.R. Caianiello, pp. 165–8. Rome: National Research Council of Italy.
73. Davis, H. 1960. *Introduction to nonlinear differential and integral equations*, pp. 185; 229–246; 501–530. Washington, D.C.: U.S. Atomic Energy Commission.
74. Casti, J. 1983. Emergent novelty, dynamical systems and the modeling of spatial processes. *Kybernetes*, 12:167 (transmitted by C. Musès).
75. Reference 11, p. lxii.
76. Reference 72, pp. 161, 163.
77. Eagle, A. 1958. *The elliptic functions as they should be*, p. 311. Cambridge: Galloway & Porter.
78. Smale, S. 1980. *The mathematics of time*, New York: Springer.
79. Ref. 67, pp. 161, 163.
80. Holling, C.S. 1973. Resilience and stability of ecological systems. *Annual*

Review of Ecology and Systematics 4:1.
81. Hughes, R.D., and Gilbert, N. 1968. A model of an aphid population (I). *J. of Animal Ecology* 37:553.
82. Gilbert, N., and Hughes, R.D. 1971. A model of an aphid population (II). *J. of Animal Ecology* 40:525.
83. Wiberg, D.M. 1971. *Theory and problems of state space and linear systems*, p. 5. New York: McGraw Hill.
84. Gaizauskas, V. 1983. Solar activity. In *Observers' handbook*, p. 49. Toronto: Royal Astronomical Society of Canada.
85. Goddard, V. 1966. Imagining into reality ... an introduction to Douglas Fawcett ... Mimeographed lecture, 12 February, 1966, Attingham Park, England.
86. Musès, C. 1977. SUPL, In *Modern Trends in Cybernetics and Systems*, vol. 3, ed. J. Rose and C. Bilciu, pp. 167–178. New York: Springer.
87. Reference 14, p. 83.
88. Musès, C. 1962. The logic of bio-simulation. In *Aspects of the Theory of artificial intelligence*, pp. 157–8. New York: Plenum. It is necessary to note here that when we did this book, we had read Heaviside's works but had not yet seen Balthasar van der Pol's magisterial treatment (in his and H. Bremmer's *Operational Calculus*, Cambridge University Press, 1964) of the Heaviside unit function $u(t)$. We were looking for an analytical form of it, not realizing that

$$u(t) = \frac{1}{\pi} \lim_{k \to \infty} \int_{-\infty}^{kt} = \frac{\sin \tau}{\tau} \, d\tau$$

was the answer; whence

$$du(t)/dt = \delta(t) = \lim_{k \to \infty} \frac{\sin (kt)}{\pi t}.$$

Van der Pol and Bremmer, however, did not realize (*ib.* pp. 62, 74) that this latter function is in fact $\delta(t)$ and that for $t \neq 0$ it is zero, since its sum of positive areas is nullified by the sum of its corresponding negative areas at $k = \infty$. The only other real contender for $u(t)$ is

$$\tfrac{1}{2} + \frac{1}{\pi} \lim_{k \to \infty} \arctan (kt)$$

but this is less elegant and also $|kt|$ must be restricted to $< \tfrac{1}{2}\pi$. It is worth observing with van der Pol (*ib.* p. 59) that *signum t* ($= 1$ for $t > 0$; 0 for $t = 0$;

and -1 for $t < 0$) is given by $2u(t) - 1$, noting that $u(0) = \frac{1}{2}$. The Möbius function may also be interpreted through $u(t)$, showing the latter's importance for number theory as well as for analysis. Finally, $\int_{-0}^{+0} \delta(t) = 1$, which mostly is not realized, as it depends on infinitesimals producing a finite effect. (See supplement to be published separately as per footnote at start of epilogue.)

89. Gilling, R.J. 1982. *Mathematics in the time of the pharaohs*, pp. 18–20. New York: Dover.
90. Reference 89, p. 19.
91. Needham, J. 1956. *Science and civilisation in China*, vol. 2. p. 341. Cambridge University Press.
92. Minsky, M. 1983. Contribution to New York Academy of Sciences conference on computer culture, 25–29 April, 1983.
93. Quine, W. 1970. *Set theory and its logic*, pp. 26–27. Cambridge: Harvard University Press.
94. Reference 88, pp. 140–141 note.
95. Halmos, P.R. 1963. *Lectures on boolean algebra*, pp. 18–20. Princeton, New Jersey: D. van Nostrand.
96. Musès, C. 1978. Hypernumbers II. *J. Appl. Math. Comput.* 4:66, note 9. The material on the hypernumber w has been updated, both for this and reference 104. In the latter in note 12, p. 147, the last two lines should be amended to read: "($\pm w$) $(-w + w) = (-w + w)$ $(\pm w) = (\pm w)^2 + (\pm w)^5 = 0$. Update [3,4,6] accordingly. Finally," etc. That is, w-algebra is distributive. However, a given point in the w,r plane may lie on more than one of the orbits of $\pm w$; thus $1 + w$ lies on the $(-w)$ orbit $x^2 - xy + y^2 = 1$, and also on the $(+w)$ orbit $x^2 + xy + y^2 = 3$. Thus the same point $a + bw$ can be one power of $+w$ and another power of $-w$.
97. Jung, C.G., and Pauli, W. 1954. *The interpretation of nature and psyche*. New York: Pantheon.
98. Checkland, P.B. 1972. Towards a systems-based methodology for real-world problem solving. *J. Syst. Eng.* 3, no. 2.
99. _____. 1977. Development of systems thinking by systems practice. In *Progress in cybernetics and systems research,* ed. R. Trappl and F. de P. Hanika. Washington, D.C.
100. Naughton, J. 1977. *The checkland methodology: a reader's guide.* 2nd ed. Open Univ. Syst. Group.
101. Checkland, P.B. 1979. Techniques in soft systems practice, Parts 1 and 2. *J. Appl. Syst. Anal.* 6.
102. Smale, S. 1980. *The mathematics of time*, pp. 128–29; 133–4. New York: Springer.
103. Eells, J. 1966. A setting for global analysis. *Bull. Amer. Math. Soc.* 12:751.
104. Musès, C. 1983. Hypernumbers and time operators. *J. Appl. Math. Comput.* 12:139.
105. Reference 48, p. 151.
106. Hughes, E.R. 1942. *Chinese philosophy in classical times*. London: Dent.

107. Musès, C. 1972. The exploration of consciousness. In *Consciousness and reality*, ed. C. Musès and A. Young, pp. 103–110. (and—in 1974 by—New York: Avon/Discus. New York: E.P. Dutton.

108. Smythe R., and Checkland, P.B. 1976. *J. Appl. Syst. Anal.* 5:1.

109. Reference 91, pp. 203–300, *passim*. This book is useful and compendious, being married only by the author's inappropriately repeated allegiances to a zealot variety of Marxism linked curiously to a kind of masochistic anti-occidentalism; while insisting unreasonably on his assumption that Chinese civilization grew up in a vacuum untouched by "Western" influence, thus precluding all Iranian, Chaldean, and Egyptian influence on Chinese (especially Taoist) thought.

110. Holling, C.S. 1982. Director's corner. *Options* (Autumn):16.

111. Kellog, R.; Knoll, M.; and Kugler, S. 1965. Form similarity between phosphenes of adults and preschool children. *Nature* 208:1129.

112. Seidel, J. 1968. *Electromedizin*, 13:194.

113. Knoll, M.; Höfer, O.; and Kugler, J. 1966. Fliegerpersönlichkeit und Phosphenhäufigkeit. *Zeitschr. f. Physik u. ihre Anwendungen*, special issue on Swiss research, p. 253.

114. Knoll, M., and Kugler, J. 1959. "Subjective light pattern spectroscopy if the EEG frequency range." *Nature* 184:1823.

115. Greguss, P., and Galin, M. 1971. The holographic concept in ophthalmology. *Proceedings of the First European Biophys. Congress*, ed. E. Broda, p. 97. Vienna Academy of Medicine.

116. Gimbutas, M. 1982. *The goddesses and gods of old Europe 6500–3500 B.C.*. Berkeley and Los Angeles: University of California Press.

117. Winn, M. McC. 1973. *The signs of the Vinča culture*. Doctoral dissertation, University of California, Los Angeles, Department of Indo-European Studies. See especially pp. 291–292, which was published in book form in 1981. See also: Gimbutas, Marija, Old Europe in the fifth millennium B.C.: the European situation on the arrival of the Indo-Europeans. In *The Indo-Europeans in the fourth and third millennia*, ed. E.C. Polomé, Ann Arbor, Mi.: Karoma. pp. 14–18, 45.

118. Gimbutas, M. 1979. In *Archives Suisses d'Anthropologie Gènè-rale* (Genève), 43:113.

119. Aurigemma, L. 1976. *Le Signe Zodiacal du Scorpion dans les traditions occidentales*, author's summaries on jacket and on p. 12. Paris: Mouton.

120. Elkes, J. 1974. Language and the human psyche. In *Consciousness and reality*, ed. C. Musès and A. Young, pp. 275–276. New York: E.P. Dutton and Avon/ Discus.

121. Chaosium Games Catalog, fall 1982, ed. Tadeshi Ehara, p. 8. Albany, California: Chaosium Inc.

122. Perrin, S., and Stafford, G. 1979. *Cults of prax*. Albany, California: Chaosium.

123. Yared, Roberta. 1982. Gaming. *Options* published by the International Institute for Applied Systems Analysis (IIASA), Spring 1982, Laxenburg, Austria. pp. 10–13.
124. Lovecraft, H.P. 1960. The festival. In *Dragons and other tales*, ed. A. Derleth. Sauk City, Wis.: Arkham House.
125. Woodward, K.L., with Gates, D. 1982. Giving the devil his due. *Newsweek* (August 30):72–74.
126. Nieburg, H.L. 1966. *In the name of science*, pp. vii, 116. Chicago: Quadrangle.
127. *Bibliotheca Islamica*, vol. 24. 1971. ed. M. Ghalib, Wiesbaden: Steiner.
128. Strothmann, E. 1943. *Gnosis-Texte der Ismailiten*. Göttingen.
129. Halm, H. 1978, Kosmologie und Heilslehre der Frühen Ismā īlīya, pp. 169–205. Wiesbaden: Steiner.
130. Musès, C., ed. 1958. Editor's introduction. *Prismatic voices, an anthology.* Indian Hills, Colorado: Falcon's Wing.
131. Khosrau, Naṣr-i, Kitāb Zād al-Mosāfirīn, Kaviānī, ed., Berlin, *ca.* 1930 and Ch. 17 of his *Kitāb-e Jāmi al-Hikmatain*, H. Corbin and M. Mo'in, eds., Maisonneuve, Paris, 1953. See also Henry Corbin's inspired exposition in his *Temps Cyclique*, Berg, Paris, 1982, p. 44.
132. Musès, C., ed. 1982. Introduction. *Esoteric teachings of the Tibetan tantra*, pp. vii–xiii. New York: Weiser.
133. *Journal American Oriental Society* 86 (1966):282.
134. Musès, C., ed. 1960. *The Septuagint Bible*, 2nd ed. Indian Hills, Colorado: Falcon's Wing. See Isaiah, 14:12–14, p. 1078.
135. _____. 1951. *Illumination on Jacob Boehme*, Chs. 3 and 5. New York: Columbia University Press.
136. von Nettesheim, H.C.A. 1531. *De Occulta Philosophia*, Antwerp. 2nd and enlarged edition, Köln, 1533, Bk. II, Ch. 22.
137. Lange, H.O., and Neugebauer, O., trans., and eds. 1940. *Papyrus Carlsberg No. 1: ein Hieratisch-Demotisch Kosmologischer Text.* Copenhagen: Einar Munksgaard.
138. Neugebauer, O., and Parker, R.A., trans. and eds. 1960. *Egyptian astronomical texts*, vol. I: *The early decans*. London: Lund Humphries.
139. Walker, P.E. 1983. Letter to the author dated 22 April, 1983.
140. Gardner, E. 1900. *Dante's ten heavens*. 2nd ed. New York: Scribner.
141. Trimingham, J.S. 1973. *The Sufi orders in Islam*, p. 163. Oxford University Press.
142. Bussell, F.W. 1918. *Religious thought and heresy in the middle ages*, p. 375. London: Scott.
143. Goyon, J.-C. 1979. An interpretation of the edifice. In R.A. Parker, J. Leclant, and J.-C. Goyon, *The edifice of Taharka by the Sacred Lake of Karnak*, pp. 80–86. London: Lund Humphries.
144. Goma'a, F. 1973. *Chaemwese, Sohn Rameses' II. und Hoherpriest von*

Memphis. Aegyptologische Abhandlungen, vol. 27. Wicsbaden: Steiner.
145. Russell, J.B. 1981. *Satan.* Ithaca: Cornell University Press.
146. Armstrong, H.W. 1978. *Did God create a devil?* p. 8. Pasadena, Calif.: Ambassador College Press.
147. Giauque, W.C., and Woolsey, R.E. 1981. A totally new direction for management education: a modest proposal. *Interface* 11, no. 4:30*ff.*
148. Toffler, A. 1981. *The third wave.* p. 317. New York: Bantam Books.
149. Oury, G.M. 1978. *L'histoire de l'Eglise,* p. 294. France: Editions de Solesmes.
150. Sassin, W. 1983. Fueling Europe in the future. *Options* (International Institute for Applied Systems Analysis), no. 1:7.
151. Kreutzwald, F. 1900. *Kalewipoeg,* p. xvi of the Introduction to Ferdinand Löwe's translation of Kreutzwald's collected oral texts (now a rare book). Reval, Esthonia: Kluge Publishers.
152. *The Sciences,* January-February 1983, p. 34.
153. Hill, A.V. 1933. Wave transmission as the basis of biological activity. *Surface Phenomena, Cold Spring Harbor Symposia on Quantitative Biology,* Vol. I.
154. Scheinmann, W.X. 1968. *Why most investors are mostly wrong most of the time,* p. 89. Scheinmann Divergence Analysis Report Corp.
155. Naughton, J. Craft knowledge in systems research. In *Progress in cybernetics and systems research,* vol. 8, ed. R. Trappl, G.J. Klir, and F.R. Pichler, p. 1440. New York: Hemisphere/McGraw Hill.
156. Anderson, P. 1984. Chapter 26. In *Self-organization,* ed. F.E. Yates. New York: Plenum.
157. Prigogine, I. 1980. *From being to becoming.* San Francisco: Freeman.
158. _____, Herman, R., and Allen, P. 1977. The evolution of complexity and the laws of nature. In *Goals in a global community: a report to the club of Rome,* vol. 1, ed. E. Laszlo and J. Bierman. Oxford: Pergamon.
159. _____, Mayne, F., George, C., and De Haan, M. 1977. Microscopic theory of irreversible processes. *Proceedings of the Natl. Acad. Sci. U.S.* 74:4152–4156.
160. Posey, C. 1982. Report in *Options,* p. 5, IIASA, Spring 1982, Laxenburg, Austria.
161. Holling, C.S. 1973. Resilience and stability of ecological systems. *Annual Review of Ecology and Systematics* 4:1–23.
162. Gilbert, N., and Hughes, R. 1971. A model of an aphid population. *J. Animal Ecol.* 40:529, 532–534.
163. Rudall, B.H. 1983. Contemporary cybernetics. *Kybernetes* 12:86.
164. Musès, C. 1984. Some current dilemmas in applied physical mathematics. *Appl. Math. and Comput.* 14:210–212.

Index

The index is representative rather than exhaustive. Proper names referred to only in secondary or subsidiary fashion, and words that are mentioned throughout, are not fully indexed. Principal page references, rather than individual pages, are given for frequently used terms. Nouns include references to their plurals and also to their adjectives, wherever applicable, or vice versa. Footnotes are designated by *n.* following a page number; end-of-chapter notes, by *n.* followed by the number of the note. *See* may also mean "see also." Arabic or Hebrew words beginning with the letter *'ayn* (') and aspirated Greek words are indexed under the following (transcribed) letter; and lit. means "literally."

Abraham, Ralph, ix, 33, 55, 56
abstraction, impossibility of pure, 13, 14
Abu'l-Fayd al Misrī, 144–145; = Dhū'l-Nūn, a ninth century Egyptian who transmitted ancient doctrines
Academy, Florentine, 17, 28–29 *n.*7; *see* Ficino, Gemistheos, de'Medici, Plato
Aden, 163 *n.*31
Aga Khan, 88 *n.*16, 155 *n.*5
Agrippa, Heinrich Cornelius, von Nettesheim, compiler of old traditions, 158
Ahriman, 135, 138; cf. Set, Satan, Lucifer
akasha, 40, 124 *n.*16
'akatastasia (Greek) = *tohu* (Hebrew)

something despoiled (at origin of current universe), 158 *n.*16
alchemy 92, 98, 123 *n.*6, 155 *n.*11; *see Kam*
Alexandria
library of, 161 *n.*26
school of, 163 *n.*29
Alfvèn, Hannes, 57
Algebra as metaphor, 13
ibn 'Alī Husain, 8th Tayyibite spiritual leader and transmitter of important ancient traditions, 130, 150
Allah, etymology of, 132
allergies and resonance, 38–39
Ames Research Center, 8 *n.*5, 174; *see* NASA
aminoacyl transferase enzymes, heart of DNA/RNA functioning, 182 *n.*8

feedfoward, 3, 67*ff.*; *see* feedback
Ferrara; *see* Councils
Fibonacci series, 68, 89 *n*.25; *see* cacti,
　　flowers, Leonardo of Pisa
Ficino, Marsilio, 17, 29 *n*.7; *see*
　　Academy, Florentine
fiʻl and related (Arabic) terms; *see*
　　azalīyat (Iranian cognate)
Filippani-Ronconi, Pio, 130
First Beginning or Intelligence (*'Aql*),
　　131–132; *see Sābiq* = *Mabda'al-*
　　Awwal = manifest personification
　　of higher *maf'ūl* phase = lower
　　resonance of *Azal* (*q.v*) and
　　personification of *Maf'ūl*
First Intelligence; *see* First Beginning
Fischer, Jaakob, transmitter of old
　　Esthonian epic, 170, 182 *n*.5; *see*
　　Kalewipoeg
five, as cosmological, 124 *n*.16; *see*
　　dua, numbers
Flavius Cladius Julianus, x
flowers, 36
　　flowers and cacti-spine spirals, 89
　　n.25; *see* Fibonacci series
four-group, 42; *see* quadron
Fourier transform, 43
fravarti, 58
fravashi; *see fravarti*
free choice, 68*ff.*; *see* randomness
freedom, less profound or powerful than
　　love, 156 *n*.14
　　and love, 172; *see* theodicy
Freher, Dionysius Andreas, 151, 158
　　n.16
Freud (Freudian), 98
Fry, Christopher, cited, 154
future, 3, 12, 68, 70, 71
　　feedback from, 57*ff.*
future directedness, 66–67, 70, 71, 189

Galileo (Galileo Galilei), 6, 29 *n*.7, 50,
　　104
games, role-playing, 126*ff.*

their psychosocial importance for
　　twentieth century, 126–127
time and, 127, 128
and the problem of evil, 126–127,
　　155 *n*.4
gamma function, 68, 183 *n*.8
gap, 136
　　as love-vacuum or scarcity, 138
Gauquelin, Françoise and Michel, 55,
　　56
Gemistheos, Georgios (Plethon), 17,
　　29 *n*.7; *see* Academy, Florentine
Gerber, Paul, 29 *n*.12; *see* perihelion
　　shift
Germer, Lester, 33
ghafla, 146
Gibbs, J. Willard, 50
Gimbutas, Marija, 114, 124 *n*.17 and
　　18
gnosis, ancient Egyptian, 146 *ff*, ch. 5
　　passim
　　Ismaili, 158 *n*.19
　　Kabbalistic, 143
　　Manichaean and Coptic, 159 *n*.19
　　official Christian, 140
　　Sumero-Babylonian, 156 *n*.16
　　Valentinian, 132
Goa (Georges Alloro), 181 *n*.4
God (or our Universe) wounded, 139
　　as hero, 135
Goddess (of our Universe)
　　as Daēna, 139
　　Egyptian priesthood of, 162 *n*.26
　　Protectress of Earth, 140
　　Sirius as her star, (note in this
　　connection that $2 \times 37 + 1 = 75$
　　primordial forms, *q.v1*.), 161
　　n.26
Gödel, Kurt, 1
Goyon, Jean-Claude, 126, 146*ff.*,
　　164 *n*.33
Grail, Grail Castle, 139
gravitation, 62–63
Greaves, James, 158 *n*.16
Greeks, 142
grunion, 35, 36, 43

About the Author

Charles Musès is one of the pioneers of new thinking in science in the twentieth century. He co-lectured and worked with the late Ross Ashby and Warren McCulloch, and with Norbert Wiener in a postgraduate course on neural cybernetics given under the auspices of the University of Naples in 1962. He was requested by the Italian government to write the official obituary for the father of cybernetics after the latter's untimely passing in 1964.

Dr. Musès fundamental papers span problems in the complex interfaces between sociology, biology, psychology, philosophy, and mathematics. He was the first mathematician to discover and develop the higher arithmetics of hypernumbers beyond the square root of minus one, and pioneered the term "hypernumber" in 1966. He is also a contributor to UNESCO's *Impact of Science on Society*, foundations editor of the British journal *Kybernetes*, and editorial board member for the *International Journal of Bio-Medical Computing*. Dr. Musès can be reached through his editorial offices at St-Antoine de Siga, 06670 France.